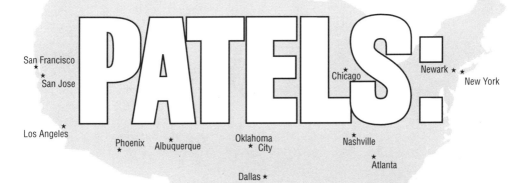

★ Portland

San Francisco

★ San Jose

Chicago

Newark ★ ★

New York

Los Angeles

Phoenix ★ Albuquerque

Oklahoma ★ City

Nashville

Atlanta

Dallas ★

Houston ★

★ Orlando

D1616322

PATELS

A GUJARATI COMMUNITY HISTORY IN THE UNITED STATES

GOVIND B. BHAKTA

ucla asian
american
studies
center
press

UCLA ASIAN AMERICAN STUDIES CENTER PRESS

LOS ANGELES, CALIFORNIA

Printed in the United States of America.

Library of Congress Control Number: 2002109745
ISBN 0-934052-39-5

Author: Govind B. Bhakta

Editor: Russell C. Leong
Assistant Editor: Brandy Lien Worrall
Cover Design: Phil Avari
Book Design: Lisa Winger

TABLE OF CONTENTS

List of Tables and Charts

Chapter 1

Chapter 3

Chapter 4

PREFACE

Do You Know a Patel?

So little is known about our Indian American Patels—their roots, their settlement in the U.S., their experiences. At the same time, Patels are highly visible on the American urban landscape, especially in the motel business across the nation.

I hope my book, *Patels: A Gujarati Community History in the United States*, will be welcomed by students, scholars, researchers, journalists, as well as the general American and Indian public, who have become increasingly interested in these Patel groups in the U.S. I am proud to bring this history—never before available in a single volume—to individual Americans and Indians, as well as to organizations and institutions across the U.S. and India. This book will provide Indo-American Patels with a source of pride regarding their identity as a community and their place in American history, in addition to allowing young Asian American Patels to learn more about the background of their ethnic group and to find role models from their community in the U.S.

Within this history, I have designated the first generation non-resident Indian Patels from Surat, Bulsar, and Navsari districts (those who came in 1960's and onwards to U.S.), as "head of the households". Their spouses are also considered first generation Patels. Their parents are documented as the grandparent generation; Lastly, the children of " head of the household" are called the " second generation". The phrase" Indo-American Patel Family Members" is abbreviated to IAPFM.

This book is a product of a seven-and-a-half-yearlong comprehensive project. The main focus of this book is to let the present and future generation know who we were, who we are, and how we can become a great community. We can begin by first setting straight the facts and figures about our Indian heritage, and then proceeding to analyze where we stand along the barometer of the present.

Particular attention is given to the traditions of the Indo-American kin communities in Surat, Bulsar, and Navsari districts of Gujarat State (India), and to their Indo-American Surti Leauva, Bhakta, Matiya, and Charotaria Leauva (SBMC) Patidar relatives in the U.S. This book will provide an extensive amount of demographic and economic statistics, and basic information on the SBMC Patels of these three districts.

Overall, this study may be considered as a case study of Patels from Gujarat. Ultimately, all sub-castes of Patels have the same ingredients culturally, socially, and philosophically. Historically, they are from the "Love" or "Kush" generations, or Leauva or Kadava Patidars. With this wealth of information, one may discern the present and future developments of this particular society. Unless and until we explain the good, indifferent, and terrible parts of our shared past, how can we follow the right path in the future? This is the main intention of this book.

My research will help the individual Indo-American Patel identify and communicate with living family members, as well as to appreciate the tremendous effort and persistence his or her ancestors displayed in overcoming circumstances in their lives to leave a legacy to their descendants. I have attempted to answer such questions as: Where did the name *Patel* come from? Why did Patels leave their homeland? In what parts of the world did they settle? How long did they stay? Where did they go when they left for other lands, and what were their new lives like? Do I know a Patel?

Hitesh Bhakta is an example of a successful member of the Patels. Although Hitesh was born and raised in Zambia, Africa, his parents are from Dighas, Surat, India. After completing most of his schooling in England where he obtained his law degree, he went on to practice law as a real estate and business litigation attorney in Southern California. Hitesh serves as a chair of the code of Professional Ethics and Bylaws Committee. He is a vice-chairman of AAHOA and an active member of AAHOA's Industry Relations Committee for the past two years. In addition, he is a member of the Board of Directors of the Indian Medical Association of Southern California and the South Asian Sheriff's Advisory Council. Over the course of his career, Hitesh has been closely involved in his family businesses and as a second-generation multi-property hotelier; he currently operates a number of hotels in California and Texas. Hitesh lives with his wife, Chitra a physician, and his daughters Alisa and Kareena.

Ramesh Patel was born in Vyara, Gujarat, India. As a child, Roy helped operate the family business. After completing his B.S. from South Gujarat University in Surat, he immigrated to the U.S. in order to pursue a career in the hospitality industry. He moved to Jackson, Mississippi in 1978 and purchased a small motel. Roy is a seasoned franchise hotelier and a successful owner/partner of multi-franchise properties with over twenty years of hotel experience. Roy's Jackson-based company owns and operates twenty hotels throughout California, Louisiana, Mississippi, and Tennessee. Roy is also a humanitarian, deeply involved in social, religious, and community service. He was founder of the Gujarati Samaj of Mississippi and served as its first president from 1998-1999. Roy is active in temple activities and the India Association of Mississippi.

These two stories are but a sampling, as there are thousands of narratives about Indo-American Patels, interwoven with the greater social, cultural, religious, and business life of the Gujarati community in the United States. This book will provide a comprehensive selection of such stories, so that the reader will be able to create an image of the significance of the Indo-American Patel community in the United States.

ACKNOWLEDGEMENTS

This book would not have been possible without the support of several individuals and organizations. I am thankful to the members of the Surat, Bulsar, and Navsari districts, the Surti Leauva, Bhakta, Matiya and Charotaria Leauva Patels, who helped me conduct the survey by completing the questionnaire for Indo-American Surat, Bulsar, and Navsari district Patidars, which included over 226 families. I am thankful to many individuals who gave their time and special knowledge regarding our Surat, Bulsar, and Navsari district Patels for providing data and perspective.

I would like to express my sincere gratitude to the following individuals for their consultation and help in reaching to the members of the Patidar group. These include President of the Matiya Patidar Samaj, Mr. K.C. Patel; Shree Ramkabir Bhakta Samaj of U.S.A. President Mr. Chandrakant D. Patel; Shree Ramkabir Temple, Inc. President Mr. Lalinbhai G. Bhakta; Mr. Hasmukhbhai B. Patel of the Surti Leauva Patidar Samaj of Southern California; Mr. Shankarbhai G. Patel, and Mr. Natubhai Patel, Presidents of Leauva Patidar Samaj of U.S.A.; Dr. Niranjanbhai D. Patel; Mr. V.C. Bhakta, Mr. Bhikhubhai U. Patel; Mr. Ramanbhai M. Patel; Mr. Ishverbhai A. Patel, Anil Patel, Mr. Harshadbhai P. Patel, President of Charotaria Leauva Patidar Samaj of U.S.A., and Mr. Anandraua Lingayat for their kind support and encouragement. For his support in promoting this project, I would like to thank an attorney friend Mr. Indra M. Gandhi. Thanks to Kanak Ratanjee for providing copying facilities. Thanks to Mr. N.D. Bhakta, as well as Nainesh M. Bhakta for the photographs and to Mr. Dwine Brinson for picture-scan help. I am very grateful to Dr. Kantibhai M. Desai of Navsari, who has given me valuable suggestions in materializing this project. Dr. Ashvinbhai Desai (Reader and Head of Comparative Literature, South Gujarat University, India) played an important part by encouraging me to write for Patels who are settled in U.S. but migrated from south Gujarat. He has worked with this project for over a year and guided me to finish this book.

Over the many years that it took me to research and write this book, dozens of friends and relatives contributed to the work. A project of this nature and size preys heavily upon one's mental health. Thankfully, at various times I was able to rely upon a good group of friends to keep me going. These include Umesh Bhakta Ashram Shala Navsari, Dhirubhai K. Patel, President of Matiya Samaj India, Dr. Rohit Bhakta, and Dahyabhai Digasvala Navsari.

Without the help from Prof. Russell Leong, editor of *Amerasia Journal* and the UCLA Asian American Studies Center, and Dr. Karen Leonard, Professor of South Asian History and Culture at the University of California, Irvine, this project would not have been possible. They have guided me in the final stages of the project development, pushing me to strive for high scholarly goals, while standing by me as friends. I would like to express my sincere gratitude to Brandy Lien Worrall for editorial assistance. I am grateful to my organizer, proofreader, and evaluator, Rhonda Higdon, graduate student of Karen Leonard, for her sincere friendship, warmth, and interest in my book and my community. She helped edit this piece for a year. Thanks for her professionalism, skill and enthusiasm. I would like to thank all well-wishers and supporters of this book for their encouragement and faith in me.

Last, but certainly not least, my wife, Sumati, and my four children—Shailesh, Jayshree, Tina, and Amit—my son-in-law Anand, and my brother-in-law Mukundbhai deserve high praise for putting up with me during this enterprise. Their patience, direction, tolerance, love, and pressure for me to finish have made me quite the lucky human being. My sincere thanks and apologies to anyone who fails to appear in this list.

INTRODUCTION

A Note to Patel Youth

Young friends, it is a matter of pride that you were born in America and possess American citizenship or residency. It is my feeling that you should make much progress, have a successful life, and in the end, be able to achieve various life goals and to reach to the loftiest levels of your potential. Our blessings are for you, but I have to speak with you of some private issues. Kindly listen. Perhaps you may have no time to listen, but you can at least read this much.

I put a question before you: Do you know your parents? I am not trying to give you "great advice," but I want to convey some truths to you. You will think "Yes" and "What kind of question is that? How could we *not* know our parents?" Friends, I do not mean it in that sense. I am asking if you really know: What is their native land? Why have they come to America? What do they want to achieve? For whom do they labor, and why? In India life was very arduous. Your parents had no economic resources on which they could rely. They made debts, studied diligently, and remained here in the United States because they had hopes of making a good life for themselves and you, their children.

In India our lives passed amid troubles and tensions. Although our childhoods passed into innumerable miseries and pains, we still wanted our children to become happy. We thought, no conflicts should ensue in their lives; they should come forward in America, achieve good degrees, and make their lives prosperous. Only with these hopes in mind can parents go on laboring day and night.

Now that the American environment is spread out all around you, you may be feeling that your parents are Indian, and you are American. You may ask yourself, "Why should I remember Indian customs and traditions? Why should I not live as an American when I have to live in America?" You are correct. I also would think likewise were I in your place. But I would ask only this: Would you want to do something for your parents who have sacrificed everything for you? The nation in which your parents had been born has a great and glorious inheritance of culture and civilization. America may have material prosperity, but India offers much cultural and spiritual inheritance. We, the older generation, only believe this. Kindly do not neglect your parents who have given you birth and took a deep and abiding interest in your cultivation.

Maybe your parents are illiterate or do not know as much as you know, but those who gave you birth are equal to the Lord God. Their service is my only religion. It is understandable that there may be differences between your thinking and their thinking, but the bridge between parents and children must never be broken under any circumstances. Young friends, kindly keep this little message of mine with you and, "You shall surely swim successfully the life-sea, and reach your goals."[1]

The struggle to reconcile two cultures is indeed prevalent in the lives of many second-generation Indian Americans. Nevertheless, evidence indicates that this struggle subsides considerably once young Indian Americans reach college age.

One survey shows that among eighteen- to twenty-five-year-olds sampled, the overwhelming sense of affiliation was with their Indian heritage. Ninety-five percent of the interviewees responded that they were Indian, without any qualification. Moreover, 70% said that they recently made efforts to familiarize themselves with their Indian language, either by speaking with their parents or by taking college classes. Also among their concerns was how to preserve and pass on Indian culture for future generations. The interviewees state that as they become older, they start to feel more comfortable with themselves and, therefore, feel a stronger affiliation, which is manifested in a number of ways. For example, many drop the Americanized versions of their names in favor of their given names.[2]

In addressing important questions and issues of both parents and the younger generations, I would like to devote this book to our youth. It is important to maintain communication among generations, to discuss our problems and differences, and to try to make compromises on some of the more conflicting elements of our disparate cultures, traditions, and experiences.

Methodology

Patels: A Gujarati Community History in the United States is designed to provide a comprehensive report on the most significant social, historical, cultural, and demographic aspects of Indo-American Patidar of Surat, Bulsar, and Navsari districts of Gujarat State, India and their family lives in the U.S. in a manner easily understandable to readers accustomed to quantitative data (with most data presented in a table format). The book is divided into ten chapters, each of which focuses upon specific cultural topics. An introductory section in each chapter outlines and provides background to the chapter. There is a glossary provided at the end of the book for readers not familiar with Indian terms and definitions.

For the survey I have selected four Indo-American SBMC communities settled in the U.S. The survey posed questions regarding the following areas: sex, age, country of origin, immigration, marriage, trips to India, residential habits, hobbies, education, language, occupation, entrepreneurships, ethnicity, networking, annual income, satisfaction with leisure, education, love life, finances, children's spousal choices, dating, inter-caste marriage, sources of conflict between children and parents, overall health, life in the United States versus life in India, social contacts, loneliness, and respect for elders. There were twenty-eight main questions, some of which are sub-divided with multiple-choice answers. Some family members skipped questions; hence, different questions yield different numbers of respondents.

The research survey was conducted by mailing a questionnaire (see Appendix H) in March and June 1995 to a total of 1,533 families of SBMC Patel communities. The lists of families' addresses were taken from the Surti Leauva, Bhakta, Matiya, and Charotaria Patidar community directories. I received a 15% survey response. One hundred and fifty-one families, with a total 572 family members, responded to 80% or more of the questions, and seventy-five families, with 278 family members, responded to 30%-60 % of the questionnaire. A total of 226 families, with 850 family members, participated in this survey. There were 226 male heads of households, with 205 wives; 274 second-generation children (over sixteen years); seventy-six grandfathers; and sixty-nine grandmothers. Respondents answers were tabulated in a table format. Initially there were 83 tables prepared for the book. But for the sake of convenience, 41 tables are now presented and the remaining 42 tables are briefly explained throughout the book in text format.

The last column of tables with number of respondents represents the participant numbers of particular member of the family group. Percents are based on the number of answers received from that particular family member's group to the total number of subjects in that particular family group. For example, for the question "trips made to India," the percent of first-generation male parents who made one trip to India is the number of answers received from the first-generation male parents who made one trip to India to the total number of first-generation male parents who participated in this questionnaire. Similarly, this applies for the first-generation wife or spouse group, second-generation children group, etc. Additionally, there is a source note appearing below the table, which is a guide to sources of statistics.

Other data presented comes from many sources. The sources include Federal Statistical Bureaus (Indian and U.S.) and other organizations that collect and issue statistics as their principal activity, including private research bodies, trade associations, and social organizations. Sources of information include the Questionnaire for Indo-American Surat, Bulsar, and Navsari districts (SBMC) Patidar in U.S., scholarly books, journals, official reports and government documents, and various social organizations, national newspapers, community newspapers and periodicals. Individual interviews, most of which are relatively up-to-date, are available from several sources, but the sources are not always in agreement. Most statistical data should be viewed as forecast or estimates.

The statistics presented were obtained and tabulated by various means. Some statistics are found in technical enumerations or censuses, while others are based on more speculative samples. Some information is extracted from records kept for administrative purposes and books. Most information is obtained explicitly for statistical purposes through questionnaires by mail. Some information is obtained by personal interviews.

This book is not only a guidebook to prepare for the twenty-first century, it is also a comprehensive source from which the reader is free to draw his or her own conclusions. There is broad coverage of subject areas pertinent to life in villages in the Gujarat state and in India, as well as the Indo-American life of the SBMC Patels in the U.S. The data in these tables are based on data obtained for only a portion of the population units of the Indo-American SBMC Patels. The list of the Surti, Leauva, Bhakta, Matiya, and Charotaria Leauva Patidar households was obtained to use as the sampling frame. The table quantities are referred to as "sample estimates."

The cultural diversity of India is reflected in the U.S. There are approximately seventy Hindu temples in the east and northeastern states of the U.S., and approximately fifty in the southern and western states (see Appendix A). There are over hundreds Indian American organizations, many of them in metropolitan areas. Over one hundred different *jatis* (tribes) of Indo-Americans are represented in the U.S. (See Appendix B) Twenty-five different Patel sub-castes have made a home in the U.S.

The Surti Leauva and Bhakta Patidar have local- and national-level organizations, while the Matiya Patels and Charotaria Patels have local-level organizations. One of the primary objectives of the Indian organizations has been to expose Indian culture to the next generation of Indian Americans, as well as to educate non-Indian Americans on Indian culture. The Asian American Hotel Owners Association

(AAHOA) provides an active forum in which Asian American hotel owners, through an exchange of ideas, can communicate, interact, and secure their proper position within the hospitality industry. AAHOA is a source of inspiration, promoting professionalism and excellence through education and community involvement. This organization has approximately 7,000 paid members. At the 1997 December convention in San Jose, California, over 5,000 people participated in workshops, discussion groups, panels, forums, and educational seminars.

As recently as 1980, there were 387,000 Indian Americans in the United States. The 1990 U.S. Census recorded 815,447 Indians Americans. The 2000 Census Bureau figures show an Indian American population growth of 49% since 1990 to a total of 1,215,000. Then and now, Indian American Patels rank first in the Indo-American population group, numbering over 300,000.

Care has been taken to present a balanced view of all topics. The author has tried not to inject his own philosophical preconceptions into the selection, presentation, or interpretation of the data; however, some bias admittedly does occur—the author being a member of the community about which he writes.

PATELS

A GUJARATI COMMUNITY HISTORY
IN THE UNITED STATES

1
_____

WHO ARE
THE PATELS?

CHAPTER 1

PATELS AND THE GUJARATI HOMELAND

In the following poem Gujarati poet Khabardar writes that Gujaratis recreate Gujarat in any place they go, in any country in which they have settled. They create the flavor of Gujarat by preserving their language, dress, customs, and culture.

જ્યાં જ્યાં વસે એક ગુજરાતી...
જ્યાં જ્યાં વસે એક ગુજરાતી, ત્યાં ત્યાં સદાકાળ ગુજરાત
જ્યાં જ્યાં ગુજરાતી બોલાતી,ત્યાં ત્યાં ગુર્જરીની મહોલાત.

ઉત્તર દક્ષિણ પૂર્વ કે પશ્ચિમ, જ્યાં ગુર્જરના વાસ,
સૂર્ય તણાં કિરણો દોડે ત્યાં સૂર્ય તણો જ પ્રકાશ :

જેની ઉષા હસે હેલાતી, તેનાં તેજ પ્રફુલ્લ પ્રભાત ।
જ્યાં જ્યાં વસે એક ગુજરાતી, ત્યાં ત્યાં સદાકાળ ગુજરાત

ગુર્જર વાણી, ગુર્જર લહાણી, ગુર્જર શાણી રીત;
જંગલમાં પણ મંગલ કરતી, ગુર્જર ઉધમપ્રીત;

જેને ઉર ગુજરાતી હુલાતી તેને સુરવન તુલ્ય મિરાત ;
જ્યાં જ્યાં વસે એક ગુજરાતી, ત્યાં ત્યાં સદાકાળ ગુજરાત

કૃષ્ણ દયાનંદ, દાદા કેરી, પુણ્યવિરલ રસભોમ,
ખંડ ખંડ જઇ ઝૂએ ગર્વે કોણ જાત ને કોમ !

ગુર્જર ભરતી ઊછળે છાતી, ત્યાં રહે ગરજી ગુર્જર માત;
જ્યાં જ્યાં વસે એક ગુજરાતી, ત્યાં ત્યાં સદાકાળ ગુજરાત

અણકીધાં કરવાના કોડે, અધુરાં પુરાં થાય;
સ્નેહ, શૌર્યને સત્ય તણા ઉર, વૈભવ રાસ રચાય :

જય જય જન્મ સફળ ગુજરાતી ! જય જય અદલ ગુજરાતી !
જ્યાં જ્યાં વસે એક ગુજરાતી, ત્યાં ત્યાં સદાકાળ ગુજરાત

Jyan jyan vase aak Gujarati tyan tyan sada kal gujarat
Jyan jyan Gujarati bolati tyan tyan Gurjarini Maholat
Utaar Dakshin Purba ke Paschim Jyan jyan gurjarna vaas
Surya tana kirano dode tyan Surya tano ja prakash

Gurjar vani Gurjar lahani, Gurjar shani rit;
Jungleman pana mangal karati, Gurjar Uadyamprit;

Aana kidha karvana kode, adhuran puran thaya;
sneh, sharyane satya tana uar, vaibhav raas rachaya:

Jai jai janma safala Gujarati ! jai jai adal Gujarati
Jyan jayn vase aak Gujarati tyan tyan sadakal Gujarat.

Translation:
Wherever Gujaratis migrate, they create a Gujarati atmosphere, and one can feel he is living in Gujarat. Wherever the Gujarati language is spoken, Gujaratis' luxurious living in palaces may be found.

North or south; east or west, where Gujaratis live, they brighten the places like morning sunrays. Dawn starts with the beautiful singing.

Gujaratis language, mixing nature, practicality, industrious life and love for the language are the property for Gujaratis, turning life upside down.

Gujaratis from Gujarat, the precious and blessed land of Krisha Dayanand dada, proudly establishes themselves in different continents.

Gujaratis are adventurous, pleasant, loving, trustful and prosperous.
Hey Gujaratis bless you! Be successful in life. Wherever Gujaratis reside, we can find a place like Gujarat.

The legend says that one of the gods of the Hindu Pantheon, Lord Krishna, who ruled from Dwarka, breathed his last breath at a place famous for its shrine. And in modern times two illustrious sons of Gujarat, Mahatma Gandhi and Sardar Vallabhbhai Patel, have influenced the course of Indian history to such an extent that the name of Gujarat will forever be remembered by posterity.

Gujarat is one of twenty-four states of the Indian Union situated on the western part of the Indian sub-continent. The Gujarat state came into existence on 1 May 1960, as a result of the bifurcation of the erstwhile Bombay state. Gandhinagar, the capital of Gujarat state, is situated on the western bank of the river Sabarmati, twenty-five kilometers north of Ahmedabad. Gujarat has a long historical and cultural tradition dating back to the days of Harappan civilization. The Gujarat state administratively consists of twenty districts, divided into 184 *talukas*, with approximately 18,114 villages.

Gujarat ranks tenth in population (with 42 million) in India. Although agriculture continues to be the primary occupation for the large majority of people, the formation of business acumen, industry, and thrift are also principal characteristics distinguishing Gujaratis. The practice of trade and the long coastline have enabled Gujaratis to carry on prosperous maritime exchange with foreign groups since ancient times. Today, large numbers of Gujaratis reside in eastern and southern Africa, in many Arab countries, the U.K., the U.S., Canada, and New Zealand.

In Gujarat, as in other parts of India, culture and religion are interlinked. Hinduism accounts for 88.9% of the population, Islam for 8.46%, and Jainism for 1.99%. Like other languages of the Indo-Aryan family, Gujarati is derived from Sanskrit through Prakrit and Apabhramsha. However, it is now known that Gujarati evolved much later. Great authors and poets such as Kanaiyalal Munshi, Umashankar Joshi, Sundaram, R.V. Desai, Pannalal Patel, and Dhumketu have had a great influence on the culture of Gujarat. Gandhiji also influenced literary life in Gujarat, as he did so in many other aspects of Indian political, cultural, and religious life.

Of all the parts of India, Gujarat can claim to have distinction in the preservation of ancient traditional songs, dances, and drama. The best known among these is the *RAS* and the *Garba*. Most art traditions trace their origins to the ancient period of Lord Krishna's rule. When Krishna became the ruler of Dwarka in Gujarat, he not only distinguished himself as a brave fighter, statesman, and philosopher, but he was also known for his appreciation for dance and music. Since then, folk dances have become a part of life for the people of Gujarat.

Even though Gujarat today has become one of the most industrialized states in the country and ranks second in terms of industrial production, the Gujarat economy remains wedded to the land because its population is based on agriculture. Principal food crops are pearl millets, sorghum, paddy, maize, and wheat. Commercial crops like cotton, groundnuts, oil-seeds, sugarcane, and tobacco account for nearly 50% of cultivated lands. Dairying, one of the most effective investments for bringing about socioeconomic changes in rural India, was given the utmost priority in Gujarat.

Surat District

Founded by Parsi refugees in the twelfth century, Surat emerged as a minor trading post during the sixteenth century, when it was plundered and razed by the Portuguese numerous times. Chandra Guptas, Muslim rulers, and Mogul kings ruled Surat until 1573 A.D. The Portuguese established a business center in Surat; later, came other Europeans and Valandas. Bombay harbor then overtook Surat and made tremendous progress in business and commerce.

Packed around a tight bend in the Tapi River, sprawling Surat was the west coast's principal port before the meteoric rise of Bombay. Until 1947, Surat was one of the ports of Bombay province. Every government activity was administered by Bombay. The 1928 Bardoli nonviolence *satyagraha* and the 1930s Mahatma Gandhi *Dandi Kuch* procession are the historical events of this district.

After independence, Surat was given a district designation within Bombay state. In November 1956 Surat district was formatted along with the other districts of Ahmedabad. In 1960 the Bombay state was further divided into Maharastra and Gujarat states. In 1964 the Surat District was divided into two districts—Surat and Bulsar. In October 1997 the Bulsar district was divided into two districts—Navsari and Bulsar.

In 1592, after a protracted siege, the town fell to Akbar, under whose patronage it became one of India's most prosperous mercantile capitals, as well as an essential embarkation point for Muslims heading to Mecca. The British first appeared on the scene in 1612, after being granted permission by the Moguls to trade in the area.

Three years later, they routed the Portuguese in a naval battle off "Bloody Point," the mouth of the nearby Sway estuary, and opened a trading factory soon after. The Dutch and the French followed but saw their *godowns*, or warehouses, sacked by Shivaji's Marathas in 1664. The British, however, came through unscathed. By the end of the eighteenth century, their hold over the town and its shipyard was finally secured.

The British were the first to establish a silk factory having arrived in 1608, and Surat remained their headquarters until it moved to Bombay in 1674. Surat is a center of the jewelry business. The production of gold and silver thread, kinkhab brocades, and wood and ivory inlay work are also important. Silk weaving is a cottage industry producing the famous Tanchoi and Ganjee saris.[3]

Surat might eventually have become western India's number one city had it not been devastated by fire and floods in 1837. Many of the Jain and Parsi merchants fled south to Bombay, precipitating a decline from which Surat has only recently recovered. Over the past decade the city's booming textile, chemical, and diamond-cutting businesses—a legacy of the Dutch trade-links—have generated a 60% growth in population. However, the resultant overcrowding and pressures on an already over-taxed infrastructure are all too evident. In the winter of 1992-1993, the packed commercial and Muslim districts around the main bazaar finally burst at the seams, erupting into some of the worst communal riots the state has ever seen.

Today, Surat consists of thirteen *talukas*—Choryasi, Olpad, Kamrej, Maangrol, Madavi, Songad, Vechal, Nizar, Vyara, Valod, Bardoli, Mahuva, Palsana. The total population of the Surat district in 1981 was 2,493,211—1,427,172 of whom were village inhabitants and 1,066,039 of whom were city residents. There were 1,284 villages and twenty-one cities, respectively.

These days Surat is one of India's fastest growing industrial centers, but it attracts little tourism, other than the occasional business traveler or die-hard colonial history buff. Apart from a couple of melancholic European cemeteries, Surat's most memorable feature is its traffic, which, even by Indian standards, is appalling.

Surat's few historical sights are much spread out. One of them is Chock, the busy riverside intersection at the foot of Nehru Bridge. Facing the old British High Court building on one side and the incongruous steeple of an Anglican church on the other, the castle is the city's oldest monument, erected in 1540 on the banks of the Tapi by the Sultan of Gujarat in an attempt to curtail the trading activities of the Portuguese.[4]

Background to Migration: Surat Village Conditions in 1981

Table 1 presents various statistical data (using Surat district as an example) meant to demonstrate the serious lack of basic facilities to which those in the first world have become accustomed on a daily basis. For example, in 1981, 95% of the sample villages had primary schools—fifty-four villages had no primary school facilities, even though these are mandatory. Only fifty-three villages had primary medical facilities available. One hundred and fifty-eight villages had basic subdivision medical facilities available, resulting in a total of only 24% of villages that had basic medical facilities available. As for water, 1,163 villages had drinking water, mainly from simple ground wells. In terms of communication service, 405 villages (46%) had postal facilities. Only 3% of villages had shopping or market facilities available.

Table 1
Number of villages and percentage of villages (in each taluka)
with various facilities in Surat District.[5]

	Choryasi	Olpad	Kamrej	Mangrol	Mandavi	Songad	Uchhal	Nizar	Vyara	Valod	Bardoli	Mahuva	Palsana	Avg
No. of Villages	89	102	69	149	133	171	37	53	148	40	81	69	49	95
Educational	94	97	90	100	95	93	95	94	97	95	91	100	94	95
Medical	37	25	29	15	25	14	24	21	20	30	31	22	31	24
Drinking Water	100	100	100	100	100	100	100	100	100	100	100	100	100	100
Telegraph/ Postal	79	59	62	41	35	19	30	38	42	55	60	55	59	48
Shopping Market	-	-	-	0.7	3.0	2.3	2.7	3.8	4.7	5.0	1.2	14	-	3.0
Transportation	94	94	91	65	68	59	84	43	70	75	93	94	86	78
Solid Road	81	45	61	19	37	32	57	43	31	45	68	44	59	48
Electric Facilities	85	68	100	40	29	15	19	45	41	82	93	67	100	60

Educational Facilities: Every village must have minimum one primary school.
Medical Facilities: May be one or more of the following: hospital, maternity ward, basic health center, or child welfare center.
Drinking Water Facility: Water facilities are mainly from well water, village level water tank system, or from the irrigation at the district level.

Navsari District

Navsari district consists of five *talukas*: Navsari, Gandevi, Jalalpur, Bansda, and Chikhli. Navsari is situated twelve kilometers from the Arabian Sea on the banks of the river Purna. According to a myth, there were nine ponds (*sarovars*) around Navsari, making it known as the city of nine ponds.

The history of Navsari dates back two thousand years. Ptolemy, the Greek geographer, recognized in his writing in 150 A.D. that Navsari was a port. According to the books *Tavarikhe Navsari* by Sorabjee Mancharjee Desai and *Navsari Province Collection* by Raybahadur Desai, Navsari was referred to as "Navsarika" during 669 A.D. Later, Navsarika became known as Navsari.[6]

In the eleventh century, Brahmins and Jains lived in the middle of town, signifying their status as respected people of the upper classes. During Chaluk ruling, Navsari was a political center of the administrative branch. The reign of Karan Vaghela (1304 A.D.) ended, and Muslim rulers came to Gujarat. During this period, the Muslim population increased, as Muslims started occupying Kaji Street, Motvad, Pirmaholla, Khatkivad, Vorvad, Kumbharvad, and Kadiyavad. During Mahamad Begdas' rule (1476 A.D.), the Makdum Shah Pir Cemetery was built on the south side of Navsari. Most of the Muslim population still lives in this section of Navsari.

In the development of Navsari, the Parsi community is the most notable. In the eighth century they came to Navsari from Iran to save their religious beliefs and subsequently mixed with various other communities. This small but peaceful, prudent, and noble community has given great contributions to the economical, social, and cultural development of Navsari and India at large. Dadabhai Navarojee and R.D. Tata are two men revered because of their contributions to the political and econom-

The center street of Navsari.

ical sectors of India. *Tarota bazar* and its surrounding area are still occupied by this community.

During Akbar's rule (1573), Mogul rulers took over most of Gujarat except Navsari. In 1618 Kekobad Maherjee took charge of collecting revenue from King Jahangir, son of King Akbar. Then came Pilujee Gayakwad and started Gayakwadi ruling to this town. They installed their offices in Junathana area and made Navsari one of the provinces of Gujarat-Bombay State. They remodeled this city, as well as Baroda and Puna. Schools, park and recreation centers, libraries, sanitation, and waterworks became developmental projects.

There are various historical reasons behind Navsari's rapid development and prosperity. In 1858 British ruling began, as they built such facilities as the post, telegraph, and railways. Mafatlal and Darbhanga also established textile mills during British rule. The Navsari Cotton Mill, Tata Metals, P.S. Industries, Gufic, N.I.F., and Naranlala Metals were a few companies that provided the main source of employment around Navsari. Wealthy farming also attributed to development. J.R.D. Tata made generous donations for schools, colleges, hospitals, and libraries in Navsari. Navsari Rotary and Lions International Institution were established during British rule.

The diamond business is currently one of the major businesses in Navsari, providing employment to surrounding communities and boosting local businesses. Shree Ardesor Desai was the pioneer of the Navsari Electric Supply Co. (1923). At that time, amongst a population of 20,000, he had only sixty-eight customers who could afford to pay for electricity!

Today, the estimated population of Navsari *talukas* totals 306,846.[7] The Navsari Nagar Palika, Dudhia Talab, Tata Hall, Bal kridangan (children's playgrounds), vegetable markets, shopping centers, colleges, and hospitals are a few of the many sites and attractions of Navsari. The J.C. Lalit Art Center, Uday Art, and Mahefil are active cultural institutions. Navsari takes pride in community harmony, having had no incidences of communal riots in memory (except minor communal tension in

2001). Jain, Hindu, Punjabi, Muslim, Christian, and Parsi all live together peaceful-ly in this town. Patels are mostly visitors to this town from around the world.

Navsari has inspired many poets and writers throughout the years. Rustam Masani, R.V. Desai, Manibhai Trivedi, Jahangir Desai, Saiyadalli, Jayant Joshi, Takhallus, A.K. Trivedi (author of several books) first Principal Garda College, Navsari, Hushnus, Ranchhodjee Paragjee, Chandrakant Pandya, and R.K. Mehta were a few among many who helped build Navsari culturally and historically. There are very few countries in which we cannot find non-resident Patels from the Navsari district, and all of them take pride in their roots.[8]

Bulsar District

Bulsar district consists of eight *talukas*: Bulsar, Pardi, Umarganwe, Gandevi, Chikhli, Vansda, Dharampur, and Navsari (which became a separate district-county in October 1997). According to the 1981 Census of India, there were 1,385,000 village residents (78%) in Bulsar district, and 388,862 people (22%) were city residents. (see Appendix C, Tables A and B for comparable data and discussion of Bulsar district's facilities and population).

Village Life in Gujarat

As the first rays of sun stretch along the fields of cotton, rice, or sugar cane and light up the more than one thousand villages of these districts, the inhabitants of each household are already waking. While women prepare breakfast (*rotla, kadi, and shak*), sweep the house, and wash pots, men return from fields where they may have stayed up all night to guard against animals and to tend their crops, watering the rice or sugar cane. The scene is alive with noise as people call loudly to each other, children cry, and dogs bark. For breakfast, even the poorest make do with a flat round of mil-let bread with tea.

"Jhupadi's" farm workers huts on the outskirts of the villages.

The village houses are constructed of roughly hewn stone and mud. Those of the higher castes have tiled roofs and floors. Some even have stone or marble pillars surrounding a sunken area beneath the open sky, where people wash and bathe. Some farmers have indulged in home improvements: extending their houses, new rooms for buffaloes, new tile roofs, open kitchens, separate rooms for individual family members, and in-door toilets, which were once considered unacceptable for sanitary and religious reasons.

On the edge of village, the mud houses of the *rathods* and *harijans* are thatched with dried grass. Their interiors are dark and small. Their owners have no land, or may have very little land of their own and must work themselves out for a very small daily wage to those landowners who need extra help in the fields.

Women working the rice fields each have their own unique technique of planting rice bushes.

Each section of the village has its own well. In the center stands the temple, and at the end there may be a *choro* and the banyan tree under which the village elders and youth, day to evening, just sit talking and killing time. There may be a small shop in the village to provide basic foodstuffs and cutlery supplies.

Paths radiating out from the village reach the secondary school, the pond for washing clothes, and the farming plots that resemble a patchwork quilt. A bullock cart belonging to the richer farmers is loaded with melons or vegetables, bound for cities ten to fifteen kilometers away. The poor women of the village carry hew-loads of kindling or vegetables to sell to households in town.

It is towards the end of the monsoon season (June to September)—a busy time of the year, and although the first rains were late, they came in sufficient abundance for the villagers to be hopeful for a reasonable harvest of rice and *jawar* or cotton. Those households that have small plots of land are striving to grow enough food to last them for most of the coming year. With plenty of land, well-to-do farmers are intent on growing sufficient yields to enable them to sell a large surplus for cash. They are the ones who can afford to hire laborers from the lower castes.

Cows and buffalo's out for their daily grazing.

(Right) "Galli" A cart basic transportation of an Indian Village.

All the work is done by hand. Every one has a role dictated by age, caste, and gender. The younger children, male and female, take care of the cattle or buffaloes, while older girls help their mothers weed the fields of millet and older boys help their fathers apply fertilizer. The grandfather of each household supervises activities, while the female head of household organizes the communal food supplies. Those too old for heavy work in the fields are doing light work around the house, like growing fruit trees or vegetable gardens, or shelling pulses and cleaning grit from rice.

Despite this description, no generalities can be applied realistically to every one of India's villages. The fabric of rural Indian life is woven from skins of half a million shades of color, every village subtly distinguished from its neighbor. Most villages are made up of many different religions and caste groups, which, although inevitably affected by the others, keep themselves relatively separate. Neighboring villages are bound together in many different ways through caste, belief, trade, marriage, and shared schools.

Many villages have enjoyed an improvement in the quality of life, for they have been affected by a range of government programs that have reached the rural areas directly. These programs—such as electricity, irrigation, transportation, building of roads, communication systems, and bank financing of tractors and other farming equipment, new hybrid seed varieties, and fertilizers—have made tremendous changes in most Indian farmers' financial lives. In 1986, 60% of the rural population had electricity, whereas only twenty years earlier, a mere 10% had this luxury.[9] Electricity brought with it the possibility of mechanized agriculture, even if only richer households could afford the new power source. Bullock carts still traverse the roads but now share them with wheels and rubber tires. Young rural men are beginning to wear trousers instead of the traditional *dhoti*, and girls are wearing machine-made skirts. Nonetheless, village life all over India remains attuned to the rhythm of the seasons, particularly to the onset of the rains.

Traditional agriculture has its drawbacks—among them, the drudgery it entails. The burden is particularly heavy for women, who have an onerous work imposed by the fields, the home, and the bearing and rearing of children. Husbands can at least console themselves, as they labor with the reflection that the land is theirs. Pride of possession colors their attitude towards the soil. "We have great affection and trust for mother earth," says the man from the farmer family. "When we are alive, it is she who gives us rice, gives us food. It is she who takes us in when we are dead. If we do not work the land, how will we get food? We worship the land. It is our life. It is beautiful. It is always beautiful."

These days, electric or diesel-operated pump sets are scattered all over the land. Tractors have replaced bullocks for plowing; bullocks carts have given way to trucks, bicycles to motorcycles, and even tractors to tractor-trailers. However, a number of agricultural operations are still done by hand.

Thanks to education and the new technologies, status is now increasingly often determined by income rather than by caste. Most of a Gujurati village is composed of more or less five castes: land lords (Patels), farm workers (Rathods), untouchables (Harijans), and some other miscellaneous castes such as barbers, potters, carpenters, and cobblers, represented by a few families. They each have their own *jatis*.

Lives and Traditions of Patels in India and in the U.S.

In India groups such as the Patels are accustomed to the lifestyle that included living in a village, as well as living in a joint household. Upon migration to the U.S., some of the traditional aspects of their life have changed. Farming, for example, is not the primary means for making a living as it was in India. The Patels live in larger, more scattered communities, as opposed to the villages where one could have face-to-face communications with fellow Patels everyday. Also, language, education, traditions, religious rituals, as well as dating and marriage, are other areas that have transformed from the time families were in India to their present time in the United States.

CHAPTER 2

PATEL MIGRATION WITHIN INDIA

Traditional accounts indicate that the Patels of Gujarat are descendants of Aryans. Therefore, the history of the Aryans is in essence the history of the Patidar of Gujarat. (See Appendix D) The Aryans lived in the highlands of Persia in Central Asia around 2000 B.C. One group of Aryans migrated towards Europe, a second group migrated towards Iran, and a third group entered India through Afghanistan and settled in the Punjab.[10]

Hardworking and resourceful people, this group quickly learned farming and animal husbandry, rearing cattle. Before long they were happy, prosperous, and culturally advanced, as the land was a fertile place for people to lead a good life. It became a kind of "stepping-stone" for a more evolved life in other regions. As a result, there was no conflict between *Dharma, Artha,* and *Karma.* Human life was harmonious and holistic.

The *Rig Vedas* describes "Purusha-Sukta," the four classes to which it was necessary to delegate the responsibilities to run an efficient community, for these very advanced thinking people. The four categories are Brahmins, Kshatriyas, Vaishyas, and Surdras. The system was not as rigid as it would later become when people were stereotyped (throughout the British regime, in processes such as tax collection registering) as belonging only to one particular caste. It was common practice for a Sudra to become Brahmin, the Vaishya to become Kshatriya, and so on. Brahmins were the advisers, preachers, educators and teachers. Kshatriyas were the defenders of an area, region or kingdom. Vaishyas were the tradesmen, shopkeepers or landowners, and the Sudras were farm helpers or involved in more menial types of work.

The Gujarati Patidars of today were Kshatriyas in that caste system. Those Kshatriyas who were specially trained to fight full-time and protect the territory were real Kshatriyas, and the rest of the Kshatriyas would fight only when they had to defend against enemy attacks. However, during peacetime, this latter group of Kshatriyas, called Kurmi Kshatriyas, subsisted on agriculture and cattle-rearing.

The Kanbi, Patel, and Patidar surnames have evolved over the years. Circa 3000 B.C. Bhagvan Ramchandra was the king of Ayodhya. His two sons, Love and Kush, ruled Punjab. The area to which Love brought peace and prosperity by proper administration was known as Leya, while the area that Kush administered was known as Karad. The Patels of today living in Gujarat are the descendants of Love and Kush. The Kurmis—inhabitants of the Leya region of Punjab—came to be known as the Leva Kurmis, who would later become Leva Kanbis. The Kurmis of the Karad region of Punjab eventually came to be known as Kadva Kanbis.

The atrocities, mistreatment, and loss of family members suffered during the attacks by King Syrus (600 B.C.), King Darius of Iran (518 B.C.), Alexander the Great of Greece (300 B.C.), and later the Shaka, Huns, and Tartar attacks on the Punjab, drove many families from the Punjab during this era. Chandragupta Maurya ruled from Bihar to Gujarat during 300 B.C. This was the time when the Kurmi Patidars moved from Leya province and Karad province of Punjab to Gujarat through Sindh, Rajasthan, to Kachha-Saurastra. Another group of Kurmi Patidars came to Gujarat Saurastra through Jaipur Rajasthan and Bhinamala.

In Gujarat, Adalaj was the first settlement place for Leauva Patidars between 400-700 A.D. They came from North India, Rajasthan, and North Gujarat. During the ruling periods of Kings Chavda, Solanki and Vaghela, these Patidars were happy. They were farmers and carried out trade with Khambhat by bullocks cart.

Around 1000 A.D. the Badhshah of Afghanistan attacked and conquered Punjab. He and his soldiers committed great atrocities on the people of Punjab. Hindus were forcefully converted to Islam. They kidnapped and raped many Hindu women, forcing them to commit suicide. Some of the women were converted to Islam, and some soldiers married them in the traditional Muslim style. Patel forefathers left Punjab to escape the atrocities of the Afghan king and his soldiers and to save their women. The people who left Punjab were Kanbis from Leya and Karad villages of the Gujaranvala district, Punjab (presently in Pakistan). Even today, there is a group of people of the Kanbi caste in the villages of Punjab.

The Kanbi people left Punjab for Marvad with what little belongings they could fit on their bullock carts. At that time Parmar kings ruled Marvad, and the fame of Rajah Bhoj was widely known. However, Marvad was very densely populated, and it was not possible to acquire enough land for all. After staying for a short period in Marvad, they left for the Kheda District, having heard that there was uncultivated land available; this brought them to Gujarat.

During the Solankis' rule of Gujarat from 600 to 1064, the uncultivated land in the *taluka* of Patlad was granted to the Patels when their forefathers made a request to the Solanki king. Land equivalent to about one *gam* (village) was granted to each family, and the Kanbi people settled on this land. Being hard workers, the Kanbis managed to cultivate the land with great bounty and skill. It was decided that a twelfth portion of the crop would be given to the king as tax in return for the land grant. However, the cost of collecting this from each farmer was very high, so the king drew up an agreement and appointed a headman for each village to control the farmers and collect their crops for the king. This land contract was kept in the custody of the elders in the headman's family. The records of the kingdom were kept on the *pat* (record or logbook), and the person who entered and kept these records was known as *patlikh*. This is one version of the name's origin: Patlik was shortened to Patal, and later became Patel.

Those who came from the Leya region became known as Leauva-Kurmi, and those that came from the villages Karad region became Karadva-Kurmi. Later, the Leya-Kurmi came to be known as Leauva Kanbi, and the Karadava name was shortened to Kadva Kanbi. The Kadva Kanbi settled in the northern part of Gujarat, and the Leauva Kanbi settled around Khambhat.

Because the people who settled in Gujarat were very industrious and intelligent farmers, Gujarat started to prosper in a short period of time. As time went by, the kings and the kingdoms changed, as did the portions of the crops given to the kings. The main industry and income of the kingdoms was agriculture. These growing kingdoms were sustained on the income from the farms, and the payments were eventually increased to one-sixth of all crops cultivated.

Between the fourteenth and fifteenth centuries, the king of Delhi, Aladdin Khilji, and his soldiers captured the Charotar part of Gujarat, thus ending the rule of the Hindu king, Karan Ghelo. Aladdin Khilji told his *subas* (clerks) that since the strength of the farmers was in their wealth, they should squeeze as much as possible from the farmers without making them completely destitute. He instructed them to leave only enough for the farmers to sow the following year's crops! Fifty percent of the crops were collected in payment from each farmer, rendering them extremely poor. Aladdin Khilji ruled Gujarat for fifteen to twenty years in this fashion.

Mohammed Bagdo became the next ruler of Gujarat in 1500. He took a third of all crops and outlawed any stealing. To improve farming efficiency, he chose the best farmer from each village and handed those farmers the bulk of the land. In return he asked the chosen farmers to improve farming, provide security for the village, and pay the kingdom on a fixed cash basis (*Bandhi Avak*). It was in this way that the tradition of giving part of the crop to the king was abolished, and a permanent land grant was established. Whoever had these titles to the land were called Patedar (another version of the name's origin), which changed to Kanbi Patidar and later became Patel Patidar. This way the Patel Patidar became the owner of each village. Henceforth, the Patel Patidar have maintained themselves as Patidar and have cultivated land by hiring farm laborers. Thus, Gujarat villages started again to prosper after these reforms were instituted.

In 1593 Akbar conquered Gujarat. Akbar had the land measured by the *Todarmal* system and established the *Vindhoti* system (land tax). Vir Vasandas, a Patel from a village near Kheda who was in charge of tax collections, held a convention to honor the mogul king Bahadur Shah, inviting all the Kanbis from Gujarat to attend. At this convention he introduced all Kanbis to King Bahdurshah as "Patidars" and had them officially entered as "Patidars" in the government records, thereby establishing them as proprietors of the land who had to pay fixed revenues to the government.

This is today's *Maheshul* system, which implements a payment share according to the number of acres owned by the farmer. When the Kanbis first came to Kheda from Marvad (one of the first villages to be established in the Petlad *taluka*, along with others), they slowly became over-populated, bringing about a shortage of houses and agricultural land. For example, in the beginning each family had about 5,000 *vigha* (3,000 acres), but when that land was passed on to the successive generations through the patrilineal system of the brother's inheritance, the share to each individual family became increasingly smaller. This, in turn, made the families poorer.

In 1666 King Aurangzeb granted the Patidar permanent ownership of the land. This law finally gave them the chance to work hard and make a good living for themselves. Since then, the Patidars stopped their nomadic wandering in search of sustenance and shelter. They settled in the villages where they obtained farms.[11]

Between 1820 and 1830, some of the poorer Patidar families decided to move from the Kheda and Broach districts towards South Gujarat. They were joined by Leauva Patidars from other densely populated villages and settled around Surat. The surrounding areas of Surat were dense forests that the Leauva Patidar cleared in order to cultivate the land. Houses were built from the timber of the same jungles, and villages were established. This is the manner by which the migration of Aryans-Kshatriyas-Patidars, which began in central Asia between three thousand and four thousand years ago, reached the southern Gujarat, Surat and Bulsar districts circa 1820. The surname "Patel" is, thus, occupational in origin.[12]

In the beginning there was a link between the Patidars of the Kheda district and those of the Surat district. However, transportation was difficult, and the link started to weaken. The main means of transport at that time were bullock carts, horses, and camels. It took ten to twelve days to travel between Charotar and Surat (the first railway came to India in 1860, with the route running between Bombay and Thane). Relatives from Surat and Charotar visited each other, but the contacts gradually decreased over the generations. In the end all links were effectively broken. From the beginning, marriages between the Patidars of Surat and Charotar were virtually impossible, as these events could entail twenty to twenty-five days of travel.

Between fifty and sixty villages were established by the Patidars who came to Surat. The group built between one to sixty houses in each village, and because there was plenty of land, they constructed large houses. The *khacho-vaado* (front and back yard) houses in Surat were large enough for each house to have its own well for water. Sheds were built for the cattle, and each had an *ukardo* for cattle manure. They also kept a *khari* (plain, clean place) in the *vaado* for bringing in the crops. All these facilities were incorporated in each house. However, in Charotar they had faced the difficulties of not having all these conveniences. The Kanbi Patidar were hard workers, and in a short time they started to live comfortably and happily.[13]

In Gujarat the Patel surname has been used widely for Patidars since 1400. Before that time, they were known as Kanbis. Out of Gujarat's 18,000 villages, there are approximately less than 10% of villages without Patidars. Patel, Amin, and Desai are the major surnames used for Patidars in Gujarat. There are around 1,500 surnames for Patidars all over in India. Most of the time, the surname of Patel suits their occupation and profession.

Five hundred years ago, all Patidar were farmers and lived in the villages of India. They did not begin to restrict themselves in marrying and dining until 600 A.D. Each group of Kadava, Leauva, or Aangana Patidar all considered themselves of the same ancestry, and no one was higher or lower ranked in caste, creed, or religion.

When the Kurmi Patidar moved from Punjab, they were worshipers of Sankar. In 156 A.D. the Kadva Patidar started praying to Umiya Mataji as their family goddess, and the Leauva Patidar chose Annapurna Mataji as their family goddess. These goddesses were the wives of Sankar and believed to be Energy and Power. The new temple of Umiya Mataji was built in Unza (north Gujarat) in 1865. Under the Solankis and Chavdas rules in Gujarat, these Patidar groups of Leauva and Anjana restricted themselves to marrying and dining only within their own groups. After 1413 the Patidars started to move from villages to rural towns such as Ahmadabad and began to adopt more upper-class lifestyles than village people. Village Patidars, impressed with city life, thought their daughters would be happier in cities when they were married. They started the dowry system to provide for these daughters in their new urban homes.

Mahatma Gandhi's personal secretary Mahadevbhai Desai once wrote about the Gujarat Patidars:

> In Bardoli Taluka, there are five main categories of Patidar: Leauva, Kadva, Matiya, Bhakta, and Charotaria. They had their own caste constitution and it worked for them. If someone has the ability to convince them to get the job done, he or she will be successful in that particular job. Bahiskar (boycott) is not unknown to them. If one is found evil for the community, he can be boy-

cotted for generations. Sardar Vallabhbhai Patel knew how to work with these Patels, and Sardar was successful in Bardoli Satyagraha during India's independence days. The women work with the men in the farms by day and do their housework in the morning and from evening to midnight. Women are polite and courageous. They are afraid of doing wrong and are religiously conservative. To fulfill promises and maintain vows are their chief qualities. Insisting on truth is in their blood.[14]

In India the Kurmi Patidar population of today totals approximately 70 million in Madhya Pradesh (Malva), 1.5 million in Rajasthan, and 1.5 million in Gujarat (14.26% among Hindus).[15]

The use of a highly sophisticated network of computer resources in Europe, North America, Australia, and Africa has allowed for the search and location of over 160 million names and address records of Patel households worldwide.[16] A Court of Arms research report indicates that there are 24,049 heads of household in the U.S. who bear the Patel name.[17]

Leauva Patidar

The Leauva Patidar community of the Surat, Bulsar, and Navsari districts has a history that goes back several centuries. Vadnager-Unza (north Gujarat) was the original settlement of Leauva Patidar. Some then moved from Unza to Adalaj, near Ahmedabad. Aladdin Khilji conquered Gujarat and ruled for about twenty years, during which time he collected half of the farmers' crops. This was well beyond their capacity to pay. The farmers grew tired of his levy and moved to Kanam, Charotar and southern Gujarat.

After Khilji's death Mahamad Begado ruled Gujarat. Under his emperorship the Patels were happy. By 1600, Patel families had become so populated that they had left only one acre of land or less to support their families. They moved to Surat and surrounding areas in southern Gujarat in search of greener pastures and spread out in more than 187 villages of Surat, Navsari, and Bulsar districts (see Appendix E). Although these Patels were originally the followers of Annapurna Ma, they are the followers of all Hindu *dev-devis* (god-goddess).

During the mid- to late-nineteenth century, the resourceful and adventurous Patidars began immigrating to South Africa, East Africa, the Caribbean Islands, and parts of the South American continent. It was not until 1911 that the Patidars began migrating to the North American continent. The first account of a Leuva Patidar coming to the U.S. is from *Marro Americano Pravas* (*My American Tour*) by Govindbhai Naranbhai Ukabhai of Ruva Bharampore. He came to the U.S. for both education and employment. Govindji Deputy was a well-known educator in the Gujarat state after returning to India in 1917. In his records he mentioned Mr. Makanjibhai Kalyanji of Bajipura and Ratanjibhai of Afva, who were also men who had come to further their educations while being employed as farm laborers.

These Patidars and their descendants reside all over the world, especially in India and the U.S. From my survey data, 2,903 families currently live in the U.S., 63% of them residing in California, Texas, Tennessee, Georgia, and Florida. The total U.S. population (with children) is 11,704.[18] It is estimated over 7,000 Leuva Patidar Families live in the U.S. Patidars are involved in various enterprises, including but not limited to lodging, engineering, medicine, science and service-related industries, everywhere from major metropolitan areas, to the heartland of small-town America.

In spite of relocation to a foreign country, they have not forgotten their rich heritage. They have been actively involved in local and national organizations, promoting cultural, religious, sporting, and festival events. In other words, they have brought their Gujarat to America.

Charotariya Leauva Patidar

There are eighty-one villages in Olpad, Palsana, Bardoli, Netrang, Navsari, Kamrej, Choryasi, and Olpad *talukas*, spread over south Gujarat (see Appendix E). Sixty-five percent of them reside in India, 22% in the U.S., and 13% in other countries. There are two regional concentrations of Charotariya Patidar Samaj in India: the villages on the east side of the Baleshver are known as *Balewshveri*, while those on the west side are known as *Choryasi*. The population of these villages of CLPS is 29,000. Forty-two percent of boys and 58% of girls are studying at the primary, high school, and college levels. In the U.S. 50 % (of 950) families are settled in New Jersey, Georgia, New York, California, and Florida. The total U.S. population (including children) is 3,092.

The CLPS have customs and religious ceremonies for marriage and death similar to the Leauva Patidars, since they have the same religious beliefs. The Charotaria Patidar Samaj Bhavan was erected in Gangadhara, Surat district in 1988, and there is one community hall in Bombay for the convenience of fellow brothers and sisters. In order to establish communication in their community, the CLPS publish a monthly magazine, *Ghadatar*.

Matiya Patidar

Between 1840 and 1850, some of the Leauva Patidar became Piranpanthi (followers of Pirana) who accepted Imamshah as their "Guru." The Piranpanthis worship the *pir* (the holy grave) of Pirana Imamshah, in addition to the Hindu gods and goddesses, syncretically. It is estimated that 90% of this *panth* is now forgotten. Once the older generation passes away, only 1% of the *panth* will remain and soon after may be completely forgotten.

The *Panch* (a group of five village elders chosen by the people) of the Leauva Patidar who were not Piranapanthi disapproved of this dual religious practice. *Panch* from fifty to sixty villages of the Surat district gathered many times to decide what to do. They ruled that those Leauva Patidar who were the followers of the Pir should renounce the Pir *panth* and be Hindus only, worshipping Hindu gods and goddesses. Whoever disobeyed this ruling would be made *nyatbahar* (outcast), and all relationships would be cut off from them. Henceforth, the Patidars who had gone on the *mat* (revolt) and continued their dual religious practice became known as Leauva Matiya Patidars and later the Matiya Patidar. They do not follow the orthodox religious, marriage, or death traditions of the Leauva Patidars.

In India the Matiya Patidars are located in Navsari and Bardoli *talukas* (see Appendix E). There are over one hundred families in Bombay and a few other families in other parts of India. Overseas, the Matiya Patidars have spread all over the world, but the main settlements are in the United States. There are 3,221 families worldwide, with 1,505 (47%) of them residing in the U.S. In the U.S. 73% are in California, Florida, Texas, and Georgia. The total U.S. population (including children) is 4,888. Only 3% remain in India; 22% reside in the U.K., 15% in South Africa, 6% in New Zealand, and 7% in other countries (Canada, South Africa, Zambia, Zimbabwe, Fiji, and Australia.)[19]

Bhakta Patels (Patidars) conduct their prayers with Bhajans before a marriage ceremony.

Bhakta Patidar

They were once known as Uda Bhagat, later as Bhakta Patidars, and then just Bhaktas. The founder of this religiously defined sub-caste was Gyaniji, a main disciple of Kabir. Gyaniji received the "Shree Ramkabir" mantra from Kabir, and he passed it on to his disciples, who were known as Ramkabir Bhakta Patidars—later shortened to Bhakta circa 1424. Kabirsaheb is the Satguru of this Bhakta sub-caste of Leauva Patidar Samaj.

Jivanji Maharaj, another follower and teacher of Kabir's philosophy, wrote about the Uda Bhaktas:

> These Bhakta will achieve their goal of liberation without going into or dealing with religious rites and ceremonies. They believe there is no difference between Ram and Kabir as the Guru is the one who shows the path to reach to the God Ram. This sub-caste does not believe in Kriya or Karma Kand (rituals). They do not worship any Goddess. They believe in (1) chanting the "Ram Kabir" Guru mantra, (2) satsang, (3) Ram-Krishna Bhakti, (4) absolute karma (work free from desires). They do not worship any deity, but they worship and sing Ram and Krishna's lila and bhajans. They chant and worship the "Ramnam" or "Ramkabir." This is a combination of having form and formless (saguna-nirguna) worship.[20]

From Kanam, Vankal, Charotar, or Champaner, the Leauva Patidar moved to Surat, Navsari, and Bulsar districts around 1620. They first settled in the villages Sarai, Dhaman, Teladi, Nizar, Sarbhon, Dighas, and Timba. These Bhakta Patels were involved in buffalo-cattle rearing and farming. They kept to themselves and believed in good behavior, good conduct, and good thoughts. Simplicity in life was their trademark. No smoking or liquor was allowed, and vegetarianism and cleanliness were associated with the *Ramnam*. They were soft in nature, so in the case of fighting or tension they would not take the shelter of the courts; rather, they could say to each other "Ramkabir!" and the matter would be ended. They also did not use Brahmin in marriage or death ceremonies.

Since the last decade, Bhaktas have also instituted more or less the same ceremonious rituals as the Leauva Patidars. Kabirvad, at the bank of the Narmda River in South Gujarat, is their place of pilgrimage. The late Shree Kalyanji Maheta, Rastra Pita Gandhiji, and Sardar Patel all maintained close bonds to this community. Bhakta women even went to jail during Gandhi's *Satyagraha* (non-violence) movement, along with their men.

Today, 1,415 (40%) Bhakta families live in the United States. Of them, 73% reside in California, Texas, New Mexico, Kansas, and Georgia. The total U.S. population (including children) is 4,341. Forty-six percent of Bhaktas have stayed in India (see Appendix E), and the other 14% are spread out in different parts of the world.

CHAPTER 3

FROM INDIA TO AMERICA

In the late 1920s an emigrant from Punjab to the U.S. had returned to his village and asserted that in America, a man could do as he pleased; there was plenty of land and money available to all. However, in India one could not borrow, as no one would advance him money.[21]

The queue at the U.S. Embassy in Bombay.

The development of the U.S. is a significant phenomenon in world history. It is an experiment in bringing together people of different cultures, histories, languages, and religious, and social institutions from all regions of the globe, to live and work together and to form a new nation. It has offered hope and opportunity for individuals to change themselves and to transform society.

Migration During 1900-1946

Nine out of every ten of the first Indian immigrants to the U.S. came from the Punjab, a farming region in the north of India.[22] They left India because land was growing

23

scarce. Farmland was being divided into progressively smaller parcels, as eldest sons inherited family farms, which is common in patrilineal societies in which inheritance is passed down in this manner. Younger sons, in response, became adventurers. Many were given the task of going to North America to earn money to help their families buy more land or pay debts back home. These immigrants had to travel first by train to Calcutta, then by ship to Hong Kong. No ships steamed directly from India to North America at this time, so Hong Kong was the true Asian departure point for these immigrants. There the immigrants left Asia and crossed the Pacific to land in Vancouver, Canada. From that destination the immigrants branched out to find work wherever they could. They worked in the forests cutting lumber, building railroads in the ever-expanding national train system, and planting and cultivating their own crops or picking the fruits and vegetables of other landowners.

However, Sikh farmers from Punjab were not the only Asian Indian immigrants who came to the U.S. in the early part of the century. Other smaller groups arrived as well. Some were merchants or religious leaders, while others were students seeking an American education. During school vacations a number of them worked as farm laborers. Between 1900 and 1946, there was a total of 11,150 Asian Indian immigrants admitted to the United States.[23]

Migration During 1948-1965

During this tumultuous period of American immigration, 6,474 Asian Indians came to U.S., and of these, 5,774 were non-quota immigrants, mostly wives, children, and other dependents of American citizens.[24] In 1945 President Roosevelt favored the "Naturalization Bill," and President Truman finally signed it into federal law, giving Asian Indians the right to become naturalized citizens. The law stated that once Asian Indians became citizens, they could bring their spouses and children into the country with them. Many families were reunited under this new law. In addition the law allowed 100 Asian Indians to enter the country each year. This was known as a "quota system" of immigration into the United States.

Period of Growth: 1965-1975

After years of unsuccessful efforts by Truman and Eisenhower, President Kennedy's vision of a system governed not by race of immigrants but by their skills became a reality. In 1965 a new law made sweeping changes in American immigration policy. The national-origins quota system was abolished, and the Pacific-barred zone provisions were repealed. A ceiling of 170,000 immigrant visas was established for eastern hemisphere nations.

This did not include parents, spouses, or children of U.S. citizens. Seven selective preference categories were established, four of which provided for the reunion of families of U.S. citizens and resident aliens; two for professional, skilled, and unskilled workers needed in the U.S.; and one for refugees.

Immediately after the 1965 reforms, Indians took the advantage of new immigration possibilities. More than any other group of Asian immigrants, Indians used the occupational and investor categories of the 1965 reforms to develop family networks in the U.S. Because so few lived in the U.S. in 1965, the occupational categories were often the only ones available. In 1969, for example, 45% entered in the occupational categories, 26.8% as investors, and 27%

under family reunification. As family networks matured, the reunification categories were used to petition for other relatives. By 1988 approximately 89% entered in the family categories and less than 11% under occupational categories.[25]

Since the enactment of the 1965 immigration law, the third wave of arrivals from India continued to increase dramatically. This pattern established in the years after World War II continued as professional men and women and their spouses and children sought out better opportunities for themselves. These Asian Indians were overwhelmingly young—three out of five were under thirty

Since the passage of the 1965 Immigration Act, many Patels have moved to the United States.

years of age, and one out seven was less than ten years old. Between 1965 and 1974, only 85,580 Asian Indians immigrated to American shores.[26] This third wave has contributed significantly to the stream of Asian immigrants arriving in the United States.

Overall, between 1900 and 1975, total 103,204 Asian Indians were admitted to the United States. However, several important amendments have modified the 1965 law, each of which has affected Asian immigration. The population of Asian Indians brought their siblings and extended family members, which make up only 9.2% of the total population.[27]

The following scenario illustrates how immigration laws since 1965 have helped Asian Indians and Asian Pacific Americans stay together when coming to the U.S.

Mr. C.B. Bhakta (sitting on far left, third row from the bottom on next page), a bacteriologist, came to the U.S. in 1956 on a student visa and later received a green card under the third preference visa category. He was a public health worker in Los Angeles from 1965 to 1995. When he arrived in the U.S., his wife and unmarried children accompanied him. After five years of permanent residence, he became a naturalized citizen. Bhakta petitioned for his parents under the immediate relative category, for his brothers and sisters under the fifth pref-

erence category, and for his married sons and daughters under the forth preference category. These siblings and married children brought their spouses and
minor, unmarried children. Some of the unmarried children married here or
brought their spouses from India. After being naturalized, in the same way, his wife
filed for her relatives to join her in U.S.

Once the new law started to take effect in late 1965, Asians quickly began to use
their citizenship status to sponsor, along with spouses and minor children, their parents, and unmarried children over the age of twenty-one, as well as married children

Immigration laws since 1965 have helped Indo-Americans stay together when coming to the U.S..

and their families. The number of naturalized Asian citizens had at first been relatively small, but the proportion of the total number naturalized jumped from 11%
between 1958 and 1968 to over 25% during the next decade. Between 1981 and 1990,
49% of all new citizens were Asian. Obtaining citizenship relatively rapidly, they
have taken advantage of their new eligibility to sponsor non-quota and first-, fourth-,
and fifth-preference applicants. Those with permanent residence but without citizenship continued to apply for their spouses and unmarried children under the second preference. If one then combines this family reunification strategy with that by

Table 2
Asian Indian Classifications upon Admission to the United States [28]

	Family Reunification	Job Preference	Investors/ Others
1969	27%	45%	27%
1985	86%	13%	Discontinued
1989	85%	1%	Discontinued

naturalized citizens, for example, for the period between 1966 and 1978, Asians constituted not only 29% of all newcomers, but also a majority of both second-preference persons and spouses, children and siblings of citizens. In fact, half of all family members of citizens admitted during the years 1966-1978 were relatives of Asians.

In 1969 the majority of Asian Indians entered the United States on the basis of employment. In the 1980s, this decreased as more and more Asian Indians entered the U.S. to be with family members and less on the basis of employment or investing.

Table 3
Proportions of Entries in Immediate Relative and Job Preference Categories for IAPFM to the U.S.

	(1) CR	(2) AR	(1)+(2) FR	JP	NP/OT	No.of Respondents
(1) Head of Household	36%	22%	58%	15%	27%	157
Spouse	25%	63%	88%	0%	11%	126
Children	15%	73%	88%	0%	12%	108
Father of (1)	57%	31%	88%	10%	2%	49
Mother of (1)	43%	54%	97%	0%	4%	54
Percent of Total	**31%**	**48%**	**79%**	**6%**	**15%**	**494**

Father of (1) and Mother of (1) Refer to the father and mother of the first generation Patel head of the households.

The above preferences are according to the Immigrant Act of 1965.

Family Reunification categories: CR=Citizen Relatives (first and fourth preferences); AR=Alien Relatives (second and fifth preferences); FR=Family Reunification; JP=Job Preference (third and sixth preference); NP=Non-Preference; OT=Other preferences such as Investors, Visitors, etc.

Reasons for Migration

Seventy-nine percent of the Patels came to the U.S. using Family Reunification strategies, 6% used Occupational Preference, and 15% were Investors or Other categories. The great majority of these new Patel immigrants still migrate for economic reasons. As we have seen in the first chapter, Indian villages often lack basic facilities. India is not a fully developed country and cannot supply enough jobs for its educated people. In 1970, for example, 20,000 doctors were out of work in India. In 1974, 100,000 engineers could not find jobs.[29] Salaries are another problem in India, where even highly trained workers are poorly paid compared to U.S. standards. The big difference in income and exchange rates make coming to the U.S. very alluring.

New immigrants are also attracted to the U.S. by the success of friends and family members who journeyed before them. Even unskilled workers and uneducated people have better earning opportunities in the U.S. than in India. Commonly, these new immigrants will visit India in a two- to three-year period after their immigration to the U.S. and spend their dollars in India. The American dollar is worth 40% more than the Indian rupee. This big difference in exchange rate astonishes relatives.

A number of migrating Asian Indians originally plan only to improve their opportunities back in India. They wish to attend universities in the U.S. and then return to their homeland. Indians with American educations are paid much higher salaries than those educated in India. Many who arrive as students decide to become citizens. The economic slowdown in India, the lack of access to domestic higher education, and the inability of the government and private industries to employ a highly trained labor force have all contributed to the emigration of skilled professionals to the United States.[30]

Illegal or Undocumented Immigration[31]

An estimated 150,000 illegal immigrants who settle in the U.S. every year are foreigners who arrive legally but stay beyond the expiration date of their visa. However, according to the INS, some slip across the border and stay permanently.[32]

Immigrants come from all over the world in many different guises. They may travel by boat or jetliner with valid business, student or tourist visas, and then subsequently ignore the expiration date of their visa. They may even forge documents or use fraudulent employment visas in order to stay. They may contract sham marriages to U.S. citizens, although this practice has been discouraged in recent years by changes in the law.

Illegal immigrants take all sorts of risks just to get to their host country, whether they hazard border patrol, pass through dangerous tunnels, or swim across the Rio Grande. The new immigrant is often so anxious to work that he or she will accept the minimum wage or less, in jobs with sub-standard working conditions or health and safety regulations, while citizens hold out for a greater salary, or will not even take the job at all.

This situation is enhanced by the new "Free Trade Zones" and other tax-free international labor zones meant to allow companies to take advantage of cheaper labor. For example, the relative cost per unit of software developed (allowing for a program's size and complexity) in India is about $125. This makes India the cheapest place in the world for software companies. The most expensive country is Japan at $1,600, and the U.S. is intermediate at $1,000.[33] Thus, the presence of immigrants and/or cheap labor affects the larger economy.

Sam Patel, who came here by crossing the Mexican border, stated: "It's very simple. The bosses look for the cheaper laborer. Everyone knows the situations with illegals, and the bosses know it too. The illegal person will work for whatever they are offered."[34]

2

HOW FAR DID THEY FLY?

CHAPTER 4

SETTLEMENT, ENTREPRENEURSHIP, AND BUSINESS

How far did they fly? Five and a half thousand, as the crow flies or: from Indianness to Englishness, an immeasurable distance; or, not very far at all, because they rose from one great city and fell to another.[35]

—Salman Rushdie, *The Satanic Verses*

How have Indians woven a tapestry of success across so many countries? The advantage of taking over the commercial outposts of the old British Empire after independence was achieved is one explanation. Facility with English and hard work are also important. Indians come from tight-knit communities that are both supportive and competitive. They find niches of opportunity among thousands of different parts that make up economies, or develop ways to coax more out of businesses—like motels and corner stores—which less patient entrepreneurs have disdained.[36] Indians have also prospered in corporate America. There are senior Indian executives at Citicorp, Ford Motors, and Novell Company.

Turn off nearly any major American highway, and you are likely to encounter Indian hospitality at a good price. Approximately 40% of all U.S. motels are owned by Indian Americans, who are the dominant ethnic group in what is known as the small-lodgings business establishments with fifty rooms or fewer.[37] They also run many franchises for larger chains like Days Inn and Holiday Inn. A few operate on an even larger scale, like H. P. Rama, who opened a 170-room hotel in Orlando, FL, and B.U. Patel, who owns the 440-room Clarion Hotel in San Francisco.

More than 100 Asian Americans from all corners of the U.S. assembled on the evening of 14 September 1996 for a special dinner and reception honoring President Bill Clinton. The event, organized by the Democratic National Committee, was part of a two-day Indian American conference to raise Asian American political consciousness and to create a unified presence on Capital Hill. Senator Kennedy was present and commended the AAHOA (Asian American Hotel Owners Association) for working so hard to actualize the "American Dream" and indicated that we should be very proud of our successes.

In a letter to AAHOA, in response to their attendance at the Washington conference, President Clinton wrote:

Asian Americans want to fulfill the American dream of owning their own businesses. Through the hard work, commitment and dedication of Asian Americans, many of these businesses have flourished into multi-million dollar ventures. . . Asian American-owned businesses have contributed to the economy and have created new jobs in communications, medicine, technology and the hospitality business. Asian Americans now own over 50 % of the economy lodging sector. Asian American businesses are growing rapidly and will play a major role in the American economy as we approach the 21st century. Asian Americans understand the meaning of community; it is a characteristic rooted in their culture and heritage. This community has become a highly recognized political voice and economic force in this country.[38]

Before 1917 immigrants from India were primarily agricultural workers from Punjab who spoke little English and lacked other employment skills. During the 1950s and 1960s, fewer Indian unskilled laborers migrated, while more and more professionals and their families left India for the U.S. While the "brain drain" already began prior to 1965, the immigration law changed and accelerated this movement. In 1967 over 50% of Indians in the U.S. came from the professional classes. In 1969 the percentage of Indians who came to the U.S. on professional class preferences declined to under 50%.[39] By 1985 the share was under 20%.[40]

Although most Indians who came to U.S. in the 1960s and 1970s were professionals, later arrivals were not as well educated. In 1980, 48.5% of all Indo-Americans held managerial and professional positions; by 1990, their proportion had dropped to 43.6%. Many new Indian immigrants, who qualified for entry under the family-sponsorship category, came from small towns or the countryside. These immigrants represent a vast spectrum of economic and professional backgrounds and work in a variety of jobs. They also have developed their own specialized niches, virtually monopolizing certain businesses or professions and slowly changing the commercial, political, and cultural profiles of the cities in which they live.

The common thread linking all immigrant work niches is the "insider's edge" on the profession. Recruitment through one's ethnic network is one of the most efficient ways for an employer to get workers. Ethnic labor, in particular family labor, is cheap and easily exploited. For example, the operation of the smaller hotels and motels, as well as restaurants and grocery stores, relies extensively upon women—often the wives and sisters of owners—who do all the work of cleaning rooms, laundering sheets and towels, and attending the hotel desk.

Additionally, in these niches, there are no linguistic, cultural, or discriminatory barriers to overcome. For example, in New York City, which has an Indo-American population of 140,985, Indian Americans have a virtual monopoly on newsstands.[41] Other small business preferences for Indo-Americans and Pakistanis in New York and California include the operation of 7-11 stores.

Hotels owned range from decrepit downtown residential hotels, to motel chains such as Days Inn and Best Western, to isolated properties on interstate routes. Perhaps a thousand of the hotel and motel owners are originally from East Africa, people who migrated either to the U.S. or to Great Britain when Indians were expelled from Uganda. As British passport holders, some of them migrated first to Britain, where they established small businesses such as grocery stores, and then to the U.S., bringing their investment capital with them. Other direct immigrants from India to the U.S. have entered the lodging business after investing savings from white-collar professional jobs, such as in pharmacy or engineering, because they did not perceive opportunities for economic mobility for themselves. And in particular, on the West Coast, many who had degrees in construction or engineering have started construction companies along with their hotel-motel businesses.

There are sectors where the recent rapid increase in Asian Indian presence is a result of prior experience. Gujarati Jains have controlled the South Asian diamond trade for centuries in India. In the U.S. they form the second largest ethnic group, after the Hasidic Jews, in the New York Diamond District. After agriculture, gas stations have been another major area of investment and employment for many Punjabis. In New York City the Department of Consumer Affairs estimates that 40% of the city's gas stations are owned and operated by South Asians. Though there are some white-collar professionals who own these gas stations, many of the Sikh Punjabi gas station owners and operators are either from farming backgrounds or from working-class backgrounds in India.[42]

This type of class and educational background reflects, to some extent, the changes in the pattern of immigration from South Asia. While low English proficiency is probably the single largest barrier facing recent immigrants, their job options are also constrained by the level of schooling and job skills they bring from their native country. A significant number of Asian immigrants come from professional or managerial classes in Asia, but there are equally large numbers who migrate with low levels of schooling and job skills.

Pioneers

In the beginning of twentieth century in North America, Punjabis were the first immigrants from India. They worked hard in the lumber and railway industries and later became landholders and farmers in Yuba City. After 1920, a few Patidars came to North America. During this period there were about 3,000 Punjabis but hardly any Gujaratis in North America.

The following section describes some of those early pioneers who made their way to North America to establish a community outside their homeland.

Kanjibhai Manchhubhai Desai

Kanjibhai came from Dighas, Surat, and left India at a young age in 1922. He started from Bombay to Brazil and then went to Trinidad. He was accompanied by Nanalal Patel, who came from Khara Butawada, also in Surat. From Mexico, they illegally entered the U.S. in 1923. They worked in Punjabi farms in Sacramento and in the Yuba City area for twenty cents per hour for about twenty years. There were a few other Gujaratis who came during the 1930s. The weather, hard work, and the economic depression in the U.S. disheartened them, and majority of them returned to India.

Kanjibhai bought his first hotel in Sacramento. Unfortunately, Kanjibhai suffered paralysis and had to move to San Francisco for medical treatment. Since he needed to stay in a hotel in San Francisco and pay rent, he decided to buy or lease a hotel in San Francisco. He and Nanalal Patel were the first Patels who leased a hotel in San Francisco. Later, they bought three hotels, but because of poor business, they had to relinquish the hotels to their original owners. Meanwhile, Kanji and Nanalal leased another hotel named "Goldfield" in San Francisco. It became a historic place for them. In this hotel they hosted distinguished guests from India like Jawaherlal Nehru, Vijiya Lakhmi Pundit, Dr. Radha Krishnan, and many other ambassadors from India. Nanalal Patel later went back to Sacramento, where he bought the Congress Hotel there.

Bhikhu

Bhikhu known as D. Lal, one of the early Indo American Patel hotel and hospitality entrepreneurs along the west coast in the 40's, began a tradition that continues today.

This is a story of a man from a small Indian village who grew up in the U.S. and died in 1996 at the age of 89.[43] Dhirajlal—better known as D. Lal or Bhikhu—left India on 21 January 1930 to embark on a journey to America. A friend smuggled him aboard a British cargo steamer, assuring Bhikhu that in a few days he would be safely transported. The steamer made its way through the Suez Canal and took port in Trinidad. For two years, he had to work at odd jobs and remained in Trinidad, encouraged by other Indians in the area. In 1932 he made his way to Jamaica. He became acquainted with a Bengali family, and with the help of this family, Bhikhu was placed aboard a ship, tucked neatly into a banana crate for the six-day trip to New York.

On the third day the ship suddenly drew into port. A Bengali man found Bhikhu in the darkness of the cargo base and told him the news. The ship had developed mechanical troubles, and all the cargo would be unloaded. Bhikhu was forced to leave, and consequently found himself in the Spanish Honduras. He had to find some work on the docks in order to buy food. He wrote to his childhood friend, Kanji Manchubhai, who had already settled in San Francisco, and asked for help. Kanji replied with the name of a friend in Guatemala who sent money to Bhikhu. During this time, he learned a little Spanish and enough English to communicate. Later, he found a Punjabi family who managed a farm outside of Honduras. Bhikhu left the city and worked on the farm for this Punjabi family for two years, earning one dollar per day.

There were few Bhakta Patels who had tried to settle before him: Madhav B. Bhakta, Sitaram R. Bhakta, Dhiraj M. Bhakta, Tulshi P. Bhakta, Morar P. Bhakta, Khusal R. Bhakta (all from Orna, Surat); Bhulabhai H. Bhakta (Syadala), and a few others from Syadala and Derod, Surat, who came to California during 1922-1923. Due to the Depression and the rough climate, they faced great difficulties in the United States. Finally, they returned to India in 1930, but D. Lal was still on his way.

Bhikhu went from Spanish Honduras to British Honduras in a small boat, where he obtained a new passport under the name of Gopalsing. He then secured a visa to Mexico and traveled there by a small boat. Arriving in Mexico City in 1937, he met a truck driver who agreed to drive him into the U.S. for $75. In the middle of the night, Bhikhu was transferred fifteen miles over the border into the land of his dreams. The journey started in January 1930 and finally ended at El Centro, CA in 1937.

From April to June, he worked on a tomato farm, earning enough money to travel to San Francisco. There he found his good friend, Kanji Manchu, from his old hometown of Digas, and they enjoyed a happy reunion. From 1937 to 1941, he worked as a fruit picker.

As one of the pioneers, Bhikhu went through rough days like Kanjibhai. D. Lal joined the military in 1941 and left to defend his newly-adopted country. For four years he served the Field Artillery in Italy and Alaska. In 1945 he returned to San Francisco as an honored soldier and was granted U.S. citizenship. In 1946 he leased a Western hotel in Sacramento with help from Nanalal Patel. The twenty-two-room property furnished hot and cold water and rented rooms for $2.50 per week or $10 per month.

Bhikhu was very homesick when he met Dahyabhai R. Bhakta (Dighas), Dulabhbhaiai G. Bhakta (Asta), and Govind D. Bhakta (Vav) in their return journey from Trinidad to India in 1947. When they stayed in his hotel, he decided to sell his hotel and returned to India for marriage in 1948. He returned to the U.S. in 1950 with wife Dhaniben and daughter Gulab. At that time, it was a twenty-eight-day trip from Bombay to Boston by steamer. He then bought a hotel in San Francisco, and in 1962 bought the Desmont Hotel. During those days, twenty-three Indian families owned most of the hotels from Third Street to Sixth Street. D. Lal was the only one who stayed at the same Desmont Hotel for more than thirty-two years, until his retirement in March 1994.

Business Across Generations

Millions of family businesses, from corner shops to liquor stores to small motels, are undergoing the major transfer of ownership from one generation to the next. Yet if history is any indication, only one-third of these companies are likely to survive the second generation. Estate planners say family businesses often lack viable succession plans, as they become embroiled in family squabbles that threaten operations. It is a very difficult process because for years, the family and the business have been intertwined. When a business owner retires, the owners need income for life. Family businesses still need heirs who are capable and willing to take over. About two-thirds of all family business owners say they will attempt to pass on their companies to relatives, according to a recent Arthur Anderson survey.

However, children may not want to take over the business. "They may be resentful of all the hours mom and dad spent at the business. While children are marked for succession, they should become familiar with the business; they should gain skills and work experience outside the company," states Danco, an economist and pioneer in family business. "The aging generation has to turn over responsibility and authority to the successors and then get out of the way. The heirs have to be accommodative to each other's need. There will be chaos if they all can't get along," says Nagar, executive director for a family business in Houston.[44]

Employment

United States immigration policy is based on family reunification, so it is not surprising that the qualifications of immigrants have changed over the past decade, according to the Center for Immigration Studies.[46] Many find positions in family-operated businesses or work in service industries, such as taxi driving, until they make enough money to pursue more lucrative ventures. More than 40 % of New York City's licensed Yellow Cab drivers are South Indians, Pakistanis, or Bangladeshis. Many Indo-Americans are self-employed. The number of Indo-American-owned businesses increased 120 % between 1982 and 1987, according to the survey of Minority-Owned Business Enterprises by the Census Bureau. The Census Bureau tallied close to 30,000 Indo-Americans owning service businesses in 1987.[47]

Table 4
Indian Immigrants Admitted to the United States by Major Occupation Group, 1991[45]

TOTAL	Professionals/ Specialty	Executive/ Administrative	Sales	Administrative Support	Precision/Craft	Operator/Laborer	Farming/Forestry	Service	Not Reported
100%	11.5%	3.9%	.7%	2.2%	.6%	.4%	32.5%	2.2%	45.7%
45064	5188	1758	313	992	281	210	14678	1011	20633

Overall 90% of Indo-American Patels are fairly to very happy with their jobs in the U.S. When American families in the U.S. were asked about their satisfaction with their present financial situation in comparison with that of one year prior, 34% replied that they were better off; 33% felt about the same; and 32% felt their were in a worse situation. When parents were asked if children will be better off than their own generation, 66% believed their children will fare better, 25% think that their children will not, and 9% held no opinion.[48]

Table 5
Job Satisfaction of IAPFM

	Very happy	Satisfied	Adequate satisfied	Somewhat satisfied	Not satisfied	Number of Respondents
(1)Head of household	43%	30%	17%	6%	4%	81
Spouse	41%	22%	23%	11%	3%	73
Children	31%	30%	31%	7%	2%	61
Father of (1)	36%	14%	43%	7%	0%	14
Mother of (1)	27%	18%	55%	0%	0%	11
Percent of Total	**38%**	**26%**	**26%**	**8%**	**2%**	**240**

Motel-Hotel Owners

Hardworking Indian Americans started off with lower-end budget hotels, triumphing over prejudice and business hostility. The next generation is manipulating Wall Street to move on to the top end of the business ladder. Table 6 shows that a significant percentage of the major chains of motels and hotels have been acquired by Asian Indian Americans.

Table 6
Percentage of Hotel/Motel Franchises of Indian American Descent[49]

All Hotels	Eco-hotel	Knights inn	Econo lodge	Days inn	Roadway inn	Comfort inn	Super 8	Travel lodge	Sleep inn
26%	46%	60%	53%	40%	35%	32%	20%	20%	19%

Tables 7 to 10 on pages 40–41, break down hotel ownership and other professions by IAPFM group; retirees, who own motels or other kind of businesses, often manage these from their homes, so they have given their home addresses only and business phones but not business names or addresses. Some of the working families have not given their employment status, but have also given their home addresses and business phones only. They were coded as "Other Business." The "Retirees" category also includes students and housewives. Table 11 describes the occupational distribution of Indo-American Patels in the United States.

Table 11
Occupational Distribution of Indo-American Patels in U.S.

Patels	Franchise Motels	Independent Motels	Total No. of Motels	Professionals	Other Jobs	Food Liquor	Other Business	Retired/ Students	Total Families
Surti	893	1388	2281	204	195	47	204	851	3782
Bhakta	277	756	1036	44	101	12	48	174	1415
Matiya	103	486	589	34	149	20	168	410	1370
Charotar	122	358	480	4	-	13	147	305	950
Total	1396	2991	4386	286	445	92	567	1740	7517
Percent	18.6%	39.8%	58.0%	4.0%	6.0%	1.2%	7.5%	23.2%	100%

"Other Businesses" may include motel businesses because some of the owners may live in the house and manage motels from the house but have not given their business names or addresses.
Professionals: Dentists, Physicians, Engineers, Pharmacists, Attorneys, Programmers, Professors, Nurses.
Other Business: Photography, Retailer, Travel Agents, Drycleaners, Gift Store, Supply, Donut, Appliance, Mail Box, Jewelers, Sportswear, Flowershops, Cabs, Gas Stations, Construction, Automobile Repair, Printing Press.
Franchises: Days Inn, Best Western, Comfort Inn, Econolodge, Super 8 Motel, Economy Inn, Travelodge, Holiday Inn, Holiday Inn Express, Budget Inn, Motel Inn, Knights Inn.
Food Stores: 7-11, Subway, Baskin Robbins, Liquor Store, Circle K.

Patels are very adventurous and courageous to take on these entrepreneurships. Perhaps they do not like to work for someone else, or their lack of English skills prevent them from adjusting to the mainstream. Whatever the reason, they have found a niche in the motel business. In this business they can hire somebody to take care of the front desk and other work around the motel. The entire family may work in different areas in the motel, and the whole family can be accommodated in the motel business. Luckily, the next generations will not have the same problems that the first generation faced, so they will have better prospects.

The new small business entrepreneurs are better educated and their businesses are more sophisticated than in previous generations. Richard O'Sullivan, a small business economist in Acton, MA, said that 64% of people starting a business in 1994 had some college education, while 16% had advanced degrees. These companies are less likely to be Main Street start-ups like shoestores or candy shops. "A tremendous shift to self-employment is under way," observes Bruce Kirchheff, former chief economist S.B.A.

Table 7
Business Distribution of Indo-American Surti Leauva Patidar in the U.S.[50]

Occupations	Franchise Motels	Independent Motels	Total no. of Motels	Professionals	Other Jobs	Food Store/ Fast food	Other Business	Retired	Total Families (Units)
Numbers	893	1388	2281	204	195	47	204	851	3782
Percent	23.6%	36.7%	60.3%	5.4%	5.2%	1.2%	5.4%	22.5%	100%

Table 8
Business Distribution of Indo-American Charotaria Patidar in the U.S.[53]

Occupations	Franchise Motels	Independent Motels	Total no. of Motels	Professionals	Other Jobs	Food Store/ Fast food	Other Business	Retired	Total Families (Units)
Numbers	122	358	480	4	N/A	13	147	305	950
Percent	12.8%	37.7%	50.5%	0.42%	N/A	1.4%	15.5%	32.1%	100%

Table 9
Business Distribution of Indo-American Matiya Patidar in the U.S.[52]

Occupations	Franchise Motels	Independent Motels	Total no. of Motels	Professionals	Other Jobs	Food Store/ Fast food	Other Business	Retired	Total Families (Units)
Numbers	103	486	589	34	149	20	168	410	1370
Percent	7.5%	35.5%	43%	2.5%	11%	1.5%	13%	30%	100%

Table 10
Business Distribution of Indo-American Bhakta Patidar in the U.S.[51]

Occupations	Franchise Motels	Independent Motels	Total no. of Motels	Professionals	Other Jobs	Food Store/ Fast food	Other Business	Retired	Total Families (Units)
Numbers	277	759	1036	44	101	12	48	174	1415
Percent	19.6%	53.6%	73.2%	3.1%	7.1%	0.8%	3.4%	12.4%	100%

Among two million new businesses formed in 1993, 20% were one- and two-person operations.[54]

"The next generation will often not follow their parents, as they are trying something new. They have already dumped traditional professions and are not following the footsteps of their parents. But the Indian diaspora will definitely get stronger and continue to grow," says Ramnath, President of Blue Chip Technology. Dr. Kiran Patel, a Florida-based Indian American who operates a string of successful hotel-motels says, "With my generation it was the ambition to be somewhere, be somebody; we were not secure, but the second generation is spoon-fed, and I do not think they will be as motivated. The primary goal was to establish oneself and that was the inner driving force for the success of Indians here."

After considering her position in the hospitality industry, Hema Patel ventured to try something new—a fine dining restaurant with a wide variety of international cuisine. She says, "For us Indians it is the desire to be successful. Wealth is a driving force as we even in India attach wealth with status. Also we would like to provide for our children, and we network closely with other Indians and provide help, even financing, even though we may not be bosom buddies. We do not work with the 40-hour clock."

Prakash Agrawal, founder of the Silicon Valley-based firm Nevmagic, says, "Basically, Indians are willing to try out new things. It is there in any immigrant's blood."[55]

Among Asian Indians overall in the work force in 1990, 30% were employed in professional specialty occupations, compared to 20% of Patels. Twenty percent of foreign-born Indian professionals are physicians, 26% are engineers, and 12% are post-secondary teachers.[56]

Self-employment is still a number one choice for second-generation Patels, as it was for their parents. The medical field, engineering, sales, and management/office-work are also attractive fields for employment for Indo-American Patels.

Table 12
Occupational Plans of IAPFM in the U.S.

	SE	ET	BM	SL	HS	SR	PR	OT	No. of Respondents
(1)Head of household	64%	14%	4%	2%	6%	5%	1%	4%	161
Spouse	H/W	5%	20%	8%	21%	33%	5%	8%	24
Children	36%	26%	10%	7%	15%	5%	0%	1%	84
Father of (1)	65%	3%	3%	0%	0%	3%	0%	3%	28
Mother of (1)	H/W	0%	0%	0%	0%	0%	0%	%	2
Percent of Total	55%	10%	7%	4%	10%	9%	1%	4%	299

SE=Self-Employed, ET=Engineers/Technicians, BM=Managers/Office, SL=Sales,
HS=Health/MedicalServices, SR=Services, PR=Semi-Skills/Productions, OT=Other Jobs,
H/W=Housewife.

Patel Hotel and Motel Owners[57]

"Together, the future is ours" was the slogan of the 1993 AAHOA Conference in Atlanta. The "Patel-Motel" has become a cliché among lodging executives and customers alike. Within big national chains, the number of owners surnamed "Patel" is staggering. One company, Hospitality Franchise Systems, had over six hundred franchises: Days Inns, Super 8s, Howard Johnsons, and Ramadas managed by Patel partners by 1994.

Gujarati motels reveal more than an immigrant group entering a discrete niche. Rather, they represent the discovery of a vast American frontier. Patels took a sleepy, mature industry and turned it upside down, offering consumers more choices while making the properties themselves more profitable. Motels that attracted billions in immigrant savings turned into real estate equity worth many billions more. That equity, managed by a new generation, is being leveraged into new businesses related to lodging (manufacturing motel supplies); some related to real estate (reclaiming derelict

housing); and some are simply cash seeking an opportunity. The Patel-Motel model is an example of the way immigrant initiative "expands" the pie.

The Patel-Motel phenomenon demonstrates how franchising can turn an outsider into a mainstream player. The earliest Patel motels date back to the 1960s, although the phenomenon as it is known today traces to the 1970s and the brutal reign of Uganda's *Idi Amin*.

H. P. Rama (from the Sarona-Pera Surat district) started his business in 1974 with a 40-room independent in Pomona, CA. Today, his Greenville, South Carolina-based company owns twenty hotels in the U.S. and in India and a factory that makes bedspreads and curtains for motels. H.P.'s father was a dry-goods salesman in Africa, but H.P. went to school in Gujarat in the early 1960s. He feels his time is not being wasted.

None of this is new to lodging—big city hotels and luxury resorts staff heavily

(left) Castle Inn & Suites, owner Bharat and Aaskis Patel.

Anaheim, California
Disneyland Park Area

Comfort Inn & Suites

Katella Parkway

(left) Comfort Inn & Suites, Owner Prakash Bhakta and family.

from university programs—but they were practically unheard of in roadside motels, pre-Patel. By buying, renovating, and reselling, the Patels did more than establish a foothold in the industry. Eventually, they would remake lodging in America, changing a centralized, highly leveraged hotel business into the lean 'n mean hospitality industry. They did it largely on their own, with their own family financing and their own on-the-job training.[58]

"They own the inner states," says John Crow of Pannel Kerr Forster International, a real-estate consultant who has worked with dozens of Patel-founded motel corporations in the southeast. "I would guess 50% or more of all new franchisees since 1992 are Indian. Altogether they have something like $10 billion in assets. The franchisers know they call the shots."[59]

The motels about which John Crow is talking are not "fleabag" mom-n-pops, but the Roadway Inns, Econolodges, Holiday Inns, and Super 8s that Americans have been enjoying for years. By 1992, more than half of Days Inns and almost one-third of the Howard Johnsons and Ramadas were owned by Indians. The starter motels bought by the first immigrants had changed hands dozens of times, but seldom left the community. By the mid-1990s, Patels had a virtual monopoly on properties of fifty rooms or less. As Patels gained experience in the motel business, they traded up to bigger properties and slowly forged a niche in their own image.

Patel success forced full-service providers to develop their own "low service," "budget," or "economy" niches. Those niches developed niches: budget for the businessman, budget for tourists with kids and without kids. Patels not only saved by shucking their restaurants and coffee shops but also by hiring other Patels. Sometimes, employee Patels work part-time in the motel, eat and sleep on the premises, and study during the nighttime shift. Besides their minimal salary, the luckiest earn equity in the motel, which could be leveraged into full ownership when the boss is ready to sell. In this way, the Patels build an empire. Cheap labor become cheap partners, and then on-site replacements, as successive waves of owners pass through the motels.

A mom and pop motel, owner, a Gujarati Patel.

40 Beautiful Rooms
Free Color T.V. in all rooms.

(left) Samoa motel, owners: Mr. K.C. Patel and his family.

Backlash

In town after town, the "native" competition erected billboards or lettered marquees with words intended to lure customers away from the "ruthless Patels." Everyone knew that "American owned" meant "No Indians." Banks and insurance companies refused Patel accounts. Throughout the 1970s and into the 1980s, franchises were closed off to Patels. "Patel meant the lowest end," says Gerry Pettit, chairman of Choice Hotels International. "People named Patel meant cooking in a curry pot and a kid getting her diapers changed on the counter, a poorly run hotel."[60]

Media treatment was even less sympathetic. Ray Amin remembers small-town papers in Tennessee wondered what "tribe" these Indians all came from.[61] A rumor spread that Native American "Indians" were behind the motel-buying spree and were planning to burn all their motels on a

National Day of a Vengeance. "I don't like 'em," an anonymous motel broker in Newport News, Virginia told the *Washington Post* in 1979.[62] "They haggle. They maneuver. They do things not customary in this country." Another broker from New Jersey asserted: "They've got different business ethics." The *Post* reported that the U.S. Department of Justice was "actively investigating" Gujarati Indians on a variety of violations.

Patels were accused of arson for profit off insurance fraud, of using their motels to launder stolen traveler checks, and of using the same surname "Patel" to circumvent immigration laws. For a time, law enforcement agencies sought a unified "Patel crime family," modeled on the Italian Mafia. According to the *Post*'s report, Patel immigrants were accused of buying motels in one family's name, then selling paper shares to others of the same name, thus a allowing dozens of Patels to enter the country behind one investor's visa.[63] Justice department officials spoke of a "motel scheme," and other newspapers launched what amounted to a nationwide Patel watch. As daily newspapers peddled the "a Patel under every motel bed" theme, industry traders erected a solid barrier of prejudice.

Since Patel motels were often bottom of the price bracket, the "American Owned" slogan was seen not as a slur but as a legitimate survival tactic employed by moteliers being overrun by foreign competition. For example, *Frequent Flyer* magazine declared in an article in the summer of 1981:

> Foreign investment has come to the motel industry causing grave problems for American buyers and brokers. . . Those Americans in turn are grumbling about unfair, perhaps illegal business practices: there is even talk of conspiracy, (never clarified, seemed to point to a "Mafia-like pool" of investors) either in New Jersey or California, which allowed these "Near Easterners" (sic) named Patel to "take over" towns like Tallahassee.[64]

A drawing of a businessman wearing a turban, with four Shiva-like arms juggling strips of motel rooms, graces the jingoistic text. "Now the average person who saves up for fifteen years to buy a small hotel can't compete with foreign investors," complained one Chicago area broker, who nonetheless was not averse to earning commissions as a broker in motel deals. *Frequent Flyer*'s overall complaint was that Patels had triggered a buying frenzy, driving the prices of properties to two or three times their previous values.

That was not only bad news for competing buyers, but also a windfall for sellers. But that was hardly the point, as this racist comment suggests: "Comments are passed about motels smelling like curry and dark hints are made about immigrants who hire Caucasians to work the front desk," the article concludes. "The facts are that immigrants are playing hardball in the motel industry, and may be not playing strictly by the rule book."

Patels laugh about such portrayals today, but at the time they were deadly serious. Even now, anti-Indian prejudice is rampant in the lodging business. In truth, the reason Patels excelled in lodging was that the "American" was being done out of his sinecure; their competition in these early years was older, poorer, and quite a bit less educated than the Gujaratis. He or she (usually both) was also childless, at least on site. It was not Patel cash as much as Patel youth and family that made the community a success and gave Patels the ability to expand holdings quickly. "We bailed those old operators out," H.P. Rama insists today. "Most of the small motels, I'd say 80%, were sold by people whose kids were not interested in running motels."[65] The astonishing key to Patel success was not that so many over-qualified immigrants settled for work in motels. It is that so many over-achievers, many with established careers, chose to leave their professions to become motel owners.[66]

Hasmukh Rama says:

> This I never anticipated, but if you look at the fundamentals of American society it makes sense. The consumer likes new things, different things. A simple idea is bought by the average American consumer, and a hotel is no different. Take the example of restaurants: you have Wendy's and McDonalds, and Burger King and Hardees. Everyone is selling beef but still everybody is doing business. Because each has its own niche. People go for it. Hotels are not quite like this, and yet it works. I still marvel at that![67]

Table 13
Characteristics of Asian Pacific American Business Owners, 1992[68]

Have Entrepreneur Relatives	Worked For Entrepreneur Relatives	Required Start Up Capital	Loan For Start Up *	Borrowed From Friends/ Relatives
35%	17%	82%	21%	12%

*Loans from spouses, personal credit, and refinancing homes included.

A sizable minority of all entrepreneurs had some exposure to the business world through relatives prior to owning their business, either by having a close relative who owned a business or was self-employed, or by having worked for such a relative. When capital is needed, Asian Pacific Americans use a strategic combination of personal savings, personal loans, and commercial loans to raise the start-up capital needed for buying the business. However, Asian Pacific Americans also have relied heavily on family and friends to help raise funds, promote corporations and facilitate transactions among firms of the same ethnicity.

Self-Employment

The vast majority of the self-employed between the ages of twenty-four and sixty-four (85%) are immigrants. While the rate of self-employment generally increases with time in the U.S., the greatest increase occurs within the first ten years. The self-employed are a very diverse group that include not only the highly educated but also those disadvantaged by a lack of education and, to a lesser extent, by a lack of English language proficiency.

One in five self-employed persons has a graduate or professional degree, but one in six lacks a high school education. Less than two-thirds are proficient in English. Education and language skills have a strong influence on earnings. In terms of a combined measure of ability, 43% fall into the "high" category, while 25% fall into the "low" category. The typical self-employed person with a low income (under $20,000) has a little more than a high school education and is not proficient in English, while the typical self-employed person with a high-income ($70,000 and over) has a graduate degree and a strong command of English.[69]

IAPFM entrepreneurs

Most of the Patel families or their heads of the household came to this country with no money in their pockets. So how could they even think about starting a business, which requires substantial amount of money? Thirty-three percent of the total survey population answered this question. Out of this, 52% said they had relatives or friends who gave them the means to pursue the same kind of business in which they were operating. Twenty-one percent had work experience in a similar business, 11% said they had special training for their particular business, 33% said they were lucky enough to get the financial help from relatives or friends to start the business, while 16 % depended on the bank loan. "Owner-carried" loans were not included in this survey.

What enables Asian Americans to become successful entrepreneurs? Part of the answer is the advantages that Asian American immigrants have over other ethnic groups in establishing small enterprises. Among these advantages is access to "human capital"—that is, skills and education, financial capital, or the money needed to establish business enterprises—in addition to "social capital"—or patterns of cooperation among group members that provide resources. Asian American immigrants either have brought these major forms of capital with them or have acquired them after arrival in the U.S.

Having group members with high levels of education or specialized skills can help the group accumulate funds for investment. Unlike earlier immigrants who were poor and uneducated and hoped to return to their homelands, more recent immigrants from Asia are from a variety of socioeconomic backgrounds and often have clear intentions of settling in the U.S. to achieve success for themselves and their families. Many have come with strong educational and occupation credentials, as well as a life-long family savings. Of the immigrants who have arrived in the last ten to fifteen years, more exhibit high levels of educational achievement than previous immigrants. Despite the high degree of professional skills and education among recent Asian immigrants, many have chosen self-employment as a way to maintain their socioeconomic status, thus avoiding downward mobility. Using their education, experience, and ties to the ethnic community, they establish businesses.

Many Asian immigrants, like some European immigrants, also share the value of thrift and stress the importance of saving money for later purchases. They tend to perceive their present frugality as a means to fulfill future goals. Thus, for many new immigrants, low-wage menial work is a part of the time-honored path toward economic independence and the upward mobility of their families in the United States. It is the ethnic solidarity and mutual trust between workers and entrepreneurs, combined with human and financial capital, that facilitate ethnic entrepreneurship among Asian Americans.

Undoubtedly, ethnic entrepreneurship can create job opportunities that compensate for many disadvantages to being new immingrants in U.S. society. The disadvantages associated with immigrant status, such as English proficiency, transferable education and work skills, lack of access to employment networks in the larger society, and racial prejudice and discrimination, often block immigrant workers from entering the general U.S. labor market.

Indo-American Patel Families who Owned Businesses in the United States

Seventy-five percent of those who answered the survey question regarding what sort of business they owned said they own motels, while 5% said they own professional services, 9 % reported sales business, and 11 % claimed to be in various business services.

"NRI," or Non-Resident Indian, is a term that over the last decade has found a firm place in India's national vocabulary. NRI continue to make their way abroad, primarily on the strength of qualities regarded as "typically Indian": hard work, discipline, self-sacrifice, and thrift. The way in which Indians have invested in unprofitable motels across the U.S. and run newsstands in New York City or late-night groceries in London is widely seen as reflective of those qualities. One American newspaper wholesaler told the *New York Times* that Indians "basically replaced the Jewish and Italian merchants and they've filled a tremendous void because nobody will put in the fourteen- and sixteen-hour days that they do quite willingly and that you have to put in when running a newsstand."[70]

By 1986, it was estimated that Indians, namely Patels, owned 28% of the 53,629 motels and small hotels in the U.S. "In Anaheim and along San Francisco and in sections of Georgia, Oklahoma and Texas," wrote journalist James P. Sterba, "it is hard to find one that isn't." Sterba's explained, "The Patels were security-conscious savers, eager to own property," and were people who took advantage of low-prices and generous mortgage financing in the early 1970s. "A motel," Sterba pointed out in the *Wall Street Journal*, "provided property, home, business and employment for a large extended family."[71]

Those motivations are widely considered representative of the new Indian approach to business opportunity abroad—a stark contrast to the earlier image of the studious Indian graduate who went from being every American professor's favorite research assistant to becoming the hardest-working salaried employee of banks, laboratories, and research corporations. Though there are still Indian doctors and scientists of considerable renown (including two Nobel Prize-winning Indo-American scientists), the new wave of Indian immigrants is demonstrating that they, too, have the entrepreneurial spirit and are prepared to take the risks that their predecessors in the professional classes largely did not.

Only 10% of households from my survey earn less than $10,000 per year, and 8% of Asian Indians overall earn less than $10,000 a year. Annually, 25% of Indo-American Patels earn $10,000 to $30,000; 24% earn $30,000 to $50,000; and 30% earn $50,000 to $70,000. Overall 40% of Patel families earn $50,000 and above, while 35% of Patel families in the U.S. earn less than $30,000. Ten percent of the U.S. Patel families earn $70,000 or more. Overall, Asian-Indians have a fifth of their households with incomes of $75,000 and above.[72] Indo-American Patels have about a tenth of their household of incomes at $75,000 or above, and that figure does not even include their assets. The median income for Asian Indian households in 1990 was $44,700.[73] In addition, according to the 1990 U.S. Census, first-generation Indian Americans have a median family income of $52,908, the highest income of any immigrant group.[74]

The first part of this group, the majority of whom immigrated in 1960s, is led by a cohort of highly educated men who came to this country because of their professional qualifications, such as doctors, scientists, academics, and other professionals. They are now in their fifties and at the peak of their earning potential—their average annual income may top $100,000. The second segment includes immigrants who came to the U.S. in the 1970s. Both men and women in this group are highly educated professionals, and their children are college-bound teenagers. The third segment consists of relatives of earlier immigrants who have been sponsored by established family members in this country. They are often less educated than members of the first two segments. This is the group most likely to be running independent small motels, small grocery stores, gas stations, or other ventures. The majority are Asian Indian Ugandans who fled that regime in the 1980s and have since established themselves in this country.[75]

CHAPTER 5

SUCCESS STORIES

San Francisco was the starting point for Indian hotel and motels entrepreneurs in the United States. These families taught other newcomers from India how to run hotels, the day-to-day operation and maintenance work. They helped newcomers find hotels or motels for themselves, and they also provided financing whenever they could. San Francisco is a centrally located, convenient place for new immigrants, with good public transportation, tourist attractions, and restaurants where Indians can get jobs.

There were approximately twenty-three Indian Patel families in the San Francisco area in early 1950s: Dhanjibhai B. Patel (known as Vakil Kaka) from Umrakh, Dahyabhai R. Patel, Shantibhai R. Patel, Lakhubhai K. Bhakta, Santibhai Patel (Siker), Sanmukhbhai G. Bhakta, Valjibhai Patel, and Ramprtbhai were among them. Most were college graduates who came to the U.S. on the immigration quota act of 1946. They lived in San Francisco as hotel/motel owner operators. These families were the backbone of the Indian urban community, helping immigrants by providing food and shelter until they found jobs. Most stayed in their hotels while attending college.

In the field of education, many Patels who came early made notable contributions to India after finishing their studies in the U.S. and returning to India and/or settling in the U.S. These included Krishnalal Shreedharni, the author of *My India: My America*; Haridas Majmudar from Vyara, sociologist and biographer of Gandhi; Makanjibhai Patel from Bajipora, Ph.D. in Agriculture; Parbhubhai from Manekpore, who founded the Gymnation in Anand; Dayarambhai from Vanesha who earned a Ph.D. from an American university and established a sugar factory in Bardoli, India; Dahyabhai from Mota, in the chemical field; Ishverbhai from Tarbhon, who established a chemical fertilizer plant in Surat; Narsinhbhai from Vaghech, former principal of Khadsupa High School and retired Professor of sociology at Indiana University; and Gordhanbhai from Kuched, Ph.D. from Georgia University.

There are number of other Indian professionals in American universities in engineering, computer science and technology, law, and commerce. Shankarbhai Patel, Hasmukh Rama and his brothers, and so many others have their Master degrees from American universities and are in the multimillion-dollar motel business. Naranbhai and Bhulabhai from Umrakh and Chandrakant from Tarbhon are directors of Patel banks.[76]

The First Wave of Patels in the U.S.

Most of the Bhakta, Leauva, Matiya, and Charotaria Patidar who came to the U.S. between the 1948 and 1970 on student, third preference (professional based), or quota bases later became citizens and sponsored their spouses and relatives. This is the more recent first group who are credited for bringing today's Patel population to the United States. It is their educational zeal, sacrifices, and determination that helped family and relatives settle in the United States. Refer to Appendix F for details of these families who came before 1970.

Dhanjibhai Patel: One of the "grand patriarchs" of hospitality

Dhanjibhai Patel stands more than vindicated in memory as the grand patriarch of Asian American hoteliers. Having mastered the ins and outs of the industry, at age seventy-six, Patel became an institution in himself.

Soon after India became independent in 1947, many Indians with entrepreneurial drive also became free to pursue careers outside the country. The Patels, the Levas, and the Desais of Gujarat trained their sight on the West and East coasts of the United States. When Dhanjibhai sought to migrate, he did not have any problems since he came from an educated and well-to-do family from Surat district, Gujarat.

Dhanjibhai Patel was one of the original motel owners amongst Gujaratis in the United States. He was very fond of reading newspapers and learning something new all the time. In 1946, he attended M.T.B. College in Surat, when he read in *Times of India* that the U.S. government was admitting 100 immigrants on greencard-based quotas from India each year. He requested application forms from the U.S. embassy in Bombay. He and six of his friends applied for immigrant visas, sending applications in a single envelope. He came to the U.S. in 1952 on a greencard.

Dhanjibhai graduated from M.T.B. College and received a law degree from Puna in Maharastra, India. He started his law career with Mr. Hazare in a law firm in Surat in 1947. In the Baroda district there were several conflicts that arose between original farm owners and Mahesuli-leased land tenants. The act provided land ownership for those who were not real owners of the land but who operated or actually farmed and paid the *mahesul* of the land. He took initiative to resolve the problem by sharing the land between the landlords and tenants.

Dhanjibhai quit his job and came to California. In the beginning his friends frightened him into thinking that one had to work in farms in order to survive in the U.S. However, he got a job as sales clerk earning ninety cents per hour. Dhanjibhai also worked with the consulate general of India in San Francisco. During this time, he took some courses in economics at San Francisco State College. He also leased a hotel there and later bought an eighty-room hotel. He bought and sold a few hotels and motels in the Bay Area. Presently, Dhanjibhai is the owner of eleven independent and franchised motels. His two sons are active in the motel and real estate businesses as well.

In India the Surat Ashram taught him to be proud of hard work, self-sufficiency, and organizational skills. He has given his selfless services to his native village Umrakh with money and time. The roads, water works, library, and Gandhi Mandir are a few examples of his services to native people.

Dahyabhai Patel: Another "grand patriarch" of hospitality

"When I arrived in San Francisco," said Dahyabhai, "I did not know what to do. It was a new country, a new environment and I was at a loss."[77] But he was inspired by the success of another pioneer in the hotel-motel industry in downtown San Francisco and decided to follow his footsteps. Explaining the attraction of the motel business, Patel stated, "It requires only a small investment. And it solved my accommodation problem because I could live and work there." In 1952 he leased his first motel in San Francisco, a 100-room property named the Monterey Hotel. He followed that up with many more properties before buying his first hotel, The Empress, in 1962.

Several decades later, he continued to be alert and savvy in his business. He oversaw the management of his hotels with the help of general managers at different locations. Unfortunately, he had to endure racial intolerance, as he recalled that guests would come to his motel but leave immediately upon noticing that he was Indian. There was always a fear of violence in those days. However, he overcame, as Dahyabhai was a jack-of-all-trades, and this versatility paid rich dividends. "I was my own carpenter, my own plumber, maid servant, electrician, washerman and what not. It was a question of survival," remembered Patel nostalgically.

Patel's success had been a catalyst for other Indian American entrepreneurs. However, his success never went to his head. His friends say he must have helped hundreds of people of his community settle down in the United States. Following his success with independent properties, he ventured to take the franchising route to consolidate his business and increase profitability and growth. "In those days, no one from the mainstream bothered to deal with us. So, it is to our credit that the mainstream vendors and franchisers now give due credence to us."

Dahyabhai was always very active in the Indian American community. He was fortunate to have seen Mahatma Gandhi and Sardar Vallabhbhai Patel very closely during his youth, and he imbibed their spirit of service. He served as host to former Prime Minister Morarji Desai and India's former Chief Justice P. N. Bhagwati when they visited the United States. Dahyabhai was magnanimous in the land of his adoption as well. He was the first to donate $10,000 and helped to raise another $220,000 for the establishment of a chair in Indian Studies at the University of California, Berkeley. While accepting this gift, Chancellor Chang Lin Tien said, "This is the first cohesive effort by any ethnic community group to raise funds for the University of California at Berkeley. The commitment of this distinguished group of friends certainly strengthens the quality of education on the campus." Dahyabhai was a member of the executive committee for two chairs at Berkeley.

The entire Indian American community has also not lagged behind in recognizing his services. Lauding his contribution in strengthening Indo-American relations, former Indian Ambassador Abid Hussain, on the eve of relinquishing charge, remarked in a letter to Dahyabhai, "I am proud of countrymen and women for having excelled both in business and professions and carved out a place of respect and prestige in the American psyche."[78] The Gujarati Cultural Association of San Jose/Fremont, The India Club of America, and the Gandhi Foundation have also bestowed honors for his services to the community. He passed away in the year 1998 but is greatly remembered.

India-Post editor Jagdish Seth asked Dahyabhai why the Gujaratis, particularly Patels, although not known for their inclination towards the hospitality industry in their home state of Gujarat, are so extraordinarily successful in the United States. Dahyabhai replied:

The Patels have been in farming back home, and they been very successful, a driven and hardworking community. India being a largely agrarian community, the hospitality industry is not significant. Land is given from one generation to another, and that is where the Patels are in Gujarat. In an interesting way, they have unconsciously replicated the same model in the hospitality industry: the hotels are like farms—a place where the families go from morning to evening and work very hard, manage people, meet deadlines, micro- and macro-manage effectively, help others to establish themselves, and eventually reap the benefits. These tasks require wisdom in operations and the discipline to do the same things day after day. The second and third generations here are inheriting these hotels and motels, and so it goes. Patels have been determined; they have helped each other to establish themselves.[79]

Kantilal C. Patel

Kantilal was born in July 1936 in Akoti, Surat, to Shri Chhotubhai and Mrs. Bhuliben. His mother instilled very high morals in him during his formative years and taught him the importance of hard work and perseverance.

Kantilal studied in Surat where he passed his matriculation. At age seventeen he was called upon to join the family business in Northern Rhodesia (now Zambia). He joined his father, uncle, and brother to develop a retail and wholesale business in Monze, Zambia, which was to become one of the largest businesses in the province. In 1972, Kantibhai became head of the family's business operation. Under his guidance and leadership, the various businesses achieved record growth.

In 1978, Kantibhai immigrated to England where he and a friend established a retail gold jewelry business. Kantibhai moved again in 1981, this time to Los Angeles, where he and his brother-in-law, Maheshbhai Shastri, along with his family, started the High Glow jewelry business. Because of their unquestionable integrity and high standards of quality and service, the business blossomed. The company opened its showroom in Lakewood in 1982 and then in Little India, Artesia, where it currently operates. Their other branches of jewelry stores are in Berkeley, CA, Georgia, Michigan, and Florida. In addition to the jewelry business, they are also in the motel business. They own several franchises and independent motels throughout the United States.

Kantibhai is a very sociable and amicable person who is actively involved within various Indian communities. He and his wife are also very religiously inclined and stress the importance of parental involvement in the academic and religious lives of Patel children.

H. P. Rama

Born in Pera Harna, Surat, he is better known in the hospitality industry as "H.P." He has owned over forty hotels in the twenty-three years he has been in the industry in the United States. His empire is spread over more than eight states. He also owns a Holiday Inn in Surat, India. He started with a 40-room motel in Pomona, CA. In 1974, very few Indians own small independent motels.[80] H.P. is considered by many to epitomize the height of success by an Indian in his field. He is the only Indian American on the board of trustees of the Educational Institute of the American Hotel and Motel Association. H.P. recently donated $1 million to the Cornel Institute in New York for a scholarship in the hospitality field.

In reflecting on his career, H.P. relates some of the moves that contributed to his success. The decision to leave California, where the market was likely to become saturated, and explore newer markets was crucial. The next move was to renovate properties. H.P. bought several run-down properties, turned them around, and later sold them for a higher price. As his experience in handling and management grew, H.P. ventured into larger properties of 100 rooms and larger.

In the 1980s, H.P. and his brothers realized that they were losing business to those who were building new hotels and decided to venture into that sector. They are growing by adjusting very quickly to market conditions in the lodging industry and keeping their knowledge constantly updated, changing their thinking as per requirements—and these are the key to success, he emphasizes.[81]

Tusar Patel

Orange County hotelier Tusar Patel, owner of the Tarsadia Hotel, is close to purchasing the far bigger Anaheim Marriott hotel. He lost a high-profile bid of $12 million for Anaheim's Grand Hotel in 1996 to Disney, who paid $13.3 million. The Anaheim Marriott, a convention-oriented facility, is Orange County's third largest hotel. The deal for the 1,033-room hotel, said to be in the $80 million range, would be the biggest move yet, as Tarsadia positions itself to benefit from the expansion of the Anaheim Convention Center and Disney's *California Adventure*, a new theme park next to Disneyland. Only the nearby Anaheim Hilton and Towers and the Disneyland Hotel have more guest rooms.

Patel has become the city's second largest property owner after Disney. His Tarsadia Hotels and affiliated companies own several Anaheim hotels, including the 238-room Jolly Roger and the 254-room Conestoga in Anaheim. Tarsadia recently purchased the 400-room Hyatt Regency Alicante and an adjacent office building in Garden Grove a few blocks from Disney. They plan to convert the office building to a 279-room all-suites hotel.

"They are very successful, and they're moving upscale," said hotel broker Alan X. Reay of Atlas Hospitality Group in Cost Mesa. They bought a San Mateo hotel that now operates under a franchise agreement with Marriott International.[82] Tusar Patel's father, Bhikhubhai U. Patel, was one of the 1970s immigrants from Zambia (who immigrated to Zambia from India in 1940s and then to the U.S.) who started a small motel in Anaheim in 1973.

Naranbhai G. Bhakta

Naranbhai was born in Mahuva on 11 November 1939. After he finished the eleventh grade, he married Savitriben Kalidas Patel. He and his brothers began their first small-scale industry, manufacturing shoes with a Ghanian partner. Like his brothers Bhaktibhai, Chhotubhai, and the late Chhaganbhai and Ramanbhai, he too has an innate ability for business. He came to Ghana in 1957 and expanded on the developments of his brothers.

After forty-two years of being in Ghana and Nigeria, their industrial portfolio includes some eight manufacturing plants and two agricultural farms. Their product range is eclectic—from leather goods, soft drinks, and pharmaceutical drugs, to water drilling, among others. Collectively, they employ approximately 1,800 people.

Through the Gopalbhai Haribhai Bhakta Memorial Foundation, the Shree Ramkabir Mandir of Carson, CA received its largest donation of $100,000 from the brothers. The foundation funds an "eye camp" every month in Mahuva, Gujarat, where several hundred people take advantage of free eye check-ups and cataract surgery. Through the Memorial Foundation, a hospital in Gujarat has received Rs. 30 Lakhs ($100,000); Rs. 1 Karor ($ 335,000) has been donated to a pharmaceutical college near Baroda, Gujarat; and the Polytechnic College in Tajpure received Rs. 50 Lakhs ($167,000). At Amalsad Arts College, a hall has been built in memory of late Chaganbhai. The foundation has been a pivotal force in uplifting many in the Surat, Bulsar, and Navsari districts and in the Gujarat state, through several hospitals, water works, and other important social infrastructures.

Naranbhai visits the U.S. almost every year. His family includes two brothers who settled in the U.S. and his nephews. His youngest nephew takes care of business in Ghana, and Naranbhai works in Nigeria. Many of his relatives and friends were able to enter into business in the U.S. through his financial support.

Bagubhai N. Patel

Past president of Leva Patidar Samaj U.S.A., Mr. Patel came from Moti Falud, Bardoli *taluka*, and is presently residing in Asheville, NC. He came to the U.S. in 1969 for further education in civil engineering. After receiving his B.S. in civil engineering, he received his M.S. in structural engineering in 1972. He has been in the motel business since 1979 and is still associated with the Leva Patidar Samaj activities. He was one of the directors of the AAHOA.

Hitesh Leva

Hitesh was one of the youngest presidents of any community-based Indian association in the country, and his radio show, "91 Namaste," is an adventure for all listeners in the Nashville area. He was instrumental in the formation of Vanderbilt University's Indian Student Association and has presented numerous workshops on Indian culture, history, Hinduism, and the *Mahabharata*. He has put together an Indian American youth conference to motivate and unite young people. He plans to attend medical school.

By organizing a conference on Indian American youth, Hitesh felt that there should be some outlet through which the youth could interact, as well as foster discussions about youth issues. The conference organizers were recently in the process of beginning a national-based Indian American Youth Association and were planning to host national conferences with attendees from all fifty states.

Ramesh Gokul (Patel)

Ramesh was the President and CEO of Knights Franchise System, Inc., a subsidiary of HSF, Inc.. According to Ramesh, recent trends in America have steered clear of introducing family ethics and values in business.[83] This trend is rapidly changing with the realization that a social value structure should apply evenly in all circumstances if a community is to survive and progress.

Since Indian Americans bring with them the old traditions of close family ties and values, it is important for the community to remember that these values apply in the business place as well. Employees should be treated as extended family. At the same time, Indian Americans need to have the wisdom to balance this idea so that the benefits and merits of this "extended family" are not overlooked.

Chhaganbhai B. Bhakta

Better known as "C.B." in the Asian Indian communities, Bhakta was born in Sarai, Navsari. C.B. received his high school diploma from Navsari High School and his two-years associate degree from M.S. University, Baroda. He came to the U.S. as a student at University of Pennsylvania in 1956. C.B. received his B.S. in public health from the School of Public Health at Berkeley in 1958. Because his visa was not renewed and there was a shortage of suitable employment, he went to the U.K. in 1959, where his wife joined him. He worked as a scientific research assistant with Leed's Hospital Board, York, from 1959 to 1960. He served as a chief bacteriologist at Marsh and Baxter Ltd., Birmingham, England, from 1960 to 1964. He returned to the U.S. in 1965 and worked for the Los Angeles Department of Public Health from 1965 to 1995, until he retired.

Community work is the very significant for C.B. He is listed in the *International Who's Who in Community Service* [84] and in the 1979 *Noteworthy Americans*, by American Biographical Institute. He received the Gold Pin Service Award of Los Angeles County in 1986 for his twenty years of civil service. He was a major architect of Shree Ramkabir Bhakta Samaj of U.S.A. in 1977. C.B. was a treasurer for the Mahatma Gandhi Memorial Foundation of U.S.A., secretary of the Federation of Indian Associations of Southern California, and teacher of Gujarati classes.

C.B. loves to educate people on how to live a healthy life. Professor Chandrakant Patel wrote in the *Naya Padakar, Purti Edition* about C.B., "One who has unanimity with mind, word, and action is a Yogi. Union of good thoughts and good behaviors make a man trustworthy in communities. Where activity, place, and society meetings are centered at one place is Chhaganbhai." [85]

A. V. Patel

Mr. Patel earned a B.S. in chemistry from Gujarat State University in 1966 and a B.S. in chemical engineering from California State University, Pomona in 1969. He then earned M.S. in chemical engineering from University of Southern California and M.S. in mechanical engineering from California State University, Los Angeles in 1972.

A.V. has owned and operated hotels and motels throughout Texas, Oklahoma, Tennessee, Mississippi, and Georgia for the past twenty-six years. He also served on the AAHOA Board as the Chair of the By-Laws Committee.[86]

Balvant "Bill" Patel

Bill is a well-established businessman and hotelier in Stockbridge, Georgia. He was born and educated in India, and at the age of twenty-three, Bill started his own business after arriving in the U.S. with his family in 1980. Bill found his opportunity in franchised hotels and later became a major partner in a hotel management corporation, which owns a Best Western, three Hampton Inns, and other franchised properties. Elected to the AAHOA executive committee in 1998, Bill is a strong and revered leader in the hospitality marketplace and the Asian American community. Bill is a trustee of Shree Shakti Mandir of Atlanta and is the past president of the Peach State Volleyball Club.[87]

Jayanti "J.P." Rama

Born in Pera-Harna, Navsari, J.P. Rama is a top hospitality executive and pioneer of the Asian American community. During the last four years, he has held positions on AAHOA's executive board, serving as chairman in 1997. J.P. has been the president of JHM Enterprises, a Greenville-based company he created in 1978. JHM Enterprises currently owns and operates twenty-one hotels, consisting of 2,842 rooms, including a Holiday Inn in Surat. J.P., a Certified Hotel Administrator, oversees operations, purchasing, development, and acquisitions for JHM, which has become a driving force in the development of the southeast's burgeoning lodging environment.

J.P.'s other affiliations include past president of Leauva Patidar Samaj U.S.A., past president of the Vedic Center in Greenville, and past member of Rotary Club International. J.P. has received numerous industry and community awards for his professional excellence and his charitable efforts. In recognition of his entrepreneurial sprit, he was the 1995 recipient of the Small Business Association "Entrepreneurial Success Award." In 1997 he was honored by the Indian American Cultural Association of Atlanta for being a successful entrepreneur and for providing strong leadership in the continued growth and success of the AAHOA.[88]

Ramesh J. Surati

Ramesh is a successful entrepreneur, as well as a strong and dedicated leader in the AAHOA. Born in Malawi, Central Africa, he was educated in the applied sciences in the U.K., earning degrees in biology and radiology. In 1980, Ramesh joined his brothers at their newly created hotel business. Through years of hard work and a success-driven attitude, he and his Nashville-based Aram Associates, LLC came to own several independent properties in Ohio and Pennsylvania and two franchises in Tennessee. Ramesh was a Chairman of the AAHOA in 1999 and Chair of the Convention Committee.[89]

Pramod R. Patel

Pramod is a third-generation hotelier and a leader in the hospitality industry. He is a graduate of San Francisco State University, with a degree in business administration, finance, and real estate. Pramod entered the hospitality industry in 1991, and by 1999 he owned ten successful properties in the San Francisco area. As a devoted hotelier and a key leader in the AAHOA, Pramod has been a director-at-large and an active member of for the last four years. Pramod is actively involved in local politics and is a founding member of the Peninsula Gujarati Association.[90]

Priya Patel

Priya is an independent young woman hotelier from San Jose, who has learned that hard work and individualism are the key ingredients for personal and professional success. Born and raised in San Jose, Priya is the daughter of a successful hotelier. Her father, Hirabhai Patel is instrumental in teaching her the hospitality business and instilling in her a positive work ethic. Priya earned her B.S. in environment science from San Jose State University, while working at several of her father's hotels in California. After graduation, Priya took a full-time position with the family company, P & S Inc., a national hotel development and management firm owning properties throughout the United States. As a leader in her community, Priya advocates for women in the hospitality industry. "I think that women should stop blaming men and get off their rears and start doing something for themselves," she said. "There are many opportunities for young, educated women in our community."[91]

Pragna Patel

Pragna Patel was born in Uganda. When she was eleven years old, her family moved to San Francisco and purchased their first hotel there. Her family then bought a hotel in Reno, Nevada, where Pragna grew up and attended college. Pragna graduated from the University of Reno in 1984 with a degree in health science and biochemistry. Pragna is the owner and manager of the 43-unit Days Inn of San Luis Obispo, CA.

Pragna believes that while it is very notable that women have labored hard in support of their families to help establish their businesses, she is glad to see young women make choices for their education and career. However, she also feels that relationships are strengthened when people have more in common, and sharing a business experience with the family and friends increases the time they have together.[92]

Maganbhai C. Patel

Patel was born in Malekpore District Navsari, Gujarat, India. His father, a school teacher and farmer, raised him in a small farming town. He took part in the non- violence freedom movement in the 40s under the leadership of Mahatma Gandhi and Sardar Patel.

He went to elementary school in the town school of Malekpore and middle school in the nearby town of Palsana. He attended the high school in Surat and he stayed at the Patidar Ashram, a boarding house. Due to economic reasons, he had to move to BABS High School in Bardoli and graduated in 1951. After graduating from High School, he had to postpone college for one year due to the poor economic conditions of the family. He worked one year at the farm with his family and his parents had him married in 1953. He convinced his uncles to support his education. He went to Baroda State for engineering. After five years, he graduated with a degree in Mechanical Engineering in 1960. After graduating, he worked as an assistant lecturer at the MS University in Baroda. While he was working in India, he was admitted to Virginia Tech in Blacksburg, Virginia.

He obtained his M.S. in Mechanical Engineering from Virginia Tech. He worked as a Development Engineer with Black and Decker and later worked for American Standard and RCA Electronic Co. In 1970 he bought a small 28 unit motel in

Bordentown, N.J., under Patel & Sons, Inc. from his savings as well as financial help from relatives and friends. He was the first educated Patel to get into the motel (not hotel) business, while keeping his engineering job.

He advised and assisted hundreds of families in a way of financial help, management, maintenance, bookkeeping, accounting and other aspects of motel business.

Surekha Patel

Born in Navsari, Surekha graduated from Gujarat University with a B.S. in chemistry in 1970. Throughout her life, Surekha has played the roles of mother, wife, businesswoman, and associate. After marrying and moving to America in 1970, she worked as chemist. Soon after, Surekha began her career and life in the hospitality industry with the purchase of her first hotel with her husband Chandrakant; both terminated their employment and began their professional careers as full-time hoteliers. Through years of dedication and a focused mind, she played an integral role in building the family business, which has cumulated into twelve hotels, totaling more than 1,500 rooms in the Dallas/Ft. Worth metroplex.

In 1987, she served as Founding Director of the State Bank of Texas, whose chairman, C.E.O., and president is her husband. She has served on the Loan Committee and Board of Directors, providing direction to the institution, which now totals more than $100 million in assets and four branches. In addition, she simultaneously began a career in marketing at American Airlines, where she continued working for ten years until her recent retirement.

Narendra "Naz" Patel

In the 1950s, Naz's parents migrated from Khoj Pardi, south Gujarat to the U.K., where Naz was born and raised. After graduating with honors in 1976, he moved to California to attend California State University of Los Angeles. He graduated with a degree in management. He was employed at Walter Heller Financial Company for the next three years, after which he decided to go into his family business. Currently, Naz and his family own and operate several motels in the Los Angeles area.

Naz is active in his local Chamber of Commerce and the Kiwanis Club, where he served as president in 1996. He is serving his third year as a Regional Director of AAHOA.

Dhiru "Robin" Prema

Robin was born in Satem, south Gujarat in 1960. He moved to England in 1965 and graduated from Birmingham Polytechnic England with a degree in mechanical production engineering in 1982. Robin relocated to the U.S. that same year to pursue his professional career. Throughout his career, Robin has developed and managed 150 people in various industries. Presently, he owns and operates several hotels.

Active in his community, Robin helped develop the Apache Business Association, which represents business in the community, helps to improve business practice, and advocates crime prevention. Robin has been a Regional Director of AAHOA since 1998. He advises AAHOA members to diversify into emerging industries, to create a fall-back plan for survival, and to continuously learn new skills and knowledge for future success.

Bhupen S. Patel

Born in Sunav, Bhupen moved to the U.S. in 1971. He graduated from Chicago Technical University in 1974, earning a degree in electrical engineering. In 1977, Bhupen bought his first lodging, the Bakers Motel, in Griffin, Georgia. Bhupen moved to Spencer, Iowa in 1982 and purchased a Super 8 motel. He and his wife Sudha have been developing properties together since 1985. Currently, Bhupen owns properties of various brands. He has been active in AAHOA for the past three years. In 1992, Bhupen received the Super 8 Special Achievement of the Year award, and in 1996 ILA honored him as their Hotelier of the Year.

Pramod K. Patel

Born in India and raised in Panama, Pramod attended La Boca College, majoring in business. After graduation, he immigrated to the U. S., and at the age of twenty, Pramod purchased a small motel in Las Vegas. His portfolio over the years has included such brands as Hampton Inn, Days Inn, and Ramada Inn. He and his family are in a development phase, constructing Hampton Inn and AmeriSuites properties. Serving his first year as a Regional Director of AAHOA, he strives to increase awareness of membership in AAHOA.

Pramod is one of the founders and a trustee of Gujarati Samaj of Oklahoma, as well as serving as president for the past four years. He was instrumental in forming the local cricket team, of which he is an acting team captain and winner of two Southwest Conference Championships.

Chhotalal B. Patel

The son of a doctor and the grandson of a teacher, C.B. Patel was born in India. He received his undergraduate degree from Gujarat University and earned a B.S. in chemical engineering. C.B. has been involved in the hotel business since 1978, and he is the owner and managing partner of several franchised hotels.

Serving his third year as a Regional Director of AAHOA, he has been a significant supporter of its educational programs. He has been a director on the executive board of the Hindu Temple Society of Mississippi. C.B. is an active member of the B.S.S. Temple in Jackson, Mississippi.

Manu Patel

Manu was born in Surat in 1945. Upon graduation from the Institute of Agriculture in Anand in 1967, he researched for two years at the Development of Agriculture. He later devoted ten years as a lecturer at the Agriculture College in Navsari.

Manu's journey to becoming a successful hotelier began upon his arrival to the U.S. in 1979. Manu worked as a night shift desk clerk, while his wife was a housekeeper at an independent motel located in Little Rock, Arkansas. Today, he owns and operates several motels in the Chicago area.

Manu has been instrumental in encouraging the growth of the AAHOA base in his region through his participation at the 1998 Super Regional Conference and the first-ever Youth Leadership Conference, both held in Chicago. As an active member of the Surti Samaj since 1988, he organizes and contributes to various activities throughout the year. As a Life Member of the Gujarati Culture Society, Manu fulfills his commitment to his ethnic community.

Rajesh " Roger" Leva

As a former AAHOA Treasurer, Roger Leva is one of the youngest to hold an officer's position and serve on the executive committee from 1995 to 1998. He has been a Director-at-Large for six years, and from 1996 to 1998 Roger served as AAHOA's Communications Chair, overseeing the monthly publication of *AAHOA Hospitality*. He currently serves as Chairman-elect for the Alabama Hotel Association.

Roger moved to Los Angeles with his family in 1975. His father purchased his first hotel there in 1976. In 1981, the Levas relocated to Mississippi. After completing high school in 1984, Roger attended flight school for two years in order to train as pilot and also went on to earn a business degree. Roger moved to Alabama in 1988 with his family, working full-time in their lodging business and charting his long and successful career. Roger's corporation owns and operates several motels in the Southeast.

Bhavesh "Bobby" Patel

Bhavesh "Bobby" Patel was born in London and moved to the United States in 1980. Bobby graduated from University of Mississippi and did his graduate studies at San Joaquin School of Law. In 1991, Bobby founded the Hotel Investment Group, a company owning, operating, and managing sixteen hotels, and controlling 1,200 rooms over the years. Serving his second term on the AAHOA board, Bobby believes in educating the membership and is dedicated to increasing AAHOA's unity and strength. He is extremely active in local politics and the Chamber of Commerse, and is co-founder of the Fresno Gujarati Association. He also serves on the Holiday Inn Franchise Advisory Committee.

Dahyabhai V. Patel

Dahyabhai was born in south Gujarat. He earned a B.S. in chemistry and physics from South Gujarat University in 1974. A year later, D.V. moved to the U.K., where he married. D.V. came to the U.S. in 1975 on a student visa and graduated from Pacific State University in Los Angeles with a B.S. in electrical engineering. He earned his M.S. in 1981. D.V. purchased his first property, the Sands Motel in Los Angeles, in 1975 while still attending college. He later moved to Tennessee to develop more hotel properties. D. V. is serving his third year as an AAHOA Director-at-Large. An executive committee member of Leauva Patidar Samaj of United States, he also is a former Secretary of the Gujarati Cultural Association in Nashville.

Hasmukh "Harry" R. Patel

Born in Surat in 1944, Harry Patel prides himself on being a successful businessman and a true lover of nature. Harry earned a B.S. in dairy technology from Sardar Patel University, and a M.S in food science and Ph.D. in microbiology from University of California, Davis. Today, Harry is the managing owner of a Motel 6 and a Days Inn in Columbus, Mississippi, and co-owner of a Best Western in Mobile, AL. A founding member of AAHOA, Harry has served on the AAHOA Board of Directors since 1995. At present, Harry is president of the Gujarati Samaj of Columbus. In addition, he has served as a regional director of the Board of India Association of Mississippi for the last three years. Serving his sixth term as an AAHOA Director-at-Large, Harry brings with him a vast amount of industry wisdom and leadership experience.

He would like to provide assistance to all members, in collaboration with the government of India, in building motels in India and increasing its tourism.

Prabhu M. Patel

Born in Puna-Kumbharia, a small town near Surat, Prabhu immigrated to U.S. in 1967 to pursue his education. He received a B.S. in mechanical engineering in 1971 from Tri-State College in Angola, Indiana. Although P.M. worked for engineering and consulting firms for the following five years, he desired professional independence.

In 1976, P.M. moved to Cherry Hill, New Jersey to create his own hotel development and management company and to scout out new independent hotel opportunities. He purchased his first property in New Jersey while still working as an engineer/consultant. P.M. moved Tennessee in 1978 and purchased another independent motel. He has sold his initial properties and now jointly owns seven franchised properties in Tennessee and California. P.M. offers twenty-four years of hospitality experience and community service. He was an active supporter of the Mid-South Indemnity Association (MIA) and was the last president of the IAHA before its merger with AAHOA.

Dhansukh "Dan" Patel

Dhansukh was born in south Gujarat. In 1965, he immigrated to the U.K. with his family. He graduated from business school with a two-year degree in 1976 and worked for Raymans Electronic until he immigrated to the United States. After working for eight months in the electronic field in San Francisco, he purchased his first motel in Pulaski, Tennessee. Today, Dan and his brother co-own and operate several hotels in Tennessee and Kentucky. Dan was a founding member of the Gujarat Cultural Association of Nashville and an active member of the IAHA until it merged with AAHOA. In his new role as AAHOA Chairman 2001, Dan is campaigning for hotel owners to become involved with AAHOA and to take advantage of the association's educational, political, and networking opportunities.

Chandrakant I. Patel

C.K. Patel hails from Vaghashi, Gujarat. His vast hotel experience ranges from his first independent property in Commerce, Georgia, which he purchased in 1982, to owning and operating full-service Holiday Inns. Today, his corporation owns and operates eleven properties in the Southeast. When hotel owners of Indian origin were having problems acquiring financing, C.K. explored solutions and opened a community bank in Atlanta in 1996. Like his forefathers, it was his passion to help others that led him towards banking. The bank has increased its assets tremendously since then. As founding director, C.K. serves on the board as Chairman of the Funds Management Committee. C.K. has been as AAHOA member since its inception and has served the AAHOA board for many years.

Dinu Patel

Dinu has been active in the hospitality industry since 1981. Today, Dinu owns and operates the Advanced Motel on the Brandford, Connecticut shoreline and is a partner in five other properties in the Northeast region. His entrepreneurship is diversified into other businesses, including a few retail operations. Dinu has also excelled academically; he has a M.S. in organic chemistry. After immigrating to the U.S., he earned a second M.S. in biochemistry from University of Scranton, Pennsylvania.

Dinu serves on AAHOA's executive committee for a fourth year and retains his position as Northeast Regional Director. Dinu is an active member of his Chamber of Commerce and the Rotary Club International. He also holds an executive committee position on the board of directors of the Connecticut Lodging & Attraction Association. Dinu has investments and partnerships in several businesses in India.

C.N. Patel

C.N. was born in the village of Saroli in the 1930s. He completed his primary education near Surat and pursued his Bachelor degree at M.T.B. College in Surat. He received his B.A. from the University of Gujarat. Although he wanted to pursue his M.B.A. in the United States, his B.A. was not recognized in the universities. C.N. decided to go to Mumbai to pursue his Bachelor of Commerce degree with a major in accounting and auditing from the University of Mumbai. He received these degrees in 1959 and re-applied to American universities. He then got his passport and applied for foreign exchange for his M.B.A. studies. However, the Indian government refused to grant foreign exchange for his studies. Eventually, he arrived in the United States in 1973. He decided to stay in Los Angeles, where he bought a cocktail lounge in partnership with a friend and ran that business successfully for three years.

He has been in the motel business since the mid-1970s and has been a reputed travel agent during the past three decades.

Shankar G. Patel

Shankar G. Patel was born at Shevni, Surat, India and migrated to U.S. in 1969. He holds a B.S. in agricultural science from India and a M.S. in Agriculture from Alabama Agricultural and Mechanical University, Huntsville, Alabama. He worked in the mid-1970s as Cost Estimator at Vapor Corporation. Later, he became involved with the motel business in which he owned and operated several independent and franchised motels, such as Days Inn and Hampton Inn, Holiday Inn Express, and Comfort Inn in Tennessee. He was a chairman of Indo-American Hospitality Association, 1994. He was a President of Gujarati Culture Association of greater Nashville. He is a founding member of Surat –Bulsar Leauva Patidar Samaj of the U.S.A., which was founded in 1991. He, was given the title of Director-at-Large of the AAHOA from 1991-1997. He was a recipient of Cecil B. Day Community Service Award in 1989. He received an Oberoi Award of Excellence in 1994.

Dinu K. Patel

Born in Bajipura, Surat, India in 1930s. Dinubhai completed his high school education at Varad, India. He received a degree in printing technology from London College of printing, London. One of his children has Masters degree in Business and other has Master degree in Science. Patel has been in the U.S. the last twenty-eight years. He has been in the printing business for the past six years and in real estate for the last ten years.

Chandrakant B. Patel

Chandrakant is a native of Tarbhona, Surat India, and resides in Irving Texas. His father was a graduate of Bombay University, and his wife Surekha is a graduate in Chemistry from Gujarat University. His daughters, Shetal and Teral, are Physician Assistants (P.A.) and his son Shushil posses a B.S. in Business degree and Rajan, his other son, is in his first year in college. He graduated with a B.S. in chemistry from South Gujarat University. He received a Bachelor degree in mechanical engineering at Mumbai University. He obtained post-graduate degrees at Stanford University in 1966 in Industrial Engineering and M.S. in Management Science from Johns Hopkins University 1968. Chandrakant has been in banking for the last fifteen years and in the motel business for the last eleven years in Dallas, Texas. He is a chairman, C.E.O., and President of the State Bank of Texas. The Greater Dallas Indo- American Chamber of Commerce named him Entrepreneur of the year in 2001. He is involved very much with humanitarian work with hospitals. He has generously donated to several hospitals in the US and in India.

Lallubhai Mathurbhai Bhakta

Lallubhai was born in Kapura, Surat in the 1930s. He received his Bachelor degree in electrical engineering from VJTI Bombay. He arrived in the U.S. in 1972. He has been in the motel business since coming to the United States. His two children are well educated. One has M.D. specialty in Pain Medicine and other has an air conditioning degree.

Dr. Khushalbhai Hirabhai Patel

Dr. Khushalbhai Hirabhai Patel was born in Sarpor Pardi taluka, Navsari. He received his education in South Africa in 1939. Today, at the age of seventy-nine, he is still active in business as well as in social activities. He obtained a B.S. in chemical engineering with Distinction from University of the Withwatersrand, Johannesburg, South Africa in 1943. Later, he tried to his further studies in India; however, Indian universities did not accept him because of the different curriculum. He applied and received a M.S. in chemistry from the University of Southern California in 1947. Dr. Patel received his Ph.D. in chemical engineering from Columbia University in 1950. Among his many accolades, he is also a trustee of Satem Vibhag Kelavani Mandal, Medical Trust, and Samastha Matiya Patidar Samaj.

Bhikhu Uka Patel

Bhikhu Patel is Chairman and CEO at Tarsadia Hotels—one of top privately-owned hotel companies in the U.S. Today, Tarsadia is recognized as a first-class developer and operator of hospitality assets. Established in 1976, Tarsadia has a well-defined vision, a strong sense of values and guiding principles, and a long range, quality-minded approach for business. By concentrating in Orange County and the key gateway cities of San Francisco, Los Angeles and San Diego, Tarsadia is enhancing its portfolio.

As an active member of the Matiya Patidar Samaj of US since 1970's, he has recently helped the Samaj to buy a Sanatan Dharma Temple in Norwalk, California. He is a founding president of the Sanatan Dharma Temple and is associated with various organizations.

Raj Patel

Raj Patel formed Premier Hospitality, which manages ten hotels in Oklahoma. The company successes include the Bass Hotels and Resorts Newcomer of the Year 2000 Award, as well as being listed as one of the Top 100 Owners and Developers by Hotel Business magazine.

Kanti N. Patel Alpesh Patel

KANA Hotels is a Knoxville-based management and development company led by Kanti (Ken) Patel, owner/operator. KANA Hotels began with a small "mom and pop" hotel in Michigan City, Indiana in 1977. Today, the company has twelve franchised hotels, with approximately 1,000 rooms located throughout the Knoxville, Tennessee area.

Mukesh R. Patel

With $1,000 in his pocket, Mukesh Patel moved to Tulsa, Oklahoma in 1991 to begin his career in the lodging industry. With the aid of his family and friends, he purchased an 86-room independent motel. His brother Paresh joined the Frontier Hotel Management Group after completing a business and finance degree at Oklahoma State University. Frontier currently owns four hotels and had a 63-room Comfort Inn under development in 2001.

Indubhai Patel

Indubhai was born in Surat, India in 1940s. He came to U.S.A. in 1963 and obtained a M.S. degree in engineering. He has a M.S. degree in Civil Engineering from Sardar Patel University, Gujarat, India. For more than ten years, he worked for engineering companies in U.S. He has been in Motel business since last twenty-six years. His two children have M.D.'s from American universities.

Dahyabhai L. Patel

Dahyabhai was born in Kaachhiawadi, Navsari, India in the 1930s. He is a high school graduate and married Santaben, who is also a high school graduate. He made his way in this country with hard work, integrity, and honesty. He has been in the motel business since 1978. He is very fond of his exotic fruit tree garden. He likes to work for the community and serves as one of the directors of Sanatan Dharma Hindu Temple, Norwak, California.

Hemant Patel

Hemant Patel was born in Navsari, India in 1966. Beginning his studies in Vidyakunj School in Navsari, he completed his secondary education in Bharda New High School, Bombay. Hemant than went on to receive a business degree in economics from Bombay University.

In 1986, Hemant moved to the United States and has owned independent as well franchised properties in Miami, Florida, since 1988. He was the first Indian to serve in every position in the Greater Biscayne Boulevard Chamber of Commerce, and finally became the first Indian to be named president of the chamber.

Hemant was instrumental in securing AAHOA's first proclamation from the City of Miami and Dade County for naming September 5, 2001 Asian American Hotel Owners Association Day. He is director at large of AAHOA for the year 2002 and a member of the Executive committee.

Govind B. Bhakta

Govind B. Bhakta was born into a farming family in Sarai Village, in the Navsari district of the Gujarat States, India. As a child, he lived under one roof with an extended family consisting of twenty-eight members. This early experience led to his conviction that the lives of youth and communities are interwined in a unique collective way. His village had sixty households with a population of six hundred people.

Mr. Bhakta attended a public school with only one teacher; at that time primary schools did not have benches; students sat on the floor made from cattle-dung daubing. He received his B.S. degree in Mathematics from Sardar Patel University and a M.S. in Statistics from Gujarat University (1960-1962). He taught mathematics and statistics at a Garada College, Navsari from 1962-1968, and immigrated to the United States in late 1968.

Govind B. Bhakta has been in the real estate business during the past twenty-eight years, owning "Mom and Pop" motels to franchised motels in the greater Los Angeles area and in other parts of the United States. Affectionately known to the Asian-Indian community as "Professor," Mr. Bhakta brings sincerity, industry, and intellectual ability to both his professional interests and community activities. He is active with the Indo American Patel community, and is working to build the community development capacity of Indo-American Patels nationally, focusing on the Los Angeles and Orange County areas. He was a founding board director of the Southern California I.H.M. Hotel/Motel Association (1986), and is a founding board director of the Shree Ramkabir Bhakta Samaj U.S.A.

For the past thirty years, Mr. Bhakta has lived in California with his wife Sumati who also has a M.S. degree in Inorganic Chemistry. His elder son, a design Engineer at SiliconTech has a B.S in Electronics and MBA from Pepperdine University and his daughter in- law is an Occupational Therapist. His younger son attends Tufts University School of Dental Medicine, Boston. His daughter is an Occupational Therapist and son in-law is in finance and possesses a MBA degree.

Mr. Bhakta is a firm believer in Herman Melville's philosophy that "we cannot live for ourselves alone. Our lives are connected by a thousand invisible threads, and along these sympathetic fibers, our actions run as causes and return to us as a result." Thus, Mr. Bhakta has made the larger Indo-American Patel community and its emergent youth his joy, passion, and lifetime work.

There are doctors, engineers, managers, computer personals, teachers, professors, and other professionals from Indo- American Patel Communities who excelled both in business and professions and made their names in American society. I congratulate them for their achievements and hope we will be able to recognize them in the future.

3

CONTEMPORARY ISSUES IN THE PATEL COMMUNITY

CHAPTER 6

SOCIOECONOMIC CHARACTERISTICS

Families

According to recent *Los Angeles Times* polls, more than half of Americans believe that the ideal size for a family is two parents and two or fewer children.[93] People born between 1946 and 1964 come from families with three or more children. A 1947 Gallup Poll, by contrast, shows that more than 67% of Americans believed the ideal number of children per family was three or more.[94]

David Blankhorn, president of the Institute of American Values in New York (a non-partisan think tank that studies family issues), states, "It has really changed an awful lot in one generation, large families were seen as a good thing in our parents' generation and now are increasingly seen as something that is eccentric and sort of out of the mainstream."[95] This is partly due to more women in the work force and more effective birth control, leading to women having a greater choice over the number and spacing of their offspring, and often having less time to take care of the young. But there has also been a change in the value of children for the family. Formerly, parents depended on their children to contribute economically to the household. Children were an investment, rather than an expense. Census statistics show that while in 1970, about 20% of American families had three or more children, by 1991, only 10% did.

According to the *Los Angeles Times* article, "Families," by Denton Robinson, the U.S. Bureau of Statistics revealed that more than ever there were childless couples, single parents, and people living alone.[96] As of March 1995, only 25% of all households were married with children, down from 40% in 1970. People living alone increased from one-sixth to one-fourth of all households. This research includes a widely cited 1988 study by the National Center of Health Statistics. The study found that children in single-parent families (including those whose parents never married) are more likely to drop out of high school, become pregnant as teenagers, abuse drugs, and get into trouble with the law than those living with both parents.

Research indicates that retired Asian American people over the age of fifty-five make up 12.6% of the total population; those between the ages of twenty-five and fifty-four are 46.4%; and those younger than twenty-four years of age are 41% of the total population.[97] Therefore, it is very important that we keep the young foremost in our minds and hearts, as they will inherit our future as Asian Americans.

U.S. Born Indo-American Families

The structure, lifestyle, and behavior patterns of American-born Indian families depend on several factors, the first among them being generational. The further removed from the immigrant generation, the more acculturated a person is to American norms. Often by the third generation, U.S. customs prevail in such issues as dating, mate choice, following wedding customs, role expectations, child rearing, and care of the elderly.

Another factor is place of residence. If the family resides in an ethnic community, the traditional customs of the homeland will continue to have a large influence on the family. If a family is isolated from members of its ethnic group, it is likely that it will follow U.S. practices more closely.

Social class is the third factor. The upper-middle class may have the time and money to devote to a stable, close-knit unit and adhere more closely to its cultural heritage, even if the extended family is not present as much. The poorer classes are often too preoccupied with economic survival, with parents working long hours and children assuming more adult responsibilities. However, cultural roots tend to run deep and even these American-born Indian families are able to retain a deep sense of family commitment.

Other Demographics

Table 14
Country in which IAPFM Last Resided

	U.S.	India	UK	Africa	OTHER	No. of Respondents
(1)Head of Household	4%	84%	4%	8%	1%	121
Spouse	1%	82%	4%	11%	2%	118
Children	34%	35%	10%	18%	4%	94
Father (of 1)	0%	97%	2%	2%	0%	45
Mother (of 1)	0%	95%	0%	5%	0%	46
% of Total	**10%**	**73%**	**5%**	**10%**	**2%**	**424**

Seventy-three percent of the Patels who currently live in the U.S. mostly hailed directly from India. American-born Patels make up 10% of the population, while 10% came from Africa, and 5% from the United Kingdom. Thus, two-thirds of the first-generation population came from India.

Age Distribution of the IAPFM in the U.S.

Among the IAPFM Patel's in U.S. 42% head of the households (include spouses) answered this question from the participating Patels in the survey. Sixty percent were in the age group 30-50 years. Seventy eight percent of their children were in the age group 15-30 years. Of the total Patels 65% were less than 50 years and older.

The period in which most Patels immigrated to the United States was in the 1970s. Because several clauses of the 1965 Immigration Act were relaxed, 18% of

Table 15
Year of Migration

	1950-60	60-70	70-80	80-90	90+	No. of Respondents
Head of Household	1%	17%	54%	24%	3%	145
Spouse	2%	14%	56%	23%	5%	127
Children	0%	12%	52%	30%	6%	117
Father of HH	5%	11%	38%	35%	11%	55
Mother of HH	4%	9%	38%	40%	9%	55
% of Total	2%	14%	51%	28%	6%	499

first-generation Patels came mostly on the third-preference visa during 1950-1970. They were mostly engineers, doctors, research-oriented professionals, or university professors. Those who came after the mid- to latter-part of the 1970s and onwards were mainly the siblings or parents of these Indo-American citizens. Some of these siblings and parents became U.S. citizens and then brought *their* children, siblings, and so on. This 18 % of first-generation Patels deserve credit for sponsoring the mass immigrants from India to the U.S.

Table 16
Number. Years IAPFM Have Lived in U.S.

	<5	5-10	10-20	20-30	30+	No. of Respondents
Head of Household	7%	16%	43%	31%	3%	89
Spouse	7%	14%	47%	29%	3%	90
Children	12%	11%	37%	36%	4%	114
Father of HH	5%	25%	40%	20%	10%	40
Mother of HH	7%	20%	22%	38%	13%	45
% of Total	8%	16%	39%	32%	5%	378

Seventy six percent of the Patel's have been 10 or more years in the U.S. Only 8 % have lived in America less than 5 years, and 24% have been for less than 10 years. Five percent of the Patels have been for mare than 30 years in U.S. Overall, 77% children have spent at least 10 to 30 years in the U.S.

Regional Distribution of Asian Indians

Early Asian Indians settled primarily on the West Coast. Those who entered before 1917 as part of the first phase settled predominantly in the agricultural areas of California. They were primarily Sikhs from the Punjab region of north India. These were the fellow Indian brothers who helped early immigrant Patels like Dhirajlal Bhikhabhai (D. Lal Kaka), Dhanjeebhai Bhikhabhai Patel (Umrakh, San Francisco),

Dahyabhai Ratanji and Shantibhai Ratanji Patel, Lakhubhai Kalidas Patel, Santibhai Patel (Siker), and others. Many of these came on the "100 quota'" category for India in the early 1950s, when they had just finished their graduation from M.T.B. College in India in the later part of the 1940s. Indians are the only Asian group not concentrated in the West, in contrast with other Asian groups.

Indo-Americans live predominantly in metropolitan areas. The only major rural agricultural Indo-American community is the Punjabi Sikh community in central California. Seventy percent of Indo-Americans live in eight major industrial states: New York, California, New Jersey, Texas, Pennsylvania, Michigan, Illinois, and Ohio. Of the 815,447 Indo-Americans counted in the 1990 Census, California had the largest number of Indo-Americans (159,973), followed by New York (140,985).

However, unlike the other Asian American groups, Indo-Americans continue to be concentrated in the northeastern states: 32% percent of Indo-Americans live in the northeast region of the United States. The distribution of states with the largest number of Asian Indians, besides California and New York, are: New Jersey (79,440); Illinois (64,200), and Texas (55,795). In eight states—Alabama, Connecticut, Michigan, New Jersey, North Carolina, Ohio, Tennessee, and West Virginia—Asian Indians are the largest subgroup of Asian Americans.[98]

Table 17
Surti Leauva, Bhakta, Matiya, Charotariya Patidar in Top Five States Across U.S.

Surti	%	Bhakta	%	Matiya	%	Charotor-iya	%
Ca	19%	Ca	33%	Ca	42%	NJ	13%
TX	16%	TX	29%	Fl	13%	GA	12%
TN	15%	NM	4%	TX	10%	NY	9%
GA	7%	Ks	4%	GA	8%	Ca	9%
Fl	6%	GA	3%	TN	3%	Fl	7%

(See Appendix G, Table C: Patels Regional Distribution in United States.)

Residential Preference

Thirty-two percent of Asian Indians live in the Northeast, 26% in the South, 19% in the Midwest, and 24% in the West (see Appendix G, Table D for the comparison of residential preference between Asian Indians and Patels). Working-class immigrants who are able to enter in the family categories have helped to sustain "Little Indias" and develop residential enclaves among Asian Indians.[99] An examination of the sixteen largest cities in the U.S. found that Asian Americans were nearly half as likely to be residentially segregated from Whites as African Americans.[100]

This settlement pattern is largely due to perceived economic opportunities. For the Indo-American Patel group, the presence of any existing community, especially from their own Patel sub-group or *jati*, was an important factor influencing residential preference.

Most married children have been listed separately; hence, they are not included in the "family with parents" category. Married children have been approximated in this way as 1,224. Note that these figures are available for Surti Leauva Patidar Samaj only. Widowed men or single men were 1.2%, and widowed women or single women were 0.5%.

Indo-Americans have the most balanced gender ratio of any Asian American community at 98:100. Up until 1980, 60% between the ages of thirty-five and fifty-four have been men. Almost 96% of them were foreign-born, most having immi-

Table 18
Profile of IAPFM Population in the United States 1996–1997

Patels	Total	Men	Women	Male Spouse	Female Spouse	Men Spouse	Women Spouse
Surti	11704	5854	5850	2343	2361	3511	3489
Bhakta	4341	2237	2104	875	753	1362	1351
Matiya	4888	2488	2400	993	946	1495	1454
Charotariya	3092	1538	1554	591	614	947	915
Total	24025	12117	11908	4802	4674	7315	7209
Percent	100%	50.4	49.6	50.5	49.5	49.5	48.8

Table 19
Number of Persons Per Household[101]

Patels	Person Households				1 Person
	5 or More	4 Person	3 Person	2 Person	
Surti	873	1367	405	229	29
Bhakta	259	443	160	436	117
Matiya	151	574	317	402	61
Charotariya	125	305	198	284	38
Total	1408	2689	1080	1351	245
Percent	20.8	39.7	16.0	19.9	3.6

Married men and women include widows. Married children figures were not available.

grated between 1970 and 1980. Yet after the 1965 increase in male immigrants, the ratio remained fairly even because the initial wave of post-1965 immigration was mainly in the male-dominated occupational and professional categories. Immigration today, however, because of gender-neutral family reunification categories, has resulted in a greater gender balance.

Overall, Patels believe in a living in a close family unit. A living situation in which the husband, wife, children, and grandparents residing in the same household is greatly encountered. Even in the U.S., extended family life in the Patel community is much more prevalent than in American culture at-large.

Research suggests that having children is important to the Patels. Excluding young couples, retirees and a few widowers, 16% of families have one child; 40% of families have two children; and 21% have three or more. One interesting find here is that among these 21% families who have three or more children, most families have three or more females and one male children. We may conclude from this that

Patels still believe a male child is necessary to continue the family name, and thus, young couples will keep trying to have a child if they have not yet had a boy.

It is also interesting to note that in all but one country (Canada), the male population in each group is slightly greater than the female population. IAPFM in the U.S. the male-to-female ratio is 50.4:49.6. In Panama the ratio is 60:40. If this scenario is true for India and other countries, it is an alarming situation for parents and children to find a future spouse for children. Thus, the Patels believe that they are fortunate in the U.S. to have an even better chance for their children to find spouses.

CHAPTER 7

EDUCATION AND LANGUAGE

In 1990, of Asian Indians in the U.S., there were 331,000 people five years and older who spoke Hindi, and 102,000 people five years and older who spoke Gujarati.[102] In order to discover why language is so important to our identity and culture, a demographic look at where we will be in thirty years is important. By the year 2020, there will be a large split within our community with respect to the issue of language. What this implies is that the majority of the community will speak English as a second language well into the next century. Also, a greater part of our culture and identity will continue to be manifested through our language—even for those who may speak English primarily and their native language secondarily. As a result, language will become a greater indicator of who we are and from where we have arrived. Therefore, the link between language and national origin will become an even stronger aspect of cultural and personal identity than it currently is.

One study by Peter Kiang and Vivian Lee notes that although three-fourths of the Asian American student population comes from bilingual families, nearly 60% indicated that they have a low proficiency in their parents' native language, compared to 66% who have a high proficiency in English. The study also notes that although 73% of the Asian American students came from bilingual homes, only 27% were identified as bilingual by at least one of their teachers, suggesting that many linguistic and cultural issues that students, who experience duality between home and school, face are often not recognized or addressed.[103]

This profile is consistent with findings by Lily Wong-Fillmore and others in a landmark study that provided evidence that as language-minority children learn English in the U.S., they "lose" their native language.[104] The study further suggests that as the home language is lost in the process of acquiring English, family relations also erode.

Responses from Paul Ong's survey (SALIC 1993) in Chinatown demonstrate the relationship between English-speaking ability and earning power. [105] Respondents rating themselves as speaking no English have an annual median income of $5,499, while those who speak English "not well" have a median income of $12,000, compared to those who speak English "very well" having a median income of $20,000.

Wherever Gujaratis have settled in foreign countries, there is the common anxiety of "Will the children of immigrant Gujaratis be able to read, write, and/or speak Gujarati? Will it stay alive, and, if so, for how long?" This is a burning problem for the Gujarati population residing everywhere.

Any two Gujaratis, be they in Paris or Mombassa, Toronto or New York, London or Johannesburg, can utter the Gujarati *boli* and understand each other. After fifty years, they may not be so much in touch with Gujarat, and yet the language maintains their *sanskar* and ties to each other. Author Chandrakant Baxi says:

> There are Gujarati literature readers who can buy cinema tickets, buy cassettes, buy whisky bottles, buy 555 cigarettes, go with friends and eat paunve-Bhaji, buy roses, weekly magazines and Sunday's purtis, arrange trips to hill stations, buy color T.V.'s, spend in thousands for their children's marriages. The ladies can buy cookbooks. Gujaratis have tremendous buying power but somehow book publishers and their distributors couldn't capture the Gujarati customers; that is the naked truth.[106]

Gujarati Language

Immigrants value their language and culture and therefore, want their children to read, write, and speak Gujarati. At the Fifth International Gujurati Convention, held in London in 1978, it was discovered that Gujaratis are settled for business or work in almost 110 countries. The pressing topic among Gujarati poets and writers was, "How to keep the Gujarati language alive in the foreign land?" Gujaratis spend a copious amount of money for temples or *Sadhus* or saints, so why will they not spend much money to promote Gujarati literature, via television, radio, or Gujarati newspapers?[107]

However, the academic achievements of Asian Indian children indicate that the non-English fluent children of Indian immigrants suffer from emotional stress while learning English during the first couple of years. Later, they catch up with the mainstream and often succeed in academics.[108] It is advisable for those who come to America speaking the Gujarati language to learn English in order to succeed in everyday life, while preserving the native language by speaking it at home and in social functions.

Twenty-five percent (1.26 million) of the country's students were limited in English-proficiency in 1995. And specifically in California, students speak more than fifty-five different languages. There, there are three main educational programs for these students:[109]

1. *Immersion*: Students are instructed in English, usually with simplified vocabulary and sometimes with the support from a classroom fluent in their home language. Students move into mainstream classes quickly but may lack a firm academic foundation. Non-fluent California students make up about 45% of this type.

2. *Transitional Bilingual Education*: Instruction in the student's home language, with special lessons in English. In the most extreme form it can take seven years for students to move into mainstream classes. Non-fluent California students comprise of 28% of this category.

3. *Submersion*: No specific attempts are made to accommodate the student in his or her home language, and no research supports this approach. About 27% of Californian students not fluent in English are taught in this way.

Learning English is a very small price to pay for the freedoms and economic successes enjoyed by immigrants from India, Chile, and Hungary, according to statements made at a congressional hearing given on the subject in November 1995.[110] Testifying before the Harle Economic and Educational Opportunities Subcommittee on early childhood, youth and families, the group said that the English language enriched their lives, and "Individuals who are not English proficient are more often than not relegated to second-class citizenship and are vulnerable to being isolated by language barriers that render them dependent on the government for assistance."[111]

"Bilingualism is a richness," says Alma Flo Adu, a linguistics professor at U.C. San Francisco and author of more than 200 children's books. She believes that language is one of the most valuable tools that people have, and that childhood is the best time to develop that tool. Children who are just learning to speak have demonstrated an ability to speak multiple tongues with the proficiency of a native.[112]

However, there are some drawbacks to exposing a child to this confusing tower of babble. For one thing, children raised with multiple languages often begin to speak a little later than those in a single language environment do. But the setback is only temporary and over time, the process of learning to make sense from such confusion can prove beneficial. Those children are better prepared to face new situations. They have already seen two viewpoints on the world, because "language is more than just a system of symbols, it is connected to culture."[113]

Children switch to English because it surrounds them on television, in the playground, and at school. Researchers agree that raising bilingual children is not easy. Parents have to be diligent if they are to keep English from dominating. Researchers suggest these methods for parents who want their children to stay fluent in their native language: [114]

1. Make sure children hear the native language at home as much as possible.
2. Give children lots of time around relatives and other children who speak the language.
3. In mixed language marriages, both parents should speak to the children in the language they are most comfortable with, but should be careful not to slip into the other language. When speaking to each other, use the "minority" language if possible.
4. Be consistent, but don't be fanatic. If you love to sing favorite songs to your children in English, for example, don't deprive them of this experience.
5. Read to your children daily in your native language.

Although 68% of Asian Indians age five and older speak a language other than English, only 21% do not speak English very well.[115] Of all Asian Indian families in Los Angeles County, 67% use a language other than English at home, and only 27% use English at home. At the age of three years and over, 90% speak English "very well" or "well," and 8% do not speak English well.

Of U.S.-born Asian Indians, 54% only speak English, 17% speak English "very well," and speak other languages. Of Asian Indians born outside the U.S., 19% only speak English, 51% speak "very well," 26% speak "not well" to "well."[116]

Growing Up Bilingual

For some young Indian Americans, the use of their native language is a daily reality. Shiva Prasad, at Cal Poly Pomona University, says:

I have been speaking Hindi for as long as I can remember. To me, it is a very vital part of who I am. I never gave it any thought and always took it for granted. It was only when I saw friends who could not speak or even understand their native language that I realized how much of a difference language really makes. I am really thankful to my parents for encouraging me to speak Hindi. It has helped me stay in touch with myself as well as my heritage.[117]

If we do not bother to pass on our language to the generations to come, the strong, rich Indian culture in which we take so much pride will be lost.

Only a few American universities offer South Asian languages. University of Michigan, for example, offers courses in Hindi, Urdu, Gujarati, Marathi, and so on, depending on enrollment. University of California, Berkeley also offers these courses, from its South and Southeast Asia Studies program. However, students in other schools often have no scholastic resource for learning their family's native languages.

Table 20
Gujarati-Speaking Patels in the U.S.

	N	VL	F	G	E	No. of Respondents
Head of Household	1%	2%	6%	57%	34%	145
Spouse	1%	0%	13%	72%	15%	127
Children	1%	17%	35%	44%	3%	146
Father (of 1) HH	0%	0%	4%	72%	24%	54
Mother (of 1) HH	0%	0%	21%	69%	10%	48
% of Total	1%	5%	17%	60%	17%	520

N=Not at all, VL=Very Little, F= Fair, G=Good, E=Excellent

Only 1% of the Patel population does not speak Gujarati at all. Five percent speak very little. Overall 94% of the Patel population speaks Gujarati fair to excellent. Eighteen percent of the children speak Gujarati very little to not at all. Eighty two percent of the children speak Gujarati fair to excellent. Writing Gujarati is more of a problem. Twelve percent of first-generation heads of the households do not know how to write in Gujarati at all. Overall, 14% of Patels can write in Gujarati very little, 17% write in Gujarati fairly well, 37% write in Gujarati well, 12% are excellent in writing. Fifty-six percent of children do not know how to write in Gujarati, 23% write Gujarati very little, and 20% write in Gujarati well to good.

Comparing speaking versus writing Gujarati among children, it is interesting to note that only 18% of children speak very little to not at all, versus 79% children who can write Gujarati very little to not at all. The situation is reversed for speech: 79% of children speak Gujarati fairly well to good, as opposed to 20% of children who can write Gujarati fairly well to good. Therefore, when one compares children to first-generation Patels, second-generation children seem to be losing their Gujarati writing skills. Speaking Gujarati still provides a very strong bond among family members, but the ability to write in Gujarati is diminishing from one generation to the next.

Because Gujarati is spoken at home and at social events, Gujarati has been in constant use. This language maintenance is a very strong indication of the Gujarati Patel families' close ties, as well as the reason why Gujarati Patels abroad feel so close to each other. They are still enjoying more or less the same extended family life they enjoyed in India.

English Proficiency

To preserve one's cultural inheritance, it is necessary to know the native language. At the same time, when it comes to earning the bread and butter, it is equally true that one must know the language used in daily life in the United States. English is everyone's language. How well do we know English?

According to survey results, 85% of first-generation Patels speak English well to fluently. Ninety-four percent of second-generation children speak English well to fluently. Ten percent of the Patels speak very little to not at all. Only 5% children over 16 years of age speak English very little to not at all.

Table 21
IAPFM English-Literacy in the U.S.

	N	VL	F	G	E	No. of Respondents
(1)Head of Household	2%	9%	15%	38%	36%	143
Spouse	17%	16%	27%	21%	19%	124
Children	1%	0%	2%	13%	85%	149
Father of (1)	22%	9%	20%	20%	28%	54
Mother of (1)	69%	7%	9%	13%	2%	45
Percent of Total	**13%**	**8%**	**14%**	**23%**	**42%**	**515**

In the case of written Gujarati, it is more challenging for second-generation children since Gujarati is their second language. Similarly, written English is more arduous for first-generation Patels because English is their second language.

A comparison of parents with children in written and spoken English concludes that language skill is correlated with environmental influences: parents' knowledge of a language, be it English or Gujarati, helps their children to learn that language more swiftly. Children are also seen to be much better adapting to written English language skills, based on their education in America, than their parents, but they are losing their Gujarati writing skills, perhaps due to lack of access to instruction, even though their speaking skills are still in use.

Education

Gaining access to prestigious institutions of higher education will continue to be a top priority for Asian American families, even if admissions into such institutions become increasingly competitive, and the cost of attending them becomes prohibitive. The number of foreign graduate students from Asian countries increased sharply during the Cold War, as higher education expanded rapidly with federal assistance, and as American industries, especially high-tech industries and research universities, eagerly absorbed them into their work forces.

Instead of returning to their home countries after the completion of their training, most of "the best and brightest" settled permanently in the United States. The sole strategy within Asian American communities was to use education to overcome poverty and prejudice for the next generation.

A small classroom of a school in an Indian village.

According to the National Center for Education Statistics, there were 406,000 Asian Americans in all types of institutions of higher education in 1988. Asian Americans represented only 3.8% of the college student population in 1988—a very substantial increase from 1.8% in 1976. Berkeley and UCLA continue to be among the most popular choices for Asian American students because of their quality, accessibility, and low cost. Other public universities, such as Michigan, Illinois, and Wisconsin, have also seen their Asian American enrollments go up for the same reasons. At Berkeley and UCLA, Asian American freshman enrollments increased to the point of nearly outnumbering the white student population. Generally speaking, children from the middle class are motivated to attend the very top public and private universities and colleges across the nation, while the children of working classes pursue higher education on the basis of their needs and academic and financial ability.[118]

However, attending higher-level universities is not without its difficulties for children of immigrants, other than the financial obligations involved. In a landmark 1992 study, the U.S. Commission on Civil Rights documented numerous cases of anti-Asian violence. The report states:

> The pervasive anti-Asian climate and the frequent acts of bigotry and violence in our schools not only inflict hidden injuries and lasting damage, but also create barriers to the educational attainment of the Asian American student victims, such as suspension from school and dropping out of school—these consequences exact a high price that not only the individual involved but also society as a whole is bound to pay in the future.[119]

A new corporate study on how immigrant children perform in U.S. schools found that they have a remarkable drive for education.[120] They enroll in primary and middle schools at the same rate as American-born youngsters, and those who enroll by the tenth grade are as likely to graduate as their American-born classmates.

Furthermore, immigrant graduates are more likely to enter college than their American-born counterparts.

These are major and even surprising achievements, considering the barriers facing most immigrant students: poor academic preparation in their native countries, the need to learn a new language and a new institutional a cultural setting. Factors such as family income, the level of education, and educational expectations of parents and children are the main determinants of whether a youngster will pursue a college education.

Asian Indians had the highest average years of schooling—15.6—among thirty-three ethnic and religious groups in 1989. These students have the fifth highest household income, and yet when their social standing is assessed, they rank below all but five of the groups.[121] Taking together those who completed sixteen years of education and those who also took graduate studies (seventeen or more years of education), Asian Indians had the highest percentage (48%) of education in Los Angeles county, among ethnic groups in 1980.

Table 22
Socio-Economic Characteristics of Indian Americans, 1980[122]

Percent Immigrated 1975-1980	(1)Percent High School Graduates	(1)Percent Completed 4 years or More of College	(2) Percent of years in professional specialty occupation	Median Household Income $
43.7	88.9	66.2	42.8	25,644

(1) Persons 25 years or over, (2) Persons 16 years or over.

Because of their top scores, a large proportion of Asian Indian students are eligible for admission to elite universities; in fact, Asian American students form a sizable proportion of the student population at some schools. In 1991, for example, California State University at San Francisco reported that 33% of their 14,672 undergraduate students were Asian Americans. Harvard, Yale, and Stanford had freshman classes in 1990 in which 20%, 15%, and 24% of their students were Asian American, respectively. The top liberal arts colleges enrolled anywhere between 7-17% Asian American students overall.[123]

A direct relationship exists between income and education. This is supported by findings of Lilly Lee's 1985 study, which indicates that income increases with the level of education held and number of years completed. In 1980, about 90% of Asian Indians age twenty-five and over with sixteen years or more education in Los Angeles County worked as a manager/professional/specialty agent, a technical /salesperson, or an administrative supervisor—all white collar jobs. Those with eight years of education or less worked predominantly in blue-collar professions.[124]

"When they go home, the kids end up living two different lives," says Dokim, director of Los Angeles-based Korean American Youth leadership program.[125] "The silver lining is that Asian American youth are constantly having to strive to achieve an identity," said Kohn, "and as they get older, they will see their parents as heroes. They will remember their hardworking spirit, family sacrifice and support of education."[126]

It is interesting to note that among first generation Indo-American Patels, the male to female spousal education varies little according to gender. It has already improved greatly from the grandparent generation to the first generation, and from the first generation to the second. It is even more apparent when one realizes that grandparents (both husbands and wives) had much wider educational inequalities. Sixty-three percent of the grandmothers have only primary education, versus 69% of grandfathers who have a high school education or more. Patel women used to be discouraged from going to school. It was the general feeling in these communities that if women go to high school or college, they might marry out of the caste when the time comes for marriage, and parents might not find a suitably educated groom for their daughters. The other belief was that housework is exclusively for women, and that their educations would distract from their other home duties.

Table-Chart 23
IAPFM Education Field (Graduate and Undergraduate combined)

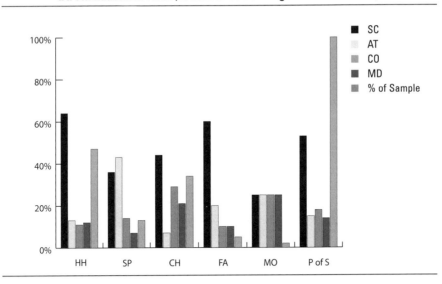

SC=Science, AT=Arts, CO=Comerce, MO=Medical, P of S=Percent of Sample

HH- Head of Household; SP- Spouse; CH- Children; FA- Father of HH; MO-Mother of HH.

Comparing the education of Asian Indians overall with the Indo-American Patel population, 21% of Asian Indians possess undergraduate degrees, compared to 29% of Patels who have the same degrees. It seems that Patels are very comparable to other Asian Indians in the U.S. in education, with a slightly higher ratio of higher degrees.

According to survey results of the Patels who received degrees, 28% of first-generation Patels received their Bachelor degrees in the U.S., compared to 35% who received them in India. Nineteen percent hold Master degrees or higher in the U.S., versus 8% who received them in India. Of first-generation women, 28% of spouses received their Bachelor degrees in the U.S., compared to 25% who did them in India. Fifteen percent of women have Master degrees from U.S. institutions, while only 5% received these in India. The story is even better for second-generation children: 62% received their Bachelor degrees in the U.S., compared to only 8% who attended Indian universities. This is indicative that since most children of the first generation are born here or mostly raised in the U.S., they prefer to be educated in the United States.

According to the above chart, 64% of first-generation Patels possess higher degrees in science, 13% in arts, 11% in commerce, and 12% in the medical field. Among first-generation spouses, 36% have degrees in science, 43% in the arts, 14% in commerce, and 7% in medicine. However, for children of first-generation Patels, 44% possess degrees in science, 7% in arts, 29% in commerce, and 21% in medicine. Children seem to be diversifying their education; less are in "hard science" positions, but more have taken over in the arts and business worlds.

Based on survey results, of first-generation Patel male household heads who received degrees, 9% received degrees during the years 1950-1959, 31% during 1960-1969, 39% during 1970-1979, 13% during 1980-1989, and 7% from 1990 onwards. For spouses, 4% received degrees between 1950-1959, 17% from 1960-1969, 48% between 1970-1979, 26% between 1980-1989, and 4% from 1990 onwards. Among second-generation children, 58% received degrees in 1980-1989 and 42% from 1990 onwards.

Table 24
Indo-American Enrollment in U.S. Colleges: 1976-1995, in Thousands

1976	1980	1985	1990	1991	1992	1993	1994	1995
10	9	15	26	29	23	36	35	34

Table 25
Indo-American Enrollment in Science, Business, and Engineering in U.S. Colleges: 1980-1994, in Percent1[27]

	Science	Business	Engineering
1980	31	16	21
1994	39	9	13

Approximately 24% of Patels who had degrees and came to the U.S. between 1950-1965 are the pioneer immigrants who brought their siblings later on and established kin networks which became the foundation for Indian immigration.

In the 1950s and 1960s, 27% of Indian immigrants entered the U.S. in professional categories, but by 1990, 90% were entering in family categories. Professionals who enter the U.S. on professional and occupational categories decreased in these two decades because a 1976 law began requiring that all professionals must first secure a job offer from their employer. The only choice left for educated persons who wanted to come to the U.S. was as a student in higher education, and later to find employment after their studies were completed. In the 1980s, roughly 50% foreign-born Indian Americans had four years or more of higher education. Table 25 indicates that after the 1976 law, more and more students—not "immigrants"—came to the U.S. in hopes of permanent settlement as scientists, engineers, or business executives.

CHAPTER 8

DATING AND MARRIAGE

Adaption and Conflict

Immigrant parents from India have to face their children's adaptation to American society and culture, a task simultaneously advantageous and problematic. Indian traditions have much to offer to the younger generations. However, though they may be well fit for the life of an average Indian, they do not accommodate as well to the life of a Western teenager. They may not even fit the average life of a modern Indian teenager, as modernizing and westernizing influences have also penetrated the culture of the urban youth in India today.

Indian traditions have become distorted in the process of merging with American culture, at home and abroad. Few of the traditional Indian experiences, confrontations, and celebrations to which first-generation parents are accustomed may ever be known to the second generation. Likewise, parents grew up with myriad social issues relating to the 1950s and 1960s in India—an important, formative experience this generation shares, but of which members of the second generation have only heard second-hand. Many of these values get passed down and sometimes, regrettably, are forced onto the second generation in an attempt to influence the children's lifestyle.

In this society first-generation parents' values are very restrictive and old-fashioned compared to those of second-generation children. Everyday social issues—dating, sex, friends, career, marriage—confronting the second generation are not well understood by the first. A majority of children are advised to forget their ethnic background and solely concentrate on their lives in the U.S. Yet in the long run, one's cultural identity and heritage will invariably intrude and remind a person about what he or she has lost. These moments often occur at critical junctures of the person's life.

Assimilation can cause a variety of anxieties. For example, one may not be able to make decisions without hesitating and worrying, "What will my parents think? What will my friends think?" More importantly, children must choose values based on a consideration of how they will affect them in the future. Sticking with one's peer group may seem like the best short-term solution, but one must take care always to consider all relationships one has and to balance one's decisions between them.[128]

First Generation Fears: Loss of Cultural Identity

Fueled primarily by first-generation fears that their children are losing touch with their ancestral roots, Gujarati schools in the U.S. are fast becoming a nationwide phe-

nomenon. "We all saw what was happening with our children and we felt we needed to get involved, few sat back and did nothing; we would lose our second generation," says Parsottam Patel, President of the Norwalk Mandir. "So many of the
first-generation parents want English as a second language class, now they are all
bringing their children to Gujarati language classes."[129]

Children of more recent immigrants pick up American ways with a speed their
parents find a bit threatening. After two and a half decades of living in the U.S., Mr.
Choo Patel watched the unmistakable Americanization of his children ages eighteen
and twenty-one. Because English is his children's first language, Mr. Choo knows
that India and its traditions are only distant stories to them. He wants them to know
something of the homeland their parents left behind. He says, "I would like them to
know the language, know a little bit about their background, know where their
grandparents came from. So that when they say 'I am an Indian-American' they
know what 'Indian' really means."[130]

Communication with people who share languages and backgrounds with us is
easy and comfortable; we fill in the blanks or adjust to our communicational errors,
having a common pool of cultural references from which to draw. However, com-
municating with people who do not share these understandings is much more difficult and uncomfortable, even frustrating at times. Words suddenly become more
like weapons in a battle, rather than a means of reaching out and sharing important
ideas or feelings. The pursuit of an education to bridge ethnic, gender, and social
gaps is often expensive, but the consequence of failing to connect with each other
also carries too high a price:[131]

> Every person. . .has an accent. Your accent carries the story of who you are—
> who first held you and talked to you when you were a child, where you have
> lived, your age, the schools you attended, the languages you know, your eth-
> nicity, whom you admire, your loyalties, your profession, and your class posi-
> tion. Traces of your life and identity are woven into your pronunciation, your
> phrasing, and your choice of words. Your "self" is inseparable from your
> accent. Someone who tells you they don't like the way you speak is quite like-
> ly telling you that they don't like you.[132]

Table 26 is the result of a survey, which asked, With whom do members of the
IAPFM socialize most frequently? The strong preference of Patels socializing with

Table 26
Friendship Networks of IAPFM in the U.S.

	Mosty Indian	Mix-any Ethnicity	Only Indian	American Only	Same Language	Number of Resondents
Head of household (1)	61%	31%	4%	1%	2%	150
Spouse	69%	23%	5%	0%	3%	128
Children	14%	83%	4%	0%	0%	139
Father (of 1)	47%	17%	25%	2%	9%	53
Mother (of 1)	47%	13%	29%	2%	9%	47
Percent of Total	48%	40%	8%	1%	3%	517

Note: "American only" denotes any nationality other than Indian.

mostly Indians may be due to lack of language ability, as they are not accustomed to speaking other than Gujarati. However, it is not perceived as such by respondents: 3% said they prefer only the company of people speaking the same language. A mere 1% answered that they prefer the company of Americans only. Children's preferences for friendships were quite different.

Dating and Sex in America

An anonymous Indo-American male, 22, said in an interview:

> I have been dating an American girl for four years. My parents don't know about it, and I don't want them to know. We sneak around and have had sex. Recently, my parents started looking for an Indian girl for me to marry. The main thing they look for is money. They don't understand my need to know and love a girl before I marry her. My mom and dad were introduced on a Monday and were married on that same Friday. I can't do that. No way.[133]

The social behavior reflected in this statement represents the crux of the difference and the source of greatest strife between the two generations of Indo-Americans. This situation induced writers such as Prakash N. Desai and George V. Coelho to conclude that, "An Indian adolescent is perhaps the greatest source of anxiety to Indian immigrant parents."[134] One may summarize that the second generation's uncertainty over these issues is, to a certain extent, a reflection of their confusion over broader identity issues. As noted earlier, immigrants who came to the U.S. in the mid- to late-1960s are not familiar with the concept of dating. In traditional families in India, it is still considered unconventional and improper for men and women to have pre-marital, romantic relationships.

The problem, according to the second generation, is that parents do not understand what it means to date. One young woman stated, "Parents think dating means having sex. That is not the case with a lot of people . . . Basically [dating is] a close friendship with the potential of evolving into something romantic or long-term."[135] Despite parental restrictions, 95% of the sample of the second generation said that they do date, but they were divided on the extent to which they inform their parents. Over half preferred not to let their parents know if they were seeing anyone.

Among the parents interviewed, 90% said they preferred their children to choose Indian spouses. Indians are not unlike other ethnic groups in their desire to keep marriage within the same group. The reasoning behind endogamy is that Indian marriage partners would make language, religious, and cultural preservation more likely. However, it is interesting to note that parents and children agree that a marriage partner should have the same ethnicity, religion, and language, in that order of importance. Similarly, "one is expected to marry within his/her caste," so that the husband's caste remains unchanged.[136]

Sex Education

Some researchers suggest that open communication has little effect on whether a child engages in sex. According to one study, just discussing the topic does not influence a child's decision. However, other surveys have found that talking to children can delay activity and help transmit important attitudes. Adolescents who use their parents as opposed to friends as a primary source for problem solving were less likely to be sexually active. This is where the Indian community has an advantage on children, as most Indian parents are very faithful in their marriage lives and are believers in monogamy.[137]

Table 27
Percentage of Teenagers Who Reported Talking with
Parents about Birth Control and/or Sex[138]

Sex but not birth control	Sex and birth control	Neither	Not sure
33%	35%	31%	1%

Noted below are some views about how parents understand their children's sexual activities:

> We feel that our lifestyle is misunderstood by our elders. Every move we make and every breath we take must be preceded with a seeking of permission and proceeded with an explaining of actions. Everything from prom night to after school activities becomes complicated. Our parents grew up in a very different country at a very different time. Most of our parents do not go to dancing with friends on weekends. Vacations were spent with the extended family. Our parents came to this country with values and habits they acquired during their own childhood and naturally, try to pass it on to us.
> Ironically, kids in India don't do things the way our parents did either. Young girls prefer to wear mini-skirts and fitted jeans rather than a salwar suit. Perhaps it's difficult for parents to accept what we do here because they have not witnessed changes in India. It is 50/50 effort. We must take the time and initiative to "educate" the older generation while our parents must make an effort to understand why we wish to make certain choices and realize that "different" does not always equal "wrong." In turn we should keep in mind that many of the values instilled upon us aren't ancient tribal rituals, but basic morals and family values.139

Dating is a complicated issue for Indo-American Patels, as they did not have this custom in their social lives in India. In the U.S. dating is a common practice, and children who grew up here want to know each other before they get seriously involved and marry. In a recent Orange County survey, 47% of American youth said they were currently dating, 32% were interested but not dating, and 21% said they were not interested in dating.[140] Having been raised in this country, children cannot be expected to act exactly as the parents did thirty or forty years ago in India, even though apprehensive parents hope their children will make the "right choice." After all, today, even in India, there are many more "love marriages" than there were in the 1960s and 1970s.

Ideal Mates

We are all in search of certain characteristics that we believe to make up our ideal mate. Many of us want that significant someone with whom to share the same hobbies and interests, while others simply hope for a genuine personality and sincere character. Whatever the case may be, each person seeks compatibility. The following are some attributes that IAPFM value: honesty, trust, and communication are all-important qualities. Some people would like to meet someone who has adjusted to two cultures, or someone who can adjust to Indian culture.[141]

The dating system is not a part of Patel culture, but the new generation is adopting this custom. However, American Patel children are not yet fully Americanized, as we can see from the following table that the dating approval is low overall in the Patel community as compared to American culture.

Table 28
How Important it is to IAPFM that a Future Mate is from any Patidar Caste

	Most Important	Somewhat Important	Not Important	No. of Repondents
Head of household (1)	50%	40%	10%	112
Spouse	53%	41%	6%	90
Children	36%	58%	6%	100
Father of (1)	34%	63%	3%	38
Mother of (1)	50%	42%	8%	24
Percent of Total	45%	48%	7%	364

Over 50% first generation head of the Patel households believe that marriage in any Patidar caste is most well-come versus 36% of their second-generation children.

Sub-caste seems an even more important issue to the IAPFM parents and grandparents, but less important to children. Based on survey results, 66% of first generation members think that marriage in one's own sub-caste is most important, 24% feel it is a somewhat important issue, and 10% think it is not an important issue. Over 68% of first-generation parents think it is very important that their children marry in their Patidar sub-caste. Thirty-two percent of children believe that it is most important for them to marry in their own particular Patidar sub-caste, while 68% children believe it is a somewhat important to not important issue.

How do Patels accept exogamy? Because of their religious beliefs and cultural and social differences among different ethnic groups, Patels often think this issue deserves thought with an open mind. Based on the survey, 2% of first generation family members agree to look for a spouse in any Indian ethnicity is the most welcome factor. Nineteen percent reported it is somewhat welcome to let the marriage take place in any Indian ethnicity. However, an overwhelming 78% said that marriage with any non-Indian ethnicity is *not permissible*: interracial marriage is not favorable for most Patels.

The decision to have a marriage within sub-caste, a Patel caste, any caste, or any ethnicity is a very contentious subject for the Patels because it is an important social, cultural and religious event. Children support that it is somewhat to most important (94%) that the marriage take place within the Patidar group. Sooner or later, Patidars should begin to consider themselves as one core group or caste, forgetting about their sub-caste differences and offering this solution to the next generation, so it may continue to identify itself as Patel.

How hard is it for Indo-American Patels find a suitable spouse in the United States? As far as first-generation Patels and grandparents are concerned, they want

Table 29
Choice of Spouse

	Most Important	Somewhat Important	Not Important	No. of Repondents
Any Patidar Group	35%	33%	7%	364
Own Patidar Group	53%	23%	13%	412
Any Indian (Hindu) Group	10%	33%	19%	290
Any Ethnicity	1%	11%	61%	250

their children to marry in the same caste to which they belonged. Twenty-nine percent of these two generations of family members think it is easy to find such a spouse, 53% said it is somewhat difficult to find, and 18% said it is hard to find a same-caste spouse for their children. Only 10% of children believe that it is easy to find a same-caste spouse in the community, 42% of children believe that is somewhat difficult, and 48% children believe that it is hard to find a spouse from the caste to which they belonged. Thus, as previously discussed, though marriage prospects overall are good for IAPFM, there may be some difficulty in sticking to same-caste preferences in the U.S., and this rule may have to be bent to allow for the different social conditions in which Indo-American children are living.

Interreligious and Interethnic Considerations

The number of second-generation Indian Americans is increasing, and many of them are dating men and women who are not of their religion. There are two perspectives on this type of relationship: the concerns of the parents and the concerns of the people involved. Some parents are surprised by their children's decisions and therefore, try emphasize the difficulties of interreligious marriages.

Interracial dating has become a fact of life, according to a *Los Angeles Times* Orange County news poll, conducted in June 1995, of 500 unmarried people.[142] Nearly 60% of respondents eighteen- to thirty-four years old say they have dated someone from another racial or ethnic group. Older singles were less inclined to "mixed race" dating—about 43% of people thirty-five to fifty-four years old had dated someone from another racial group, and only 15% of those fifty-five and older had done so.

Below is the view of an Indo-American high school student on "My Culture Is Also My Religion":

> While growing up in America, I remember it being hard enough growing up as an Indo-American. But it was even harder growing up as an Indo-American with two different religions. My father is a Catholic Christian, while my mother is a Brahmin Hindu. When I was younger, I did not know that these two religions were so different. I didn't even know that either religion existed independently. As I grew older, I realized that these differences were vital and opposite in my family and life. Since I had to grow up with two different religions, I looked to my culture as yet another religion that I had to confront. To me, religion is not simply a part of life, but a way of life. Many people adjust their life styles according to their religions, but when I

was younger I did not understand that my parents were trying to do that in my life, while also instilling cultural traditions.[143]

This young woman reflects what may happen in our community, as a shift from emphasis on "religion" to "culture" takes over in the minds of our youth, who grow up in a diverse society. Her confusion over separating her "Indianness" or national identity from her religion (in this case, two different religious influences) highlights the modern dilemma of the confused Indian. No wonder, then, that in important life decisions such as marriage, parents and children often cannot see eye-to-eye.

Marriage and Other Important Rituals

A colorful photograph of Ganeshjee for the occasion. Ganesh— invoked at the beginning of most ceremonies as a remover of obstacles.

In Hindu belief there are four *Ashramas*, or stages in life. The first is *Brahmacharya*, the period of studentship. The second is *Grihastha*, the stage of the householder. The third is *Vanaprastha*, the stage of the forest-dweller or hermit. Last is *Sannyasa*, the life of renunciation or asceticism. Each stage has its own duties. The practice of the four *Ashramas* regulates the life cycle from beginning to end. The first two *Ashramas* pertain to *Pravritti Marga*, or the path of work; while the two latter stages of *Vanaprastha* and *Sannyasa* are the stages of withdrawal from the world.

The second stage, *Grahastha* or householder, is entered into at marriage, when the student has completed his or her studentship and is ready to take up the duties of household life. Among all the *Ashramas*, this is the most important, because it supports all the others. Marriage is a sacrament in Hinduism. The wife is a husband's partner in life. She is his *Ardhangini*, or other-half equal. He cannot do any religious ritual without her. Marriage is a ceremony whereby two souls are brought into union spiritually, mentally, and physically, in the sacred bond of matrimony.

Marriages for Patidars have three parts: (A) customs of preparation; (B) marriage songs; and (C) marriage ceremony.

Major Customs of the Patidar Marriage

1. *First meeting*: Between prospective marriage partners.

2. *Betrothal*: *Cha-Pani* or *Chandala* (tea and *tilak* meeting).

3. *Sankalpado*: Sweets for prospective bridegroom, as well as determining the date for marriage.

4. *Kankotri*: The marriage invitation to the bridegroom's father.

5. *Ganesh Puja* (Ganesh worship): All *Puja* begins with Ganesh, for he dispels the darkness of ignorance and obstacles. No other God will accept any offerings before Ganesh.

6. *Mandap Ropan (Vedi)*: Beginning of *mandap* (canopy) making; four pillars (bamboo) are erected at each of the Four Corners and blessed.

"Pithi-vidhi" mixture turmeric and curds are massaged into the couple three days before the wedding is to take place.

Women welcome the "Jan"— bridegroom's relatives.

Men welcome "Jan"— the bridegroom's relatives.

"Pallu-vidhi"— the part of the ceremony, where the bridegroom's group give gifts to the bride to-be.

7. *Pithi*: Anointing of the bride and bridegroom who are being wed. The custom consists of using a paste made out of turmeric powder and curds. This normally should be massaged all over the body for a month (now, often three or five days) before the wedding, as this was meant to tone the muscles, strengthen the bones (or, in modern terms, "give a facial") to the body to improve appearance.

8. *Ganepat*: Family Goddess worship, establishing Ganesh, and food for the guests.

9. *Grahshanti (Santek)*: The religious ceremony is performed to satisfy the planets.

10. *Jan*: The marriage group goes to the bride's parents' town.

11. *Jan welcome and reception*: Brothers or cousins of the bride exchange coconut with the bridegroom, and they make sure he is the same bridegroom the sister has chosen. Then the bride's father, his relatives, and well-wishers come to receive Jan.

12. Utaro: A temporary lodging house for Jan.

13. *Kalvo-Breakfast*: At the lodging place, the mother of the bride offers a light breakfast to the bridegroom before the marriage ceremony.

14. *Pallu Vidhi*: The bridegroom's mother, her relatives, and well-wishers come to offer ornaments and clothing for the bride at the bride's residence.

15. *Jamanvar*: The wedding feast. Five hundred to 5,000 invited guests are served fifteen to twenty courses of vegetarian dishes with sweets and spicy foods.

16. *Varghodo*: The bridegroom goes to the bride's house on the special riding-horse for the marriage ceremony. This is one of the most colorful events of the marriage.[144]

Major Songs of Patidar Marriage Ceremonies

1. *Mara navala vevai*–My distinguished, the father-in-law of my daughter.

2. *Kanku chhanti kanlotri mokli*–A red goodluck paste is sprinkled on the invitation and sent to the *vevai*.

3. *Ji re pagarane vhela padharajo*—Please come early to this auspicious occasion.

4. *Kesariyo jan lavyo jan lavyo re*—The red pasted *vevai* brought the Jan.

5. *Radhaji re ghanu harakhya che manna*—Thank God, this is the happiest day in our life.

6. *Rukhmani lakhi kagal mokale*—The bride sends the letter to the bridegroom asking him to come and pick her up.

7. *Baharo ful barsao mera mahebub aaya hai*—The bride requests the grandeur nature to sprinkle flowers as her beloved husband comes to pick her up.

8. *Var Kanyanu sunder jodu*—Everyone present in the wedding wishes for the happiness of the couple.

9. *Khot padase have tari; Samaju balaki jaya sasre*[145]—This is the most emotional song, as the bride is leaving her parents, relatives and friends, and going to her in-laws' house, which is new to her.

Stages of the Patel Marriage Ceremony

1. *Welcome (ponkhana Var preksan or Parchhan)*: The bridegroom is welcomed by the bride's mother with a flower garland, and she escorts him to the mandap. The father of the bride washes the right foot of the bridegroom with milk and honey. The bridegroom is welcomed and treated as Maha-Vishnu (Supreme God) and the bride as Laxmi (Supreme Goddess). *Madhu parkh* (yogurt, honey, and ghee) are traditionally used in welcoming the son-in-law.

2. *Arrival of Bride*: *Mama* (the maternal uncle) and friends carry the bride to the mandap. This is followed by the garlanding ceremony.

3. *Kanyadaan*: Consent of the parents is obtained for the wedding to proceed.

4. *Ganth Bandhan* (Joining of Hands): The end of the bride's sari is knotted with the groom's cloth piece to symbolize their sacred union.

5. *Pani-Grahana* (Proffering of bride's hand): The parents of the bride offer her hand to the bridegroom and request him to accept their daughter. They present her with clothing and jewelry.

6. *Vaivahik-Homa* (invoking the sacred fire): The sacred fire is invoked and oblations are poured into it. Agni (fire) is the mouth of Vishnu and symbolizes illumination of mind, knowledge, and happiness.

7. *Shilaropana*: The bride places her right foot on the stone. The bridegroom tells her to be as firm as the stone in his house, so that they can face the onslaughts of enemies and the difficulties of life together.

Traditional luncheon setting served during a wedding celebration. Plates and bowls made out of dried khakhra leaves stitched together.

8. *Laja Homa* (Putting parched rice in the sacred fire): Three oblations are offered to the sacred fire. The brother of the bride puts parched rice into the bride's hands, half of which slips further into the bridegroom's hands underneath. Mantras are chanted. The bride prays to Yama, the God of Death, that he grants long life, health, happiness, and prosperity to the bridegroom.

9. *Agni Parikrama (Mangal Pherah)*: This is the most important part of the ceremony, as it is believed by all Hindus that the bride is protected by the moon for the first seven years of her life, followed by the sun for the next seven years, and *Agni* for the following seven years. Therefore, the bride and the groom have to perform *Agni Parikrama* (walking around the fire), going around four times. The first three times the bride leads, and the fourth time the bridegroom leads, approaching the fire with seven steps.

10. *Saptapadi* (Taking seven steps): The bride and the bridegroom take seven steps around the scared fire. At each step they invoke the blessings of God for food, strength, family, prosperity, progeny, enjoying life together, performing religious rites together, and for a life-long friendship.

11. *Saubhagya Chinha* (Blessing the bride): The bridegroom blesses the bride by putting *kumkum* or *sindhur* (vermilion red powder) at the parting of her hair or forehead, and by giving her *mangalsutra* (a sacred necklace).

12. *Surya-Darshana* (Looking at the sun): The bridegroom accepts the bride as his wife in the presence of the Sun and tells her to look at it, or at *Dhruva* (the star of steadfastness) and *Arundhati* (the star of devotion), if the marriage is performed at night. He asks her to be firm in her love and duty and to be as devoted to him as Arundhati (Vashishtha's wife) was to the sage, Vashishtha. The bride tells the bridegroom that she sees them and promises to be as steadfast and as devoted as they are.

13. *Haridaya-Sparsha* (Touching of hearts): The bride and the bridegroom touch each other's heart. The bride tells the bridegroom: "I touch thy heart unto mine. God has given thee as my husband. May my heart be thine and thy heart be mine forever."

14. *Anna-Prashana* (Feeding the bridegroom): The bride feeds the bridegroom and tells him: "By feeding this sweet food I shall bind thy heart with the thread of truth, sincerity and love."

15. *Purnahuti-Posh Puja and Aashirvad* (Completion of ceremony): After the final oblation is poured into the sacred fire, the priest blesses the bride and the bridegroom. Flower petals and rice are distributed to the guests, who shower them on the bride and the bridegroom and bless them. With these blessings, the marriage ceremony is completed.

16. *Kanyadan* (Gifts): The *Saga Sambandhi* (friends and well-wishers) give gifts to the bride on this auspicious occasion to wish her good luck.

17. *Kanya Vidaya* (bride and jan-groom's group send-off): This is the most emotional and heartbreaking scene in a marriage ceremony. After raising the girl in the family for twenty years or more and loving her more than themselves, her parents, family members and friends break down in tears as they send off this piece of their heart.

Many Asian Indian Patels in the United States follow Hindu Customs during special life occasion, such as this wedding.

18. *Welcome to the bridegroom's home*: Parents, family, and neighbors bless the bride and groom, and they get blessings from their family God and Goddess, too.[146]

Arranged, Traditional, and Modern Marriages

When a young son or daughter completes an education, starts a career, and is ready to get married, immigrant Hindu parents experience a great deal of enthusiasm, apprehension, and anxiety. Due to their traditional cultural backgrounds and maturity, the parents' viewpoints are relatively more conservative, rational, and less emotional than those of their youngsters. A young adult who may or may not be born in the U.S. but has been raised in the dual cultural environment grows up as a young person full of dreams and desirous of fulfilling them. After raising children and

"Vehechen" traditional gift giving at a wedding ceremony.

supporting a family, parents have experienced the difficulties of married life and have overcome many of their own shortcomings. They want their children to have the benefit of their understanding when choosing among available alternatives. A young adult, on the other hand, is full of dreams, attracted by physical appearance and first impressions, and gives less thought to the long-lasting and profoundly important aspects of marriage. These two viewpoints are not really in conflict with each other but nonetheless need negotiation to arrive at the selection of a compatible spouse.

There are many misconceptions about arranged and "traditional" marriages. Arranged marriages take place after an agreement among parents, without seeking the prior consent of bride and groom. A "traditional marriage" may be suggested by either the parents or by the bride and groom themselves, and later be approved by others.

Traits for which Indian parents typically seek in a bride for their son include: kind and pleasant personality, a noble or honorable family background, an adequate education, a thorough cultural and religious background, a good homemaker. The order of importance of these characteristics will vary in each case.

What traits would a Hindu parent prefer for a groom for their daughter? Nobility, and financial security, plus the moral and ethical strengths: kindness, maturity, education, and mental compatibility are factors that no parent can overlook.

Many parents are less worried about their son's marriage than their daughter's marriage for several reasons. First, there is the perception that a son will be more judged by his career, whilst a daughter will be more judged by her good family life—even though many young Indo-American women are being educated just as much as their brothers. Secondly, there is a traditional tendency to "marry up" one's daughters, so that a husband's caste is not altered in his marriage with the joining of the two.

In the U.S. there are two distinct categories of parents:

1) Those who have children born here or who immigrated with very young children. This category is divided into two groups as well:

   a) Those who raised children in an Indian cultural and religious environment. These children have gone to Sunday schools and are involved in Hindu religious activities, and generally have maintained good communication with their parents. These youngsters may prefer to marry a spouse raised and born in the Hindu culture.

b) Those who invest little time in Hindu traditions and culture in their children, and the youngsters belonging to this group may have more intense influences from their peer groups than parental influences.

2) Then there are those parents who immigrated with their teenage children. These parents are more vulnerable to potentially challenging situations, if continuation of Indian disciplines is not followed in these households. While these parents work very hard to make ends meet, their children are able to enjoy more liberties than they did at home. On the other hand, they may also be more agreeable to the Indian marriage process, since they were raised with it during their young, impressionable stages there.

Children of those who arrived in the 1960s and 1970s are reaching their middle twenties, the magic age for marriage There are four distinct categories of marriage among these youngsters:

Carriage— bride send off (kanya-viday) by bride's group.

1) The traditional marriage, in which youngsters, based on their own acquaintance or parents' suggestions, express preferences for a spouse, and with the blessings of all parties concerned, they marry.

2) The transnational marriage, in which a young man goes to India or overseas and marries. The groom who highly values Hindu culture and wants to raise a traditional family prefers this arrangement. The spouse may be financially less supportive initially but is culturally more in tune with traditions. However, there are always exceptions in this category for young women raised in urban environments and influenced by western lifestyles.

3) There is a similar but less common marriage for girls, in which a girl who has immigrated not many years ago visits India and finds a suitable spouse through her kin-networks there. In this case extra caution is required to prevent the possibility of a non-compatible situation. Indian boys, raised in a male-dominated society, who are not well versed in communication skills and unfamiliar with the gender balance in the U.S., may not be able to accept less submissive spouses, while the wife would expect to enjoy equal rights in the marriage.

4) Finally, there are interfaith or interracial marriages. Although their popularity is very limited, some men have married Caucasian women, and some women have married Caucasian and African American young men. There are many successful interracial and interfaith marriages, but there are added factors of possible incompatibility. Unlike in India, a person in the U.S. does not live in a closed society and is not subject to peer pressure to conform to traditional norms.[147]

An analysis of 1980 U.S. Census data by Little India Data Service shows that 24.6% of Indian men and 8.3% of Indian women who got married in America married outside their own ethnicity. This figure is the second highest figure for Asian American men, the top being Filipino men (35.6%). The figure is relatively low for Indian women, who seem to be the least likely to marry out of their group.[148]

There are additional challenging situations for young women who become career-oriented. When well advanced in a career, there may be a limited number of available bachelors. Parents may be torn between encouraging a daughter in her career and marriage. Eventually some young women may settle for interfaith or interracial marriages or remain single for a long time.

Arranged Marriages

According to Hindu scriptures, marriage begins the householder stage of life, or Grahastha.[149] The couple recites vows to heaven and earth, and pledges friendship and kindness to one another. It may take the sacred "seven steps" to achieve this. After all, the essence of the Hindu marriage is to create a mutual bond of love and respect that is conducive to the intellectual, emotional, and spiritual growth of the individuals involved. Hinduism defines marriage as a holy union of two souls facilitating further uplifting towards the divine, and at the same time propagating the human race.

Indian marriages that end up in divorce are minimal compared to rates in Western nations. Arranged marriages are popular in the Indian community. For some, it may be parental pressures that force them to find a partner in this manner; for others, it may very well be a path they have chosen on their own to find their partner. For parents, it is usually the only way they know from their own experiences. Yet, for the younger generation, it is an option.

Puneet Sehgul questioned young Indian women in order to learn their views on this contentious subject. She spoke with a few who commented, "Arranged marriages are interesting." Other comments include: "You don't really know someone unless you date them," and "I would prefer to meet people through normal circumstances like at parties or through friends." Dating builds more of a natural relationship, allowing young couple to grow with an individual without parental expectations interfering. Compatibility in intellect, backgrounds, interests, etc., is indeed a hard treasure to find. Whatever choice each individual makes, it will always be a challenge to find the right person for the future.[150]

Marriage in the United States

Of the 2% of single first-generation Patels, some may be widowed or divorced, and others may be looking for their marriage partners.

Most Hindu Patels believe that marriage is the way to achieve the ultimate goal of *Nirvana*. According to Hindu Indian culture, no girl should die without marrying, and every man and woman should have a child, so when a man dies his body can be

Table 30
Patels' Age of Marriage

	SINGLE	<10	10-20	20-25	25-30	30+	Number of Respondents
(1)Head of household	2%	3%	9%	71%	12%	2%	91
Spouse	0%	6%	52%	33%	8%	1%	88
Children	48%	1%	8%	34%	8%	1%	119
Father of (1)	0%	10%	62%	26%	3%	0%	39
Mother of (1)	0%	14%	71%	7%	7%	0%	42
Percent of Total	16%	5%	31%	39%	8%	1%	379

cremated under the ritual ceremony carried out by his eldest son or whichever son is present at the time of the funeral. This is the way one can get salvation or rest in peace.

There was a time, fifty or sixty years ago, when children used to get married at the age of two. Parents carried them on their laps, and marriage ceremonies were performed. Later, when they reached the age of sixteen, the bride joined the groom and started family life. In this situation there were very few divorces. Of the first generation Patels 71% of the men married between ages 20-25 years whereas 52% women married between the age of 10 to 20 years. Twelve percent of grandparents married when they were less than ten years old. Sixty-six percent were betrothed by the ages of 10 to 20 years.

Patel Mate Choices

Survey results indicate that 64% of IAPFM believe that the looks of the spouse are important, while 32% of family members consider looks of the spouse very important. Fifty-six percent of family members (including children) give the future spouse's intelligence very much importance, while 42% said it is of medium importance as an attribute. Almost half of first-generation Patel husbands and wives gave the most importance to intelligence as a factor in selecting in-laws. Among children, 79% said intelligence is a very important factor in their spouse selection, while 21% said it is of medium influence.

How important is the financial standing of the prospective families? Nine percent of family members give the most importance to money, when the arranged or traditional marriage takes place in the family, while 50% said it is of medium importance, and 42% said it is not important at all. Comparing the first generation with the second generation, 34% versus 68%, respectively, said that the financial status of the spouse's family is not important.

The following is a summary of the Patels' thoughts about values in the prospective spouse. Fifty percent of family members agree that strong family tradition of both the bride and groom is the most important ingredient in selecting a spouse family, while 44% said it is of medium importance, and 6% said this is not an important factor. Over 50% of members of all three generations agree on the issue of families' traditional values being the most important requirement to tie the families together.

Looks

Table 31
Summary of IAPFM Important Traits in Future Spouse

	Most Important	Average	Not Important	Number of Respondents
Looks	32%	64%	4%	443
Intelligence	56%	42%	2%	448
Financial status	9%	50%	42%	436
Traditional values	50%	44%	6%	446

Patels Findings

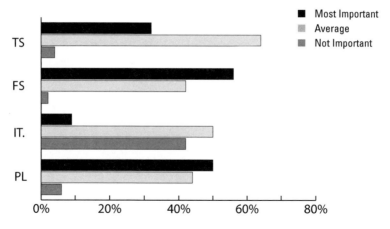

TS: Traditional Values, FS: Financial Status, IT: Intelligence, PL: Personal

Table 32
Qualities in Ideal Mate: Findings of Orange County Residents[151]

	Very Important	Somewhat Important	Not Important
Looks	16%	58%	26%
Intelligent	60%	36%	4%
Financially well-off	7%	46%	47%
Shares your values	69%	26%	5%

Orange County Residents Findings

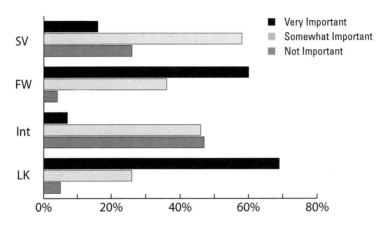

SV: Shares your values, FW: Financially well-off, Int: Intelligence, LK: Looks

Intelligence and sharing of values rated as the most important qualities when look-ing for a spouse, as opposed to looks and financial status in both Orange County res-idents and Patels.

CHAPTER 9

THE GENERATION GAP

Bicultural conflict can create a wide gap between immigrant parents and their children. Immigrants who arrived as children more quickly absorb American ways of thought and practice. Asian American children naturally begin to question their parents' ways. When parents arrive in the United States, by contrast, their work schedules often limit their time for English classes or to become involved in American pastimes and activities. Since their English proficiency is low or lacking, they must sometimes rely upon their children to be intermediaries in their contact with the English-speaking world. With children leading and parents following, a reversal of parent-child role ensues, and respect for parents may decrease, many times due to misunderstandings. Whereas parents once commanded respect and obedience, they now experience dependence upon their children, a position that is uncomfortable for them and strange for their children.

An interviewer once told the story of a Korean immigrant family in which the children had all but lost the ability to speak Korean after just a few years in American schools.[152] The parents could only speak English with difficulty, and the grandmother who lived with the family could neither speak nor understand it. She felt isolated and unappreciated by her grandchildren. The adults spoke to the children exclusively in Korean. They refused to believe that the children could not understand them. They interpreted the children's unresponsiveness as disrespect and rejection. It was only when the interviewer, a bilingual Korean-English speaker, tried to question the children in both languages that the parents finally realized that the children were no longer able to speak or understand Korean. The father wept as he spoke of not being able to talk to his children. One of the children commented that she did not understand why her parents always seemed to be so angry.

The Elderly

When there were only few Asian American families in the U.S., the elderly members of the family tended to return to their native country in the mature years of their lives. Today, however, the migration stream is reversed: more older Asians continue to arrive, even into their sixties and seventies. In 1990, Asian Pacific Islander (API) males sixty-five years and older comprised of 5.6% of the U.S. population and API females made up 6.8%.[153] Unfortunately, it is more difficult for older people to adapt to new ways and to acquire a new language. If they live with their adult children, they are somewhat protected, but there are still problems—one is the ever widening gap between them and their grandchildren.

Asian American children usually lose or never acquire fluency in their parents' native language, and often grandparents cannot speak English, so this situation results in little communication between them. In addition, Asian American children may not have learned to respect the elderly in the same way as is practiced in Asian countries. If the family lives far away from an ethnic community, the elderly suffer loneliness. Even if living with their children, the elderly are often left home during the day as the family goes off to work or school. They cannot talk to their neighbors and are afraid to venture out, remaining isolated. Coming from Asian countries where people live closely packed together, this can be depressing and alienating

Loneliness

Table 33
IAPFM Report Feeling Loneliness in American Life

	Often	Sometimes	Rarely	Never	No. of Resondents
(1) Head of household	6%	33%	35%	26%	78
Spouse	3%	40%	33%	25%	73
Children	1%	13%	53%	33%	97
Father of (1)	16%	68%	12%	4%	25
Mother of (1)	19%	56%	22%	4%	27
Percent of Total	6%	33%	37%	24%	**300**

The grandparent generation has a much harder time to adjusting to life in the United States. They miss their native land and their old companions. While most family members are busy with their own work, grandparents do not have any activities to pass their time. In comparison, IAPFM agree with Orange County residents answered this question of how often they feel loneliness in the following manner: 35% said they feel loneliness sometimes, 39% rarely, 20% never, and 7% a lot of the time.[154]

Problems with Parents

One of the reasons behind miscommunications between first-generation parents and second-generation children is that both groups have grown up in such vastly different environments. Below are some perspectives of second-generation children on their problems with parents:

Everyday life in our parents' hometown and ours are on opposite ends of the spectrum. I can recite verbatim the lectures regarding how hard the schoolwork in India was back then, and how easy we have it here. I get interrogated on "What is this rap music? Why don't you listen to classical?"

Our parents seem to see the extreme opposite side of everything and sometimes assume that we are being sucked in. If a girl calls, many parents are about ready to move. A good number of situations, relationships, and attitudes that we teens see as innocent, our parents view as a cause for war. Our parents would collapse if they found out that you know of "that part of the school" where our peers smoke. We beg our parents for a little freedom, and they see it as consenting to fatherhood.

These expectations are magnified because we are Indian. As a community, we have this reputation of excelling in our studies and are forced to find a happy medium where we are not wearing neon green pocket protectors but are still successful. Times have changed, but many attitudes have remained firm. The difference between our generation and our parents' generation is too sizable to grasp. Our parents need to see that we are dedicated to our education even though we want to have fun once in a while. They need to realize that even though we are not doctors by the age of 12, our lives are not wasted.[155]

Table 34
Cause of Tensions: Arranged Marriages

	Most Important	Somewhat Important	Not Important	No. of Repondents
(1) Head of household	40%	49%	11%	117
Spouse	36%	54%	9%	96
Children	44%	44%	13%	96
Father of (1)	50%	40%	10%	40
Mother of (1)	38%	46%	17%	24
Percent of Total	**41%**	**47%**	**12%**	**373**

First and second generation Patels are equally affected by arranged marriage problems. When looking at the causes of friction for career choice within a family, 30% of first-generation Patels believe that the main cause of friction in the family is due to job or career choice issues, while 55% believe it is somewhat important. Ninety-two percent of children believe that their career choice is somewhat important to the most important issue in their problems with parents' wishes versus their own decision making.

When looking at parental control cause of tension, 89% of first-generation Patels feel that parental control is a somewhat to the most important cause of tension in their homes. About the same percent of second-generation children believe that

Table 35
Summary of Causes of Tension Between IAPFM Parents and Children

	Most Important	Somewhat Important	Not Important	Number of Repondents
Arranged Marriage	41%	47%	12%	373
Career Choice	33%	56%	11%	351
Parental Control	25%	59%	16%	350
Children's Behavior	38%	49%	13%	330

parental control is a somewhat important to the most important cause of friction between the children and parents in these families. In other words, these two generations agree that they do not agree over issues of control.

Fifty-two percent of first-generation Patels feel that their children's behavior is a somewhat important cause of difficulties between them, and 33% believe it is the most important cause of tension. Among the second generation, 83% of children of Indo-American Patels responded that their behavior is somewhat important to the most important cause of strife in their families.

It is interesting to note that 41% of Patels believe that arranged marriages is the cause of friction within an Indo-American Patel family, while only 25% responded that parental control was the greatest cause of friction.

Social Life

Table 36
Frequency of Time IAPFM Spend Socializing with Friends

	Once a a week	Few Times a month	Once a month	Never or Hardly	Number of Resondents
(1) Head of household	51%	27%	21%	1%	73
Spouse	47%	36%	16%	1%	76
Children	37%	38%	22%	2%	91
Father of (1)	46%	31%	19%	4%	26
Mother of (1)	55%	32%	9%	5%	22
Percent of Total 4	5%	34%	19%	2%	288

"Visiting friends or relatives" means casual visits within the nearby vicinity in which they live. Of course, they probably visit relatives or friends at home in India when there is a marriage or death, or visit family members who may reside even 3,000 miles away in U.S., either on vacations or for important ceremonious occasions.

The grandparent generation has roughly the same tendency as the first generation to visit friends. They may be less likely to have friends in the United

Table 37
Frequency of Time IAPFM Spend with Relatives

	Once a a week	Few Times a month	Once a month	Never or Hardly	No. of Resondents
(1) Head of household	26%	44%	30%	0%	70
Spouse	22%	48%	30%	0%	77
Children	15%	25%	60%	1%	89
Father of (1)	41%	36%	23%	0%	22
Mother of (1)	45%	32%	23%	0%	22
Percent of Total	24%	38%	38%	0%	280

States. An additional problem for them is that they mostly depend upon their children's driving.

Comparing first-generation Patels with second-generation children, 70% of first-generation Patels visit relatives a few times a month to once a week, while 40% of second-generation children visit relatives a few times a month to once a week.

However, comparing the first generation with the second generation on socializing, 80% of the first generation visit friends a few times a month to once a week,

Table 38
Summary: Time Spent with Friends and Relatives

	OW	FM	OM	NV	No. of Respondents
Friends	45%	33%	19%	0.3%	288
Relatives	24%	37%	38%	0.2%	280

OW- Once a week, FM- Few times a month, OM- Once a month, NV – Never or hardly.

Table 39
Love Life Satisfaction of IAPFM

	Very Satisfied	Satisfied	Adequate Satisfied	Somewhat Satisfied	Not Satisfied	No. of Respondents
(1)Head of household	35%	42%	12%	10%	1%	81
Spouse	29%	39%	23%	8%	1%	75
Children	46%	26%	13%	11%	4%	46
Father of (1)	48%	19%	14%	19%	0%	21
Mother of (1)	41%	18%	18%	18%	6%	17
Percent of Total	**37%**	**34%**	**16%**	**11%**	**2%**	**240**

Table 40
Patel Life in U.S. Compared to Life in Native Countries

	Excellent	Good	Fair	Poor	No. of Respondents
(1) Head of household	20%	54%	25%	2%	133
Spouse	22%	56%	20%	2%	116
Children	63%	31%	6%	0%	131
Father of (1)	24%	36%	36%	5%	42
Mother of (1)	17%	47%	25%	11%	36
Percent of Total	**33%**	**46%**	**19%**	**2%**	**458**

while 75% of the second generation visit friends a few times a month to once a week. The first and second generations are about equal in their time spent with friends, but the second generation is a bit less with respect to visiting relatives: 40% visit with relatives a few times a month to once a week, while 75% visit with friends that often.

Overall, most Indo- American Patels are satisfied or very satisfied with their love lives. When comparing U.S. women to the Patels women, 43% of the U.S. women reported they are not satisfied in their love lives, compared to 2% of Patel women who reported the same.

Comparing all three generations: 25% of first-generation Patels think they have a fair to poor life in the U.S., 6% of second-generation children feel this way, while 39% of the grandparent generation reports similar feelings. The grandparent generation is much less happy than their succeeding generations, while first-generation parents also seem to be less happy than the second generation. One is almost always more attached to one's native land, or where one grew up, and that makes it more difficult for the elder generations to adjust to their adopted land. Even in the Moghul emperor's time, it is said that King Barber used to return to his native land from India to taste watermelon.

Bonds with the Native Land

Modern communication systems and jet travel have made the diasporic situation both easier, and in some ways more difficult, than in the past. Now we are more frequently able to renew our contacts with home, our family, and our village. However, it is also more difficult now than this would seem, because it is precisely this tantalizing access that complicates the agonizing conflict between adjustment to the world around us and loyalty to our cultural legacy—a loyalty that fades with each succeeding generation born in the diaspora. As we are cut off from the native land, the source of daily cultural self-generation, we have to preserve what we can of our heritage and merge with others around us, whether they be Americans in Queens or a pan-Indian potpourri in Delhi.

In addition to their attachments to other Indians abroad, Indian immigrants continue to maintain strong ties to India. Given that this group of immigrants came to the U.S. beginning in the mid-1960s, many have now spent more years of their lives living abroad than they have spent living in India. Yet, the bonds with India seem unrelentingly strong. Many still have extended families living in India. One hundred percent of adult sample[155] had visited India with their spouses and children at least once since immigration.

Interest in Indian politics and affairs also remains strong, reflected by the familiarity level of the sample with numerous publications for Indians in the United States. Although no one in the sample had acted on the original intention of returning permanently to India within a few years, over 70% said they had entertained the idea of ultimately resettling in India. Only one person, however, said that he was definite in his intentions to return.

As one would expect, the ties that children of immigrants feel to their homeland are not as strong as those felt by their parents. At the same time, it seems that the ties immigrants themselves retained with India have not weakened notably: many still visit India regularly and have family there.[157]

Visits to India: Between Indian and American Lives

Visiting India can be a wonderful experience. What do Indo-Americans think about their voyages to the homeland? Neil Shah, a junior at Northridge, CA, says, "India is a growing nation which is beginning to adopt western ways of living, working, and thinking. People are accepting more modern living standards. Yet, beneath this surface of modernization, India's deeply rooted culture, values, and religious practices strongly exist within the lives of its people." It is this combination of westernization and cultural heritage that gives Indo-American reason to settle in India. Even members of today's younger generation have formulated their own thoughts about settling in India permanently. Some would not live anywhere but in the U.S., while others would jump at the chance to live in India. Neil Shah visited India for the second time. When he left India this time, he brought with him not only a humble appreciation for what God has given him, but a sense of his identity. He began to learn about India instead of shrugging it off as an inferior, third-world counterpart of America.[158]

Mohin Mehta says, "However dirty, noisy, overpopulated India is, it is our own. We are not aliens or outsiders there. It was once our home. The ties are invisible, but strong. The reality may be attractive to some and disgusting to others. It all depends on one's priorities in life." She is left without a sure feeling about where she should live, but hopes that someday, she will feel 100% secure in her decision whether she chooses to reside in India or in America.

Arti Kamboj prefers the U.S. because she can experience different cultures, and women have more opportunities for learning here than in India.

Priti Choksi, however, would consider settling in India because she loves the social structure, the environment, and the warmth within people. Because she grew up in India, the best memories of her childhood are in India. Yet one thing she dislikes about India is the country's work ethic: she feels there is a great deal of procrastination, red tape, and bribery in the workplace.[159]

During her visit to India, Ms. Gupta quickly realized that India is not without its share of problems. With an enormous population and limited resources, homelessness and begging are common, which can be shocking to Americans. She was riding in a car when a young girl came to her and asked for some money. As she handed fifty *paisa* to the girl, she realized that there were countless others all over India who live in the same manner. After living in India for a few weeks, she thought that the people of India had lost their sense of civic duty. The streets of India have become the garbage cans for the Indians living there. However, amidst all of India's many troubles, she was struck by the enormous and deep beauty of the culture.

Ms. Gupta's next excursion took her to rural India. Her first instinct told her that she would never fit in their world. However, she soon realized that she had never felt so much at ease with anyone before. The whole village, which consisted of about 500 people, gathered to greet her. They offered a huge home-cooked Indian meal and demonstrated unbelievable hospitality. They may not have had much more than huts and their land, but she knew that it was all truly theirs. They had built the huts with their own hands, and the food that they set before them was produced after months of hard work in the fields. They offered them everything they had and expected nothing in return. She believes these people are the epitome of India.

Ms. Gupta's trip to India helped her to learn a lot about her heritage. To most people, India may be just another third-world country, but she knows that there are few places as deep in culture and history. There is a certain beauty that is unique to India, one that makes her sure that she will return again soon. As she left India, she felt a close bond to what she is proud to identify as her native land.[160]

Overall, how do other Asians feel about their native land? Ninety percent of Asians who have been in the U.S. seven years or less keep in touch with friends and relatives often, while 77% of Asians who have been in the U.S. eight to fifteen years still keep in touch with friends and relatives. After sixteen or more years in the U.S., the percent drops to 64 %.[161]

How does this compare with overall visits to India for either business or pleasure purposes? How often do Patels travel back to India?

Table 41
Patel Trips to India

	1	2	>4	None	No. of Respondents
(1)Head of household	20%	24%	46%	10%	147
Spouse	22%	30%	42%	7%	125
Children	22%	40%	21%	17%	152
Father of (1)	30%	21%	47%	2%	47
Mother of (1)	32%	27%	41%	0%	37
Percent of Total	**23%**	**30%**	**37% 1**	**0%**	**508**

Parents must be the main motivators who insist that children visit their ancestral land. Second-generation children, whether born in the U.S. or in India, will still have a strong affection for their ancestral land. Though they may initially feel uncomfortable with the poor sanitary conditions and poverty in India, India's great culture and unity in diversity will attract them forever.

Ninety percent of the first generation Indo- American Patels have visited India at least once after their arrival in U.S., 44% of them made trips to India more than four or more times during their life time stay in U.S. Even 83% of their children have made trips to India once or more with their parents or by themselves.

CHAPTER 10

OTHER TRADITIONS

Other Patidar Festivals

Patidar celebrate all Hindu festivals. These Indian festivals enlighten people about their religion and culture. Festivals bring to memory the heroes of the past. One can then follow in their footsteps and thereby improve one's way of life. Festivals rouse a nation towards progress. People are usually too involved in their daily work, which makes them tired in mind and body. Festivals can enliven and refresh our minds and bring us joy.

Ram Nauvami

Every hill and rivulet of Bharat (India) bears the imprint of the holy feet of Rama and Sita. Sri Rama reigns supreme to this day in the hearts of Indian people, cutting across all barriers of province, language, caste, or sect. Sri Rama's story, the *Ramayana*, has been sung and resung in all the languages and dialects of Bharat. The devotion to *dharma* came first in Rama's life, and considerations for his personal joys and sorrows came last. He would always be the first to openly appreciate the unique and noble traits in others' characters. Even for Kaikeyi (his stepmother), who was responsible for his banishment to the forest, Rama had only words of kindness. As for Ravana, the abductor of his wife, Rama's unstinted praise of his erudition and powers uplifts the story of the Ramayana to heights unsurpassed in the annals of human history. The birthday of Sri Rama in the last week of April signifies an event worthy of remembrance by everyone—whatever his or her nationality, ethnicity, or religion—who cherishes these time-honored and sublime values of human culture and civilization.

Janmastami

Krishna is worshipped in various incarnations. One of these, his most mature, serenely philosophical form, is depicted in the *Bhagvad Gita*. Another aspect of Krishna is that of a mischievous child, who steals butter from the pantry. Another is his romantic aspect in which heats dance to the flute-call of Lord Krishna. Men and women, young and old, rich and poor, all rejoice; for it is during the month of August/September Shravan Vad Aathem that we have the celebration of the birth of Lord Krishna, *Janmastami*.

Flowers, fruits, and sweets are offered at every shrine. Temples are decorated with sandalwood paste and even the fields are clothed with golden grain, for it is the rainy season "of mellow fruits and mists." Families recite from the *Mahabharat* for eight days. They feed the priests and the poor. Many fast all day. Now, as dusk falls, the temple bells herald the coming of Bhagavan (Lord) Krishna: incense is lit, and people gather to sing the *bhajans* (devotional songs) and hear the story of his birth. *Puja* (ritual worship) is performed, ending at midnight, the mystical hour of Krishna's nativity. Afterward, *prasad* (foods offered to the deity) of sugared dal coconut chips is distributed, and children especially look forward to the next day, with its delicacies, processions, songs, and dances.

Krishna was born in Mathura, by the banks of the River Jamuna, near the forests of Brindaban. He came in answer to the prayers of the oppressed people of the wicked King Kansa. In the final act of the life drama of Sri Krishna, he conveyed to his beloved disciple Arjuna the immortal teaching that has come to mankind as the *Bhagavad Gita*. The divine incarnation, Bhagavan Krishna, lived and taught more than 5,000 years ago, but the soul-melting melody of his flute of divine love ever calls mankind to seek God in the silence of meditation.[162]

Maha Sivaratri

In the months of February/March, honors Lord Shiva's birthday. Shiva has several personalities. The most prominent are a personification of the awesome and terrifying aspects of nature, a lord of animals, a great ascetic, and a master of arts—as the king of Dancers whose cosmic dance provides the rhythm of the universe. People in North India drink *bhang* and celebrate his birthday.

Patel celebrate their Indian heritage in the Navrati Garba.

Navarathri, or the Nine-Day Worship of Devi

This holiday is known as the "Festival of Nights," honoring the goddesses, beginning on the ninth day of the month of September/October. Total worship lasts for nine days, out of which the first three are devoted to Durga (the goddess of Valor).

"Mother" is adored as Power and Force–or, Durga, the terrible. One prays to Mother Durga to destroy all impurities, vices, and defects. The next three days are devoted to Lakshmi (the goddess of Wealth), who exemplifies Purity itself. The last three days are dedicated to Sarswathi (the Goddess of Knowledge). She bestows the knowledge of the Supreme Nada (voice) and then gives full *atman gnan* (self-realization), as represented in her pure, dazzling, snow-white apparel.

The tenth day is known as *Vijaya Dasami*, or Dasara. Dasara is another name for the nine-day Navarathri festival. Dasara is a celebration of the victory of Goddess Durga (Kali) over the demon in the form of a buffalo named Mahishasura. Dasara marks the triumphant ovation of the *jiva* (soul) at having attained *jivanmukti* (salvation), through the descent of knowledge by the grace of Goddess Sarswathi.

Ganesha Chathurthi

Ganesha is a fat and jovial deity invoked at the beginning of most ceremonies as a remover of obstacles. He is the leader of the army of Siva, his father; but in truth he is the Lord of the divine force inside and outside the human body. Ganesh's festival, *Chatrthi Vikram Sanvat Bhadarva vad aathem,* is held in August/September. Chathurthi is celebrated around the world with Hindus as the birthday of Lord Ganesh, the elephant headed God of wisdom and remover of obstacles. One of the most important parts of the festival is making clay images of Ganesha and worshipping them for seven or ten days. On the last day, these images are ceremoniously immersed in the ocean or in a lake.

Hanuman

Hanuman is the monkey god who helped Rama. He is one of the most popular of village deities and often is found as a household god. Hanuman is also known as Maruti (the son of Marut, the god of wind) and has a colorful personality encountered in the great epic, the *Ramayana*. He is also worshipped as the god of physical strength. Hanuman's birthday falls in *Chaitri sud Punama* (March/April).

He has carved out for himself a permanent place in every Hindu's heart because of his deep love and worship of his master Rama. His love expressed itself in unquestioning obedience and devoted service, often involving great sacrifice. He was gifted with tremendous strength and swiftness in movement equaling that of the wind. Hanumana was instrumental in searching for Sita and locating her. When Laksmana was struck unconsciously by the weapon *sakati*, discharged by Induragit (Ravan's son), it was Hanumana who came to the rescue by bringing a life-saving herb from the hill Susena. Unable to identify the necessary herb, Hanumana brought a hill itself! And thus Laksmana was revived. He is now worshiped as an ideal embodiment of strength, self-control and continence, along with a high sense of duty, sacrifice and supreme devotion.

Diwali—India's Festival of Lights

Probably the most popular and most colorful Indian festival, Divali is celebrated for as many as five days from the end of *Asvin vad barash* (Indian calendar of the last month) to the beginning of *Katrik sud Padv*, the Hindu new year (October/November). Bazaars are besieged for new clothes, jewelry, and household articles. To Lakshmi (the goddess of good fortune, prosperity, grace and beauty) coins, fruits and sweets are offered. Diwali signifies the triumph of light over darkness, good over evil, truth over falsehood. It was during Diwali that Rama and Sita returned to their capital Ayodhya, following Rama's victory over Ravana. Jubilantly and with great festivities, the inhabitants of the capital received the royal pair by lighting rows of small oil lamps along balconies and windows to welcome Rama and Sita home. The lamps that are kindled during Diwali symbolize the divine purifying light, which the great Rabindranath Tagore must have had in mind when he wrote, "In my house with thine own hands light the lamp of thy love!"[163]

The Holi Festival

Long ago a demon king, Hiranyakashipu, ruled the world. He proclaimed himself as God and made everyone pray to him, but his son Prahlad persisted in worshipping Lord Vishnu instead. As per order of Hiranyakasipu, a female demon named Holika, who believed herself to be immune to the ravages of fire, carried Prahlad into a fire. Due to the blessing of Lord Vishnu, Prahlada came out unharmed by the fire, whereas Holika was burnt to ashes. The Holi festival celebrates this mythological event. During the day following Holi, celebrated in *Falgun sud chaudas-Punam dhuleti* (February/March), people throw colored water and bright herbal powder at one another.

The Raxa Bandhan

During this celebration, a sister ties a *Rakhi*, a handspun cotton thread dyed yellow with turmeric, around the wrist of her brother. He, in return, gives her a present of clothing, cash or jewelry, and becomes responsible for her safety. This symbolic exchange is carried out during Raxa Bandhan, in the month of Shravan/August.

Patidar's Rituals

The two most popular rituals are *puja* and *yajna*. Some of the *samskaras*, or ritual sacraments, practiced by Patidar are:
1. *Jatakarma*: Birth ritual involving the preparation of the astrological chart of the child.
2. *Namakarana*: Naming the child.
3. *Chudakarana*: First cutting of the hair.
4. *Vidyarambha*: Learning of the alphabet.
5. *Upanayana*: Holy thread ritual.
6. *Tirth Yatra*: Visiting holy places.
7. Viveha: Marriage ritual.
8. Anthyesthi: Funeral rites and shradha.

Cultural Activities, Music, and Dance

The roots of Indian music are found in some of the oldest texts of the Hindu religion, the *Namskaras*, which date back to several thousand years. Artistic experience is generally equated with religious experience in India, and music has been described as one of the quickest paths toward the realization of divinity.

Styles practiced include Vedic music, ancient classical music, North Indian classical music, and South Indian classical music. Folk dances of Gujarat are: Diva dance, Garba dance, Tippani dance, Raas, and Supda dance.

Dance was part of drama, and the drama itself was danced. This composite whole was *Natyaa*, and it consisted of music, dance, and communication through expression. Bharta Nattyam combines the qualities of geometry and architecture.

Classical music played on a tabla, as a prayer to the Lord Krishna, by Parth and Puja.

The dance form used all major and minor limbs. Every part of the foot, toe, heel, and arch are used. The training of the facial muscles is a significant part of *Kathkali*. It is a vital form of theatre with deep roots in classical tradition.

Instruments used for these expressions include: Santoor, Sarangi, Flute, Tabla, Sarod, Sitar, Satara, Ghatam, Mradangam, Pakhawaj, Violin, Vina, Rudra Vina, Vichitra Vina, Shahnai, and Harmonium.[164]

Unlike *Natyasastra*, the *Sangita ratnakara* is devoted entirely to music. The much larger number of modes indicates expansion of the musical practice itself, now called *ragas*. The instruments generally support the singer. The principal melodic instruments of Hindustani music are the sitar, sarod, sarangi, sahnai and flute, harmonium, vina, dilruba, guitar and violin.

The instrumental forms of music resemble vocal forms for the most part, although an intermediate section between *alap* and the composition *jor* is especially developed instrumentally, particularly by the plucked stringed instruments.

Northern Indian *ragas*: Bhairav, malkos, hindol, dipak, Sri and megh. Each has a number of *raginis* and *putras*. This emphasizes the fundamental musical basis of strong main *ragas*, showing archaic poatatonic bone structure, with related modes, often more dedicated or having specialized character. *Kathak* dances and *Bharat Natyam* dances are well known in south Indian classical music. Great *bhaktas* poured out their religious emotion in *krtis* and other musical forms of impressive architectural scope.

Fewer musical instruments are used in Carnatic classical music than in the Hinustani tradition. The instrumental style is even closer to the vocal, and there is no such independent instrumental composition as in the North Indian *gat*.[165]

Traditional Rituals and Habits

Traditional Dress

With the infinite variety of regional cultures in India, there is a corresponding variety of traditional clothing. Predominant dress for Asian Indian women is the *sari*, a garment made of six yards of fabric (silk, cotton, georgette, or chiffon) draped and pleated around the waist over a long petticoat, with the end gathered on one shoulder. A snug matching blouse, a *choli*, is worn underneath. Styles of draping the *sari* vary from region to region; the fabric may be painted by various methods or woven in a variety of colors and designs.

For women from the Punjab, and now mostly all Indian women, the predominant dress is a long chemise called a *kurta*, worn over either baggy trousers, called *salwar*, or tight-fitting trousers gathered in to pleats at the ankles, called *churidar*. A matching scarf, *dopatta*, is draped around the shoulders. This type of dress, commonly called "Punjabi dress," has been adopted all over India. It is especially favored by young people, as it is easier to wear and more comfortable than a *sari*.

Most Asian Indian men in the U.S., as well as most men in India, have adopted western style of dressing, with traditional national dress reserved for ceremonial occasions. For men, *dhoti*, a *kafani*, and a white cap was the traditional dress back in pre-independence days. The *dhoti* was especially made from the *khadi*—handmade cotton thread—and became a symbol for Ghandi's *Satyagraha* (self-rule) campaign.

The survey reports that 30% of first-generation women still wear the traditional *sari*, while 61% wear the traditional dress once a while. The grandmother's generation more strictly wears traditional dress, at 82%. About half of daughters wear an Indian dress once in a while, for ceremonies occasions and gatherings. Similarly, first-generation fathers sometimes wear the traditional dress.

Food

What is it about the cuisines of India that binds people with ties of affection and even addiction? In the subcontinent of India and Pakistan, the cuisine is noted for its skillful blending of spices and herbs. This method of seasoning and preserving foods has spread widely through most of the countries of Southeast Asia. The reign of the Moghul Empire brought about a period of magnificence and opulence in the cuisine of Pakistan and India, which has never been paralleled. Strong Persian influences added a touch of elegance and refinement. Delicious rice pilafs, braised and tandoori roasted lamb, koftas, kabobs and the use of saffron, dairy products and edible gold leaf to decorate foods are Moghul touches. In the southern coastal areas of India, seafood dishes are unequalled in variety and quality. Steaming, deep-frying, and sautéeing are common cooking methods.

Food also plays an important role in the fabric of Indian lives during public festivals and more personal celebrations, such as births, marriages, graduation from school, and reunions. Food and drinks are always pressed upon the guest and cannot be refused. There are fifteen official languages recognized by the government, and two hundred and twenty-five dialects. Therefore, the names of foods will change depending on which part of the country you are in, as will the names of many dishes.

The most marked division in Indian cuisine is the prevalence of wheat products to the north, and the large rice culture of the central river basins and southern areas. This division is further fragmented by cultural and religious differences. Three major religions have played an important role in the development of Indian and

Pakistani cuisine. Muslims eat no pork and often no seafood, preferring beef and lamb. The majority of Indians are Hindus who refrain from eating beef. Indian Buddhists are staunch vegetarians. Indians traditionally eat their foods by scooping up small portions with their right hands. The left hand is considered unclean for eating. However, spoons and forks are commonly used in India today.

Rigid strictures of Hindu scriptures, aimed at purity of mind and spirit, demand that meat, fish, fowl and even eggs are all dietary taboos. The result of such restrictions has been the development of a vegetarian cuisine of amazing diversity and imagination. Vegetarians reclaimed and adapted many Persian rice dishes, and Hindus and Muslims alike became partial to many lavish sweets that originated in Asia Minor, such as *halva*, *burfi* (an Indian milk sweet with almonds and pistachios), *gulab jamuns* (solid balls of reduced cream), and many more. Grains and legumes are extensively used together with all manner of vegetables, herbs, and spices.

Apart from the rich foods of the Moghuls, the majority of Indian food is light and flavorful with its

A Gujarati Thali

artful combinations of spices and herbs. When properly cooked, it provides a delicious balance of ingredients, textures, and aromas. Curries, or *turrkarhis* as they are also called, are merely dishes made aromatic with spice powder or paste mixes, and then stewed with a generous amount of water or other cooking liquids. *Tandoori* cooking means oven roasting or baking.

Indian rice dishes also deserve a category of their own. There are *pulao*, grand *biryanis* and the *kitchdis*, or combinations of rice and lentils, sometimes together with vegetables. Indian meals are rounded out with fresh *chatnis*, *raitas*, and salad—combinations of fresh vegetables and fruits in yogurt—and with Indian unleavened breads such as *chapatis*, *parathas*, *puris*, *naan* and *luchi*.

In many areas of India, the diners sit on the floor, and the individual portions of dishes are arranged on a tray, on a low table or on the floor. Northern Indians use unleavened bread as an implement to scoop up food. A circular tray, called a *thali*, is the meal server in southern India: small mounds of each of the foods composing the meal are decoratively arranged around a central portion of rice.

Emerging cooking trends from the East have greatly influenced America's tastes. In larger American cities, Asian grocery stores have opened wherever there is a substantial immigrant population, and Asian herbs, spices, and sauces have begun to appear in larger supermarkets, alongside rice, noodles and soy sauces.

Hinduism accounts for 89% of the popular religion in the state of Gujarat. Gujarat is perhaps the only state in India to have such staunch vegetarians. The majority of Patels (including children) in Surat, Bulsar, and Navsari districts are vegetarians, as Gujaratis of all castes and creeds are. Among first-generation Patels in the U.S., the ratio of vegetarians to non-vegetarians is roughly 60:40.

Patels are very fond of snacks, which in Gujarat are known as *farsan*. Patels use sugar, red chilies, and lime juice in almost every dish, which gives Gujarati food a unique combination of sweet, sour, and hot tastes. *Farsan*, sweet-meats, and pickles are slowly gaining popularity with all groups of people.

The majority of Patel dishes contain one or more of the following:

Raitas: Chili, cucumber, onion, mixed vegetable.

Rice (pullao): Masala pullao, biraj, khichdi, potato, vegetable.

Puries, Theplas, and Rotlies: Methi puri, masala, jeera puri, wheat flour rotli, methi thepla, bhakhari, bajra rotli.

Vegetables: Dudhi, cabbage, potato, gavar, vangan, corn-yogurt, suran, tomato, parval, karela, papdi, cauliflower.

Curries: Buttermilk, bhndi, doodhi.

Dals: Toovar, moong, vegetable, mixed.

Farsan: Masala tikki, uraddal, peas kachori, chili, potato kachori, aluvadi, dahi vada, cauliflower handva.

Sweets and desserts: Mohanthal, copra pak, golpapdi, dudhpak, magaz, lapsi, kansar, and shrikhand.

Leisure Time

Many cultural groups have expressed concern regarding the issue of access versus control of public institutions for ethnic groups. Several years ago, most would have been pleased with mere access to public facilities, no matter who produced the work. Now, after a history of unfortunate experiences, Asian Americans are asking for control of their own cultural activities and cultural symbols.[166]

In this survey, extracurricular activities, which give Patels a more meaningful life, were sports, music, reading, travel, and cooking.

Table 42
Hobbies of IAPFM

	Sports	Music	Travel	Reading	Cooking	No. of Respondents
(1)Head of household	29%	23%	21%	24%	3%	297
Spouse	4%	17%	21%	17%	41%	269
Children	27%	25%	19%	18%	11%	435
Father of (1)	18%	18%	34%	30%	0%	77
Mother of (1)	1%	10%	20%	20%	49%	70
Percent of Total	19%	22%	21%	21%	17%	1148

GLOSSARY

Artha: Wealth.

Ashram: One of the four divisions of life according to Hinduism.

Ashvin vad barash: The twelfth day of the ninth month of the Vikram Sanvant; second dark half of a lunar month.

Atmagyana: Self-realization.

Average: A single number or value that is often used to represent the "typical value" of a group of numbers. It is regarded as a measure of "location" or "central tendency" of a group of numbers.

Bhagvad Gita: A religious poetic work of Hinduism which is a part of the great epic the Mahabharata.

Bhajans: Devotional songs or prayers.

Bhang: A drink containing hemp.

Choli: Blouse.

Choro: A public platform; a meeting place for villagers.

Churidar: Tight trousers.

Dandi-kuch: A place in Navsari district, where Gandhi started his non-violence movement for India's freedom.

Demographics: Numerical data to describe the characteristics of a group.

Dharma: Conformance to duty and obligations of life as determined by karma and divine will or moral law.

Dhoti: Man's garment.

Dopatta: Scarf without collar.

Festivals: A day of public celebration.

Deity: God or Goddess.

Entrepreneurships: The process of organizing, starting, and running a business.

Garba: Singing of chorus songs by women in a circle.

Guru: Teacher.

Gut: Musical mode.

Harijans: Persons belonging to a caste believed to be untouchable.

Holi: Ceremonial bonfires ignited as a part of the celebration.

Household Income: Total money income received in a calendar year by all household members sixteen years and older.

Jati: Race or tribe.

Jawar: Kind of grain; millis.

Jiva: Soul.

Kachho-Vado: A backyard.

Kadi: Soup made from plain yogurt.

Kafani: A long robe or shirt

Khadi: Yarn made from cotton on a spinning wheel.

Karma: Spiritual merit or demerit acquired in previous incarnation and which is currently being acquired in one's present existence.

Kartik Sud Padv: First day of the first month of the Vikram Samvant; bright half of a lunar month.

Kathkali: One of the modes of scientific dance.

Krtis: To compose.

Kurta: Long shirt.

Mahabharata: Dhrtarastra and Pandu were brothers born in the Kuru dynasty, descending from King Bharat, a former ruler of the earth, from whom the name Mahabharata derived.

Mahesul: Collection of taxes.

Mandap:A decorative canopy

Mantra: Chant.

Mat: Opinion, vote.

Namskaras: Bowing in reverence.

Nationals: People who receive the protection of a country and owe allegiance to that country, but are not formally citizens.

Naturalize: To admit as a citizen.

Nyatbahar: To expel from a caste.

Out-Marriage: Marriage to a spouse outside one's own ethnic group; exogamy.

Panch: A body of arbitrators (usually five members).

Panth: Literally, "road" or "path," but is used in this text to designate the system of religious practice and belief of the Patidar and other families described.

Pantheon: Official gods of a group of people.

Pir: A Muslim saint.

Prasad: Eatable offered to a deity.

Pravritti: Worldly activities.

Puja: Worship.

Purtis: A complement.

Putras: Sons.

Ragas: Pleasant sound modes of scientific music.

Raginis: One of the chief modes of scientific music.

Rakhi: A thread tied around the arm in full view as a protection against misfortune or for prosperity.

Ramayana: An epic based on Ram's biography.

Ramnam: A chanting word having miraculous power.

Ras: Singning of chorus songs with wooden or iron sticks by men and women.

Rathods: A caste.

Rayata: Dish made from onion, yogurt, and tumeric.

Rig Vedas: One of the branches of spiritual knowledge from the sacred book, Veda.

Sadhus: Hermits.

Sakati: The divine mother.

Salwar: Trousers.

Samskaras: Purification; culture; effect of the deeds of past lives.

Sari: Traditional dress for Indian women made up of six feet of garment and wrapped around the body.

Satguru: A teacher with a well-balanced state of mind; a virtuous teacher.

Satyagraha: Non-violent struggle for righteousness.

Sect: A group within a large religious body that follows specific teachings or rules.

Shak: Edible vegetables.

Talukas: Sub-districts.

Thali: Dish.

Todarmal: King Akabar's executive officer.

Ukardo: A dunghill; a heap of rubbish.

Varna: Literally, color. The four mythical caste groups in Hinduism: Brahman, Kshatriya, Vaishya, and Sudra.

Vindhoti: Land tax.

Yajna: A ceremonial performance of a sacrifice.

INDIAN/HINDU TEMPLES AND TEMPLE ASSOCIATIONS IN THE UNITED STATES

Eastern Region

Jain Center of Allentown, Allentown, PA; Jain Center of Greater Boston, Wesley, MA; Sri Dasavathara Temple, Wappingers Falls, NY; Sri Rajarajeshwari Peetham, Stroudsburg, PA; Hindu Temple Socitety of Mississippi, Brandon, MS; Yoga Research Foundation, Miami, FL; Jain Center of Conecticut, Brockfield, CT; Jain Center of New Jersey, Essex Falls, NJ; Sri Venkateswara Temple, Marrieta, GA; Shri Venkateswara Temple, Pittsburgh, PA; Vivekananda Vedanta Society, Chicago, IL; New Mathura Vrindavan, Moundsville, VA; Jain Center of Cincinnati/Dayton, Cincinnati, OH; Hindu-Jain Temple, Monroeville, PA; Sri Paschima Kasi Viswanatha Temple, Flint, MI; Sri Siva Vishnu Temple, Lanham, MD; Sri Venkateswara Temple of Greater Chicago, Aurora, IL; United Hindu Temple, Morris Plains, NJ; Hindu Temple, Memphis, TN; Hindu Temple of Toledo, Toledo, OH; Jain Study Center of North Carolina, Garner, NC; Mangala Mandir, Silver spring, MD; Swaminarayan Temple, Flushing, NY; The Hindu Temple of Atlanta, Riverdale, GA; Jain Society of Cleveland, North Royalton, OH; Jain Society of Metropolitan Washington, Reston, VA; Muni Shushil Jain Ashram, Staten Island, NY; Hindu Temple of Greater Chicago, Lemont, IL; Sri Mangal Mandir, Olney, MD; Himalayan International Institute of Yoga, Science, & Philosophy, Hinsdale, PA; Light of Truth Universal Satchidanada Ashram, Buckingham, VA; Murugan Temple of North America, Laham, MD; Hindu Temple, Inc., Raleigh, NC; Hindu Cultural Society, Brentwood, TN; New England Hindu Temple, Wellesley Hills, MA; Raj Rajeshwari Peetham, Stroudsburg, PA; Siddhachalam, Blairstown, NJ; Hindu Cultural Center of Tennessee, Nashville, TN; Hindu Temple of Nashville, Nashville, TN; Hindu Temple Society, Youngstown, OH; Ganesha Temple, Flushing, NY; India Cultural & Religious Center, Smyrna, GA; Jain Society of Long Island, Kings Park, NY; Jain Society of Rochester, Penfield, NY; Hindu Mandir, Garfield, NJ; Hindu Temple Society, Poland, OH; Hindu Temple Society, Inc., Augusta, GA; Hindu Temple Society of Northeast Ohio, Warren, OH; India House of Worship, Silver Spring, MD; Arsha Vidya Gurukulam, Waylorsburg, PA; Bharatiya Temple, Lansing, MI; Connecticut Valley Hindu Temple Society, Hartford, CT; Hindu Temple, Bevercree, OH; Manav Seva Mandir, Bensenville, IL; Hindu Temple & Cultural Center, Columbia, SC; Bharatiya Vidya Bhawan, Woodside, NY; Hindu Centre, Charlotte, NC; Hindu Society of Greater Cincinnati, Cincinnati, OH; Jain Center of South New Jersey, Voorhees, NJ; Sant Nirankari Mission (USA), Carpentersville, IL; Arya Samaj, Jamaica, NY; Balaji Temple, Aurora, IL; Bharatiya Temple of Central Ohio, Columbus, OH; Capital District Hindu Temple Society, Loudonville, NY; Hindu Cultural Society of Western New York, Getzville, NY; Hindu Society of North Carolina, Morrisville, NC; Aurun Jain Cultural Center, Daytona Beach, FL; Hindu Community Organization, Dayton, OH; Hindu Temple Community Center, Jackson, MI; Jain Community of Buffalo, East Amherst, NY.; Hindu Temple of South Florida, Davie, FL; Shiva Vishnu Temple, Parma (Cleveland), OH; Sri Lakshmi Narayan Temple, Liberty, OH; Swaminarayana Temple, Whekawkan, NJ; Ved Mandir, E. Brunswick, NJ. [167]

Western Region

This Ramkabir temple was built in Carson, California, so that Ramkabir Bhakta Patels could continue to worship in their traditional way.

A.I.S.A.; Adelaide Hills Meditation; All the World Fellowship; All World Gayathri Pariwar; American Hindu Federation; American Indian Senior Association; Anand Foundation; Art India; Anand Sacramento Center; Anand Yoga Centre; Arizona School of Meditation; Arya Samaj of Southern California; Asian Indian Chamber of Commerce; Auckland Satsang Ramayan Mandal, Inc.; Australian School of Meditation; B.S.S.; Baguio Yoga Center; Balaram Eco Sena; Banaras Hindu University; Bengali Association of Southern California; Bhaktivedanta Ashram; Bharatiya Culture Center; Bhartiya Vidya Bhavan—Institute of Indian Arts and Culture; Caires; Canadian School of Mediation; Chaitanya Mediation Center; Chaitanya Saraswati Mandala; Charotar Patidar Samaj; Chinmanaya Mission; Crescent Presentations; Cultural Association of India; Dakshini Bengali Association; Earth Aware Monstery; Earth voice; East West Community Church; F.I.S.I.; Federation of Indo American Association of Southern California; Federation of Hindu Association; Fiji Women's Society Inc.; Food A Gift of the Heart Foundation; Force Lo Publications; Gandhi Peace Foundation; Gauranga Mission; Gayatri Pariwar Yugnirman; Hariball Polsks Association Math; Hariball Taiwan; Hariball Vrindavan Trust; Himalayan Association; Hindu Swayamsevak Sangh; Hindi Samaj Seva Indian and Hindu Conference Center; Hindu Religious Freedom Foundation; Hindu Religious Society; Hindu Society of South Australia, Inc.; Hindu Temple and Culture Center; Hindu Temple Geeta Bhavan & Hindu Community Center; Hindu Temple Society of Southern California; Hindu Matiya Patidar Samaj; Hotel Motel Assoc. of Southern California; Hyderabadi Association; India Association of Southern California; Idrettsskade Association of Lviv's; India Association of San Joaquin Valley; India Muslim Association and Indian Council for Advancement and Support of Education; Indian Cultural Society Conejo Valley; Indian Dental Association; Indian Medical Association of G.L.A.; Indian Medical Association of

"Aarti"—an evening prayer by Patel devotees at the temple.

Southern California; Indian Prof. Toast Masters Club; Indo-American Community of Cerritos; Indo-American Business and Prof. women Interfaith; Indian Pharmacy Association; International Society of Krishna Consciousness; International Swaminarayan Satsang (Ontario) Nitai Gaur World Mission; International Swamngarayan Sanstha; Jagriti Awakening; Jodhpur Alumni Association; Kamavati Alumni Association; Karnataka Cultural Association; Kashmir Overseas; Krishna Yoga Mandir; L.A. County Association of Indo-Americans; Life Force News AZ Organization; Little India Chamber of Commerce; Maharastra Mandal; Nama; Mandal Media Chaitanya Misjoinen; Mandala Publishing Group; Mantra Meditation Hawaii; Mayur Regional School Charitable Stock of Supporting of Health Lifestyle; Misja Czaitanil; Mungir Temple Trust; National Council of Hindu Temples (UK); National Societies Ukerian-Indian Association; Nedia Meditation Center; Newziland School of Meditation; OHM; Olsztyn University of Agriculture and Technology; Pandit Brij Bhusan Lal Vrindavan Institute for Vaisnava Culture and Studies; Punjab Folks Cultural Society; Radha Krishna Temple, Norwalk; Radha Raman Temple; Radha Raman Temple; Plamntia; Rajasthani Association of North America; Rajput Association of North America; Ramkabir Bhakta Samaj of U.S.A.; Ramkabir Temple Inc.; Rana Samaj, USA; Sahara; Sant Nirankari Mission; Santan Mandir Cultural Center; Santnam Mandir Sabha; Sarvanand Ashram; Science of Identity Foundation; SEVA Official Translation Service; Shiva Temple, Morltebello; Sri Laxmi Narayana Mandir; Sri Shree Radha Krishna Cultural Center; Sindhi Association of Southern California; Southern California Gujarati Cultural Society; Sony Association, Sri Krishna Education Foundation, Sri Laxmi Narayan Temple, Sri Mandir Temple of San Diego; Sri Radha Raman Temple; Swami Narayan Hindu Temple; Tamil Students Club; Taranaki Indian Association; Telugu Association of Southern California; The Brahmacharini Asrama, Ltd.; The Buddha Center; The Chaitanya School of Meditation; The International Sivananda Yoga Vedant Center; The Vedic Culture Association, Transcendental Sound Hawaii School of Mediation;

Transcedentalny Dzwiek; Tudomanya Egyesulet; Ukraian Meditation and Martial Arts League; United India Association; Universal Manav Dharrna Center; Universal Senior Association; University of Agriculture and Technology in Olsztyn Add Meditation to Your Life; University of Bredford Peace Studies Department Ma Day School; Upasana, Vaishnav Church of the Republic of Columbia; Vaishnava Internet News Agency; Vaisnavas Bay of Plenty (Rotorua) Indian Association, Inc.; Valley Hindu Temple; Vanik Vaishnav Samaj; Varsana Ecological Gardens; Veda Vision; Vedant Society of Sacramento; Vedic Dharma Samaj; Vedic Heritage Foundation; Vedic Temple; Veerashiva Samaj; Vishva Hindu Parishad European Coordination Committee (World Council of Hindus); Vrindavan Para la Cultural y Estudios; Vrinda Academia; Wellington Indian Association, Inc.; World University of Ramanuja Sampradaya America; World Yoga.[168] Sanatan Dharma Temple, Norwalk, California.

*Note: I have not included the Indian Student Association of U.S. universities, which may be in the hundreds.

APPENDIX B
PATELS (ASIAN INDIANS): 100 SURNAMES

Patel, Singh, Shah, Desai, Sharma, Kumar, Mehta, Gupta, Rao, Qarikh, Jain, Prasad, Amin, Joshi, Das, Gandhi, Bhatia, Bhatt, Vargese, Chaudhry, Sandhu, Agrawal, Iquabal, Srunivasan, Arora, Gill, Sinha, Chandra, Mahlhotra, Parekh, Kaur, Trivedi, Ghosh, Qureshi, Verma, Dhillon, Dave, Mathur, Doshi, Sidhu, Lal, Sethi, Pandhya, Khanna, Bhakta, Subramanian, Kapoor, Agrawal, Murthy, Anand, Lyer, Mistry, Vyas, Krisnan, Grewal, Nair, Menon, Naik, Kularni, Banarjee, Chawal, Modi, Srivastava, Shukla, Sen, Mukherjee, Dalal, Aggarwal, Puri, Garg, Soni, Parmar, Mohan, Datta, Prakash, Ahuja, Mishra, Raman, Kapadia, Chowdhury, Verma, Goel, Kurian, Kothari, Basu, Rana, Bhat (2), Sood, Pillai, Misra, Chopra, Mathai, Patil, Ramchandran, Ansari, Thakkar, Mehra, Kohli.

BULSAR DISTRICT'S FACILITIES AND POPULATION BREAKDOWN BY EDUCATION AND EMPLOYMENT

Table A

Number of Villages and Percentage of Villages(in each taluka) with Various Facilities in Bulsar district

Facilities	Bulsar	Pardi	Umarganw	Gandevi	Navsari	Chikhli	Vansda	Dharmpor	Total
No. of Village	87	79	49	53	139	84	94	236	821.0

Numbers are in the form of percentages

Facilities	Bulsar	Pardi	Umarganw	Gandevi	Navsari	Chikhli	Vansda	Dharmpor	Total
Education	100	100	100	100	96	100	100	87	96.0
Medical	39	34	43	40	35	44	28	14	30.0
Drinking Water	99	100	100	100	100 1	00	100	100	99.9
Telephone-Postal	83	77	74	83	71	79	49	29	60.0
Shop-Market	3	11	14	4	-	11	10	6	7.0
Transportation	93	91	94	96	94	93	79	53	80.0
Solid Road	62	71	73	77	73	69	51	24	55.0
Electric Facility	86	85	98	96	91	93	72	20	68.0

Source: Compiled from 1981 Census of India, Bulsar District. Bulsar and Navsari are now two (as well as talukas) out of twenty districts in Gujarat where government offices are located.

Educational Facilities: Every village must have minimum one primary school.

Medical Facilities: May be one or more of the following: hospital, maternity hospital, basic health center, or child welfare center.

Drinking Water Facility: Mainly from water well, water tanks system from the village, or from irrigation.

Table B
Taluka's Village/City Population and Percent of Families in Villages (City and Village Combined), Their Education, Their Employment Status, and Among the Employed, Field Of Employment (Bulsar District)

(Taluka)

Facilities	Bulsar	Pardi	Umarganw	Gandevi	Navsari	Chikhli	Vansda	Dharmpor	Total
City Population	102812	42086	10868	69406	135093	5849	8533	14116	388862
Village Population	175221	163452	132859	120643	224704	208180	137258	222959	1385274

Numbers are in the form of percentages

Facilities	Bulsar	Pardi	Umarganw	Gandevi	Navsari	Chikhli	Vansda	Dharmpor	Total
Families In Village	62	77	91	64	65	97	94	94	78
Village Education	54	47	36	58	54	45	30	17	42
City Education	67	60	59	64	62	70	55	55	63
Working	38	43	44	37	38	46	52	53	43
Not Working	62	57	56	63	62 5	4	48	47	57
Farmer	22	36	37	14	11	47	61	74	36
Farm Worker	22	20	27	27	32	31	21	18	25
Artesian / H/W	3	2	3	3	2	2	3	1	2
Other workers	53	42	33	56	55	20	15	7	37

Source: Bulsar and Navsari are now two districts (as well as talukas) of twenty districts of Gujarat where Government offices are located.
Census of India, 1981, Bulsar District. p. 26, Table12, P.P 4, 31-32, table21, PP.6-11.
Working And Not Working Percent is With Respect To Total Population In The Taluka. H/W - House wives.
Education- those who can read and write with understanding and with former education back ground.

KURMI KSHATRIYA PATELS PEDIGREE

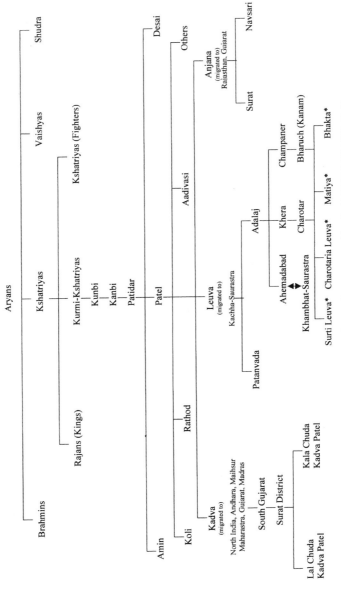

APPENDIX - D

Kurmi Kshatriya Patels Pedigree

Aryans

Brahmins — Kshatriyas — Vaishyas — Shudra

Rajans (Kings) — Kurmi-Kshatriyas — Kshatriyas (Fighters)

Kunbi
Kanbi
Patidar

Koli — Patel — Desai
Rathod — Others
Aadivasi — Anjana (migrated to) Rajasthan, Guiarat
Surt — Navsari

Amin

Kadva (migrated to) — Leuva (migrated to) Kachha–Saurastra

North India, Andhara, Maihsur
Maharastra, Guiarat, Madras

Patanvada — Adalaj — Khera — Champaner
Khambhat-Saurastra — Charotar — Bharuch (Kanam)
Ahemadabad — Matiya* — Bhakta*
Surti Leuva* — Charotaria Leuva*

South Gujarat

Surat District

Kala Chuda
Kadva Patel

Lal Chuda
Kadva Patel

*These Patel's Ancestors moved from Punjab (600 B.C.-200 A.D.) to Kuchha-Saurastra. From there to Champaner, Adalaj area (800 A.D.) and then to Khera, Vadodara area (800 A.D. - 1200 A.D.) and finally to Surat-Navsari area (1430 A.D.)

Source: Natver Patel, Patidar Samaj Darpan, Ronak Printers, Bardoli, P24 and RatiKumar Mekvan, Patidar Gauravsali Mahaguiarat, Ridhsiidhi Publications, Baroda. Patel, Gokaldas S. Patel, Mahendra G. Gujaratna Kurmi Kshtriya Patidarono Eithas, Ahmedabad 1989

APPENDIX E
PATIDAR VILLAGES IN INDIA

Surti Leauva Patels Residing in Villages of Surat, Bulsar, and Navsari Districts of Gujarat (187)

Adada, Afva, Afva-Isroli, Amadpore, Ambheti, Arak-Sisodra, Asta, Astagam, Astan, Baben, Babla, Bagumara, Bajipura, Barasadi, Bardoli, Bhamadia Bhamaiya, Bharampore, Bharmre/Manekpore, Bhutsad, Bhuvasan, Bid-Ghej, Bilimora, Bodlai, Butwada, Chanvai, Chikhali, Chikhali-Dungar, Chikhli-Derod, Chokhad, Chovishi-Moti, Chovishi- Nani, Dandeswar, Dastan, Degama, Derod, Devadh, Dhaman, Dhamdod, Digas, D\Adada, D\Nagod, Donja, Dumbhal, Dungar, Dungar-Chikhli, Dungari, Fadel, Falod-Moti, Ghej-Bid, Godadha, Goji, Golwad, Gorgam, Gunaswel, Haladhava, Hathuka, Isroli, Isroli- Afva, Jalalpore, Jamania, Jatpor, Kadod, Kalakva, Kani, Kani-Mahuva, Kantali, Karachka, Kareli, Khadsupa, Khambda, Khaparia, Kharvasa, Khoj, Khoj-Pardi, Kikwad, Kolasana Kothamdi, Kuched, Kumbharia, Kurel, Lakhanpore, Madhi, Manekpore, Mangrolia, Matvad-Kurel, Minkach, Minkachha, Mori, Mota, Mota-Surat, M.\Vaghchhipa, Moti Munsad, Nagod, NagodAsta, Nandida, Nansad, Nasura, Navafalia, Navagam, Navsari, Navsari-Timba, Ninat, Niyol, Nizar, Nizar-Umrakh, Nog-ama, N. Afva, Orgam, Orna, Panaj, Pardi, Pardi-Arak, Pardi-Khoj, Pardi-Nogama, Pardi-Pata, Par-sivad, Patharadia, Pathron, Pera, Pinsad, Pinsad-Nizar, Pinsad-Pata, Pipalghaban, Pisad, Puna, Rajpura, Ranirajpura, Ratanya, Rumla, Rundhvada, Ruva, Sadakpor, Sadlav, Sadodra, Sandalpore, Sanjan, Sarai, Saravni, Sarbhon, Saroli, Sarona, Segva, Sejvad, Sevani, Shahu, Shamalfalia, Shampura, Sisodra, Sisodra-Arak, Siyod, Soyani, Supa, Surat, Surkhai, Syadla, Tankal, Tarsadi-Tarbhon, Trbhon-Khadsupa, Tarbhon-Viraval,Tarsadi, Tighra, Timba, Timbe-rva, Timberva-Falod, Timberva-Sakri, Toli, Tundi, Uchharel, Umrakh, Undach, Vachharvad, Vadhvania, Vadoli, Vaghech, Valod, Vandervella, Vanesa, Vankaner, Vanzana, Vapi, Varad, Velanpore, Vihan, Viraval, Vyara, Zervavra.

Charotaria Patidar Residing in Villages of Surat, Bulsar, Navsari Districts of Gujarat (81)

Abrama, Ahemadabad, Ahva Daang, Althan, Althan-Vanz, Ambada, Ancheli, Ancheli- Navsari, Antroli, Baleshwar, Bardoli, Barasadi, Beed, Bharthana, Bombay, Chalthan, Chasvad, Chhinam, Dastan, Deladva, Dhamdod, Dhatva, Dindoli, Dungra, Ena, Gangadhara, Gangpur, Gothalwadi, Kadodra, Kadoli, Kanav, Kani, Karachka, Kareli, Katargam, Kathor, Kavitha, Khambhasla, Kho-lvad, Kikvad, Kolasana, Kosmada, Kuembodia, Madhi, Mahuva, Malekpore, Mangrolia, Mirapur, Mohni, Mota, Nagod, Navsari, Niol, Palsana, Parvat, Piprod, Pisad, Rundhi, Sandhiyer, Saniya Hemad, Saniya Kanade, Sarbhan, Sejvad, Sevani, Simlgam, Soyani, Surat, Syadla, Tavdi, Ten, Tundi, Utara, Vadodra, Vadoli, Vanesa, Vanz, Varachha, Vihan, Vyara, Kanthraj, Zarna.

Matiya Patidar Residing in Villages of Surat, Bulsar, Navsari Districts of Gujarat (30)

Akoti, Ahemadabad, Bamni, Bardoli, Butwada, Delhi, Ghodoi, Haripura, Itarwa, Khadsupa, Kac-hhiawadi, Munsad, Mumbai, Navsari, Orgam, Pardi, Palsod, Rayam, Shiker, Sankari, Satem, Sisodra, Samthan, Singod, Surat, Vankaner, Varad, Vadodra, Vasar, Vyara.

Bhakta Patidar Residing in Villages of Surat, Bulsar, Navsari Districts of Gujarat (86)

Ahmedabad, Ambabari, Ambheti, Arak-Sisodra, Asta, Asundar, Bajipura, Bardoli, Bhesdhara, Bhestan, Bilimoa, Chalthan, Degama, Delad, Derod, Dhaman, Dhatva, Dighas, Charanvada, Ghaluda, Ghata, Jatbharthana, Kapura, Kharjai, Kotmunda, Lotarva, Madhi, Khadsad, Mahuva, Mahuvas, Malekpore, Mandvi, Manpur, Moti Bhamti, Mumbai, Nansad, Navsari, Netrang, Netrang-Raj, Orna, Padgha, Pathradia, Ankleshvar, Atkhol, Baladva, Bedoli, Bhenskhetar, Borkhadi, Chasvad, RajChikli, Cingalvone, Devnagar, Dolatpur, Ghanikhut, Kabirgam, Kambodia, Kamria, Kamrej, Kelvikuva, Kodvav, Moriyana, Navanagar, Panchem, Panvadi, Poona, Rajpara, Sarigam, Sevad, Shir, Sukhvana, Vaghandevi, Zarna, Vansda, Roopvada, Sampura, Sarai, Sitapur, Surat, Syadla, Tarsadi, Uva, Valod, Vav, Vesma, Vyara.

APPENDIX F
FIRST-WAVE PATELS

Surti Leauva Patidars in the U.S. before 1970
(Estimated 73 Families)

Ambubhai K. Patel; Ambubhai N. Patel; Amrut K.Patel (Tarbhon); Amrut K. Patel (Umrakh); Amrut R. Patel; Bhagu N. Patel (Saroli); Amrut V. Patel; Arvind K. Patel; Bhagu N. Patel; Champak V. Patel; Chandrakant Patel (Tarbhon); Chhitubhai P. Patel; Chhitubhai V. Patel; Chhotubhai B. Patel Dahyabhai B.Patel; Dahyabhai M. Patel (Khoj); Dahyabhai M. Patel; Gaman B. Patel; Ganshyam C. Patel; Govindbhai Patel (Chicago); Hasu G. Patel (Ninat); Hasmukh G. Patel; Jairambhai Mavji Patel; Jivanbhai G. Patel; Jivanji M. Patel; Kantibhai V. Patel; Maganbhai P. Patel; Magan R. Patel; Manibhai S. Patel; Mohanbhai G. Patel; Nagarbhai G.Patel; Nanubhai Govindji Patel; Naresh D. Patel; Naresh V. Patel; Narottam C. Patel; Narshinhbhai B. Patel; Raman M. Patel; Ranchhod Lakha Patel; Ranchhodji Patel; Ratilal N. Patel; Sombhai Patel; Sombhai G. Patel (Pinsad); Surandra P. Patel; Thakorbhai K. Patel

Charotaria Leauva Patidars in the U.S. before 1970
(Approximately 30 Families)

Amratbhai Ishvar; Anadbhai Chitu; Anandbhai Chitu; Babubhai Bhikha;Babubhai Thakor; Balubahi Chhotu; Bharatbahi Khusal; Chhaganbhai Bhaga; Champakbhai Gokal; Dalaptbhai Chhotu; Girdharbhai Dahya; Harishbhai Ranchhod; Ishvarbhai Amaidas; Ishvarbhai Parbhu; Jagubhai Dullabh; Jelabhai Bhaga; Kantibhai Chhagan; Khandubhai Bhikh; Khandubhai Dayalji; Madhubhai Thakor; Maganbhai Chhotu; Mavjibhai Lallu; Naginbhai Jetha; Parbhbhai Lallu; Rameshbhai Nathu; Ramubhai Lallu; Santilal Parsottem; Sharadbhai Khandu; Thakorbhai Vitthal; Virendrabhai Chhagan

Matiya Patidars in the U.S. before 1970
(Approximately 75 Families)

Ambubhai Prabhakar; Amrut Dahya; Amrutbhai Chhitu; Amrutbhai Khusal; Amrutbhai Ranchhod; Anil Prabhakar; Arvind Lallu; Arvindbhai Chhotu; Balubhai Parbhu; Bhikhubhai Ragha; Bhulabhai Dullabh; Bhulabhai Madhav; Bhulabhai Ranchhod; Bhupendra Magan;, Chhitubhai Nathu; Chhotubhai Govind; Chunibhai Dahya; Dahyabhai Morar; Dahyabhai Ranchhod; Dhirubhai Govind; Dhirubhai Khusal; Dhirubhai Magan; Dinubhai Chhotu; Dinubhai Dahya; Dr.Arunbhai Rambhai; Natubhai Lallu; Jagdishbhai Naran; Govind Ramji; Govindbhai Dahya; Hasubhai prema; Hira Galal; Ishvarbhai Govind; Ishvarbhai Hira; Jayantibhai Bhagvan; Jitubhai Lalu; Kanji Dhana; Kantibhai Kanji; Kantibhai Vallabh; Kantilal Madhav; Kantubhai Uka; Kishorbhai Govind; Lallu Ranchhod; Manibhai Sombhai; Naginbhai Lallu; Naginbhai Ranchhod; Nandu Madhav; Nanu Chitubhai; Nanubhai Govind; Nanubhai Morar; Naranji Rama; Naranlal Dhana; Natvarbhai Parbhu; Praffulbhai Manu; Rama Madhav; Ramanbhai Dahya; Ramanbhai Daji; Ramanbhai Lallu; Ramanbhai Parbhu; Ramanbhai Ranchhod; Raman Sukha; Rameshbhai Lallu; Ramesh Ranchhod; Rameshbhai Chhotu; Ramubhai Kanji; Ranjitbhai Madhav; Sankarbhai Kanji;

Santilal R.Patel (Siker); Shantilal Ramji; Sirishbhai Hansji; Sumanbhai Lalu; Sureshbhai Sukal; Vallabh Dhana; Vijaybhai Kana

The following Patels came to the U.S. around 1925 for educational purposes:

Dulabhbhai Patel, from Karchka, received business training in the U.S. and started a real estate loan business and went into the farming business.

Govindji Patel, from Ruva, received his M.S. and served as an educational inspector in Baroda State.

Dr. Makanji Patel, from Bagipura, received his Ph.D. in Agriculture. He served as Vice Principal in Puna College and later as a head of the Microbiology Department at B.P. Baria College, Navsari.

Nathubhai (Martinet) Patel, from Afva, received his M.B.A. and went in business in Bombay.

Parbhubhai L. Patel, from Manekpore, received a M.S. degree and served as a professor at Anand Agriculture College.

Anand Santilal N. Patel (Matiya–Vankaner); Mohanbhai K. Patel (Matiya–Vankaner); Ishverlal P. Patel (Tarbhon); Dahyabhai J. Patel (Mota); Dayaram K. Patel (Vanesa); Dahyabhai J. Patel; Thakorbhai D. Patel (Charotaria-Ten) all came to the U.S. for education and returned to India.

The following Patels came to San Francisco via Trinidad:

Dhirajlal Bhakta from Orna, Kanjibhai Manchhubhai Desai-Patel from Digas, and Naranjibhai L. (Matiya) Patel, India. All three friends were pioneers who encouraged their Leauva, Matiya, and Bhakta Patels who came to the U.S. on different visa status to settle in the hotel business.

The following Patels came to the U.S. without legal status. They worked in farms and made their way to settle in the U.S.:

Babubhai D. Patel (Gogi); Bhikhubhai Patel (Vachharvad); Bhulabhai Bhakta (Syadala); Chhotubhai P. Patel (Kadva Patel) from Kamrej; Dahyabhai L. Patel (Vasarvad); Kunverji Patel (Tarbhon); Maganbhai Gopalbhai Patel (Asta); Maganbhai R. Patel (Ambheti); Maganbhai Nichhabhai Patel (Zervavara); Narshinhbhai Gokalbhai Bhakta

The following immigrated to the U.S. on the 100-quota category (1946–1953):

Ambubhai P.Patel; Bhavanji J. Patel; Bhulabhai V.Patel; Dahyabhai R. Patel; Dayaraam Khatri; Dhanjibhai B. Patel; Gopalji G. Patel; Govindbhai N. Patel; Kantibhai C. Patel; Kalyanji Patel; Lallubhai Patel; Maganbhai R. Patel; Mohanbhai Khatri; Muljibhai M. Patel; Narottam P. Patel; Ratilal Khatri; Shantilal R. Patel (Bajipora); Shantilal R. Patel Matiya (Shiker); Thakorbhai Patel (Khoj); Uttambhai Gandhi.

Bhakta Patidars in the U.S. before 1970
(Approximately 56 Families; Includes Single-Person Families)

Amrutbhai Morar; Ashokbhai Rambhai; Ashvinbhai Dahya; Bhagabhai Karsan; Bharatbhai Dharmavir; Bhikabhai Duralbh; Bharatbhai Valjibhai; Bhulabhai Jivan; Chaganbhai Bhula; Chandravadan Chiman; Chandubhai Prabhu; Dahyabhai

Gordhan; Dhaniben Dhirajlal; Dhirajbhai Narshin; Dhirajbhai N. Desai; Durlabhbhai Hari; Gokalbhai Khushal; Gokalbhai Makanji; Gopalbhai Bhagvanji; Govindbhai Bhakti; Hasubhai Dayaram; Hasumatiben Vasant; Ishvarbhai Bhulabhai; Kantibhai Khushal; Khushalbhai Rambhai; Lakhubhai Kalidas; Lokpati Bhikhabhai; Madhavbhai Gordhan; Madhubhai Gokal; Mahendrabhai Bhikha; Mahendrabhai Dahya; Manubhai Dahya; Manubhai Lallu; Mohanbhai Gordhan; Mohanbhai Govind; Mohanbahi Makan; Mohanbhai Morar; Mukuundbhai Jivanji; Pravinbhai Madhav; Rambhai Kalidas; Ramanbhai Dahya; Rameshbhai Dayaram; Rambhai Bhikha; Ranchhodbhai Morarji; Ratilal Bhikha; Dr. Ratilal Dhiraj; Ravindrabhai Gordhan; Sanmukh Prabhu; Sanmukh P. Desai; Sanmukhbhai Govind; Sanmukhbhai Lallu; Shantilal Bhaga; Sureshbhai Dhiraj; Sureshbhai Madhav; Vallabhbhai Chhotu; Yagnesh Ramanlal

IAPFM U.S. DISTRIBUTION

Table C
Surti Leauva, Bhakta, Matiya and Charotariya Patel Households in the United States

Groups	Surti Leauva	Bhakta	Matiya	Charotar	Total
Alabama	85	8	4	16	113
Arkansas	70	6	6	2	84
Arizona	13	37	30	3	83
California	559	469	634	86	1748
Colorado	13	0	4	4	21
Connecticut	0	0	20	30	50
Florida	184	26 1	94	71	475
Georgia	204	48	121	110	483
Iowa	9	14	2	3	28
Illinois	49	16	10	11	86
Indiana	62	3	10	5	80
Kansas	14	51	24	1	90
Kentucky	72	1	9	6	88
Louisiana	72	2	2	5	81
Massachusetts	3	9	6	30	48
Maryland	16	4	1	26	47
Michigan	34	4	8	14	60
Minnesota	1	33	1	0	35
Missouri	27	36	8	11	82
Mississippi	91	13	21	13	138
North Carolina	154	0	23	19	196
New Jersey	19	16	26	121	182
New Mexico	10	61	10	13	94
Nevada	1	37	11	0	49
New York	14	3	12	89	118
Ohio	103	10	28	38	179
Oklahoma	87	22	33	24	166
Oregon	38	15	10	24	87
Pennsylvania	25	6	10	27	68
South Carolina	109	6	15	13	143
Tennessee	219	34	45	35	333
Texas	443	412	145	39	1039
Virginia	78	1	12	27	118

Groups	Surti Leauva	Bhakta	Matiya	Charotar	Total
Other States	25	12	10	34	81
Total	**2903**	**1415**	**1505**	**950**	**6773**

Source: 1996 Directory - Shree Ramkabir Bhakta Samaj of U.S.A.; 1997 Hindu Matiya Patidar Samaj U.S.A. Directory; and 194-95 Charotaria Leauva Patidar Seva Samaj International Directory. 1997 Leauva Patidar of USA Directory Surat-Bulsar- Navsari Districts- Counties. Does not include Hawaii or Alaska.

Table D
Asian-Indians and Surat -Bulsar -Navsari District's SBMC Indo American Patels In, North East, Mid West, South, And Western Part of United States:

	N.E.	M.W.	South	West
Asian-Indians	32.0 %	19.0%	26.0%	24.0%
SBMC Patels	7.3%	9.8%	50.8%	32.2%

Source: The Statistical abstract of the U.S., 1996, Asian-Indians: Population, by Selected Ancestry Group and Religion: 1990, 53

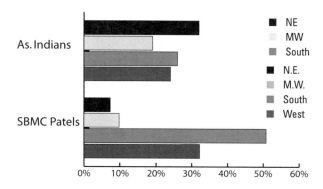

N.E. (North East) - - ME, NH, VT, MA, RI, CT, NY, NJ, PA:—-
M.W. (Mid West)- -OH, IL, MI, WI, MN, IA, MO, ND, SD, NE, KS.
South—-DE, MD, DC, VA, WV, NC, SC, GA, FL, KY, TN, AL, LA, OK, TX, MS.: —
West—- MT, ID, WY, CO, NM, AZ, UT, NV, WA, OR, CA, AR.

APPENDIX H

SURVEY QUESTIONNAIRE

Complete This Questionnaire For Indo-American Surat - Bulsar Districts Patidars

QUESTIONS સવાલો

	1	2	3	4	5	6
WORK SHEET	Sex	Age	1. The Country you born ?(US, INdia, UK, AFrica). 2. When did you move to U.S. ? 3. Immigrate to US based on: CR- Citizens Relatives (brothers-sisters), AR- Alien's Relatives (sp'se-child'n) JP- Job Preference(3rd-6th), NP-Students,Vistr's, invst'r, 4. The Country of last residence ? US, IN, UK, AF.	How long and How many Places Stayed In India,Abroad, and U.S. over 1 year? (US, IN, UK, AF)	*Marrital Status* Single(S), Married(M) at What Age?, Divorce(D), Widowed(W).	How many times you or your children visited India? Number of times 1,2,4 more or,None
કાર્ય પૃષ્ઠ	જાતિ	ઉમ્મર	૧–જન્મ સ્થળ?(US, IN, UK, AF). ૨– અમેરિકા કઇ સાલમા આવ્યા ? ૩– અમેરિકાના રહિસ કઇ રીતે બન્યા? CR –સગાના સીટીઝન(ભાઇ – બહેન) બેઇઝ, AR- રેસીડન્ટ એલીઆન(સ્પાઉઝ,બાળકો), JP- જોબ પ્રેફરન્સ.(૩ કે ૬), NP- નોન પ્રેફરન્સ.૪– છેલ્લે કયા દેશના વતની હતા ?	એક વર્ષથી વધારે, ક્યાં અને કેટલો વખત US, IN, UK, AF, મા રહયા ?	અપરણિત (S), પરણિત(M) કેટલી ઉમ્મરે(Age), છુટાછેડા (D), વિધુર (W)	તમે અથવા આપના બાળકો અને આપ કેટલી વખત ઇન્ડીયા ગયા? ૧, ૨,૪ કે કદી નહિ.
		Please Answer the above questions In The Following boxes		ચેક માર્ક કરી નીચેના ખાનાઓમા જવાબો આપો		
Your History (Head of the-Household) આપની વિગત	[]M []F	[]<10 []<20 []<30 []<40 []<50 []<60 []<70 []>70	1 [ ] US [ ] IN [ ] UK [ ] AF 2 [ ] Year 3 [ ] CR [ ] AR [ ] JP [ ] NP 4 [ ] US [ ] IN [ ] UK [ ] AF	[ ] US [ ] Yrs. [ ] IN [ ] [ ] UK [ ] [ ] AF [ ]	[ ] S [ ] M [ ] at age [ ] D [ ] W	you with child'n [] 1 [] 2 [] 1 [] 2 [] >4 [] > 4 [] none [] none
Wife's History પત્નીની વિગત	[]M []F	[]<10 []<20 []<30 []<40 []<50 []<60 []<70 []>70	1 [ ] US [ ] IN [ ] UK [ ] AF 2 [ ] Year 3 [ ] CR [ ] AR [ ] JP [ ] NP 4 [ ] US [ ] IN [ ] UK [ ] AF	[ ] US [ ] Yrs. [ ] IN [ ] [ ] UK [ ] [ ] AF [ ]	[ ] S [ ] M [ ] at age [ ] D [ ] W	you with child'n [] 1 [] 2 [] 1 [] 2 [] >4 [] > 4 [] none [] none
Children's History Over 16 # 1 બાળકોની વિગત	[]M []F	[]<10 []<20 []<30 []<40 []<50 []<60 []<70 []>70	1 [ ] US [ ] IN [ ] UK [ ] AF 2 [ ] Year 3 [ ] CR [ ] AR [ ] JP [ ] NP 4 [ ] US [ ] IN [ ] UK [ ] AF	[ ] US [ ] Yrs. [ ] IN [ ] [ ] UK [ ] [ ] AF [ ]	[ ] S [ ] M [ ] at age [ ] D [ ] W	you with child'n [] 1 [] 2 [] 1 [] 2 [] >4 [] > 4 [] none [] none
Children #2 બાળક #2 Over 16	[]M []F	[]<10 []<20 []<30 []<40 []<50 []<60 []<70 []>70	1 [ ] US [ ] IN [ ] UK [ ] AF 2 [ ] Year 3 [ ] CR [ ] AR [ ] JP [ ] NP 4 [ ] US [ ] IN [ ] UK [ ] AF	[ ] US [ ] Yrs. [ ] IN [ ] [ ] UK [ ] [ ] AF [ ]	[ ] S [ ] M [ ] at age [ ] D [ ] W	you with child'n [] 1 [] 2 [] 1 [] 2 [] >4 [] > 4 [] none [] none
Children #3 Over 16	[]M []F	[]<10 []<20 []<30 []<40 []<50 []<60	1 [ ] US [ ] IN [ ] UK [ ] AF 4 [ ] US [ ] IN [ ] UK [ ] AF 2 [ ] Year 3 [ ] CR [ ] AR [ ] JP [ ] NP	[ ] US [ ] Yrs. [ ] IN [ ] [ ] UK [ ]	[ ] S [ ] M [ ] at age [ ] D	[] []
Your Father's History: આપના પિતાની વિગત (કોઇ પણ સ્થળે રહેતા)	[]M []F	[]<10 []<20 []<30 []<40 []<50 []<60 []<70 []>70	1 [ ] US [ ] IN [ ] UK [ ] AF 2 [ ] Year 3 [ ] CR [ ] AR [ ] JP [ ] NP 4 [ ] US [ ] IN [ ] UK [ ] AF	[ ] US [ ] Yrs. [ ] IN [ ] [ ] UK [ ] [ ] AF [ ]	[ ] S [ ] M [ ] at age [ ] D [ ] W	you with child'n [] 1 [] 2 [] 1 [] 2 [] >4 [] > 4 [] none [] none
Your Mother' History: આપની માતાની વિગત	[]M []F	[]<30 []<40 []<50 []<60 []<70 []>70	1 [ ] US [ ] IN [ ] UK [ ] AF 4 [ ] US [ ] IN [ ] UK [ ] AF 2 [ ] Year 3 [ ] CR [ ] AR [ ] JP [ ] NP	[ ] US [ ] Yrs. [ ] IN [ ] [ ] UK [ ]	[ ] M [ ] at age [ ] M [ ] AGE [ ] D	[] []
No.of children under 16 : [ ] M [ ] F						
Adition'l Space						

ANSWER ZONE જવાબો માટે નો વિભાગ

Complete This Questionnaire For Indo-American Surat - Bulsar Districts Patidars

Q U E S T I	7	8	9	10	11
	Hobby: SP-sports, MU-music, TR-travel, RW-read'g/writ'g, Ck-cooking.	**Educ'n Attainment:** PS-Primary School, HS-High School, AS-two ys collg. Dipl., CD-College Degree, GD-Masters, P.hd., etc.	**The (yr) year, (dg) degree-diploma received.** Field of study-(sb) Subjects, S-Science, L-Arts, C-Commerce, etc. (mark one each for the above) and Country educ'n received (US, IN, AF, OTher)	**How well do you SP-Speak and WR-Write,** GU-Gujarati and EN-English? N-Not at all, VL-Very Little, F-Fair, G-Good, E-Excellent. (choose one each for the above)	**Estimate the no. of Patidar Fm-Families** live in a 5 M-Miles and 100 M-Miles area, from your residence?(mark one each)

Pl. answer the above questions in the following boxes

Your History (Head of House):

7	8	9	10	11
[ ]SP [ ]MU	[ ]PS [ ]HS	jyr[ ] jdg[ ] jsb[ ] US	[ ]GU [ ]SP	[ ]N [ ]VL [ ]F [ ]G [ ]E	5M[ ] <10	100M[ ] <10
[ ]TR [ ]RW	[ ]AS	jyr[ ] jdg[ ] jsb[ ] IN	[ ]GU [ ]WR	[ ]N [ ]VL [ ]F [ ]G [ ]E	[ ]<25	[ ]<100
[ ]CK	[ ]CD	jyr[ ] jdg[ ] jsb[ ] AF	[ ]EN [ ]SP	[ ]N [ ]VL [ ]F [ ]G [ ]E	[ ]<50	[ ]<200
	[ ]GD	jyr[ ] jdg[ ] jsb[ ] OT	[ ]EN [ ]WR	[ ]N [ ]VL [ ]F [ ]G [ ]E	[ ]<100 Fm	[ ]>500

Wife's History:

7	8	9	10	11
[ ]SP [ ]MU	[ ]PS [ ]HS	jyr[ ] jdg[ ] jsb[ ] US	[ ]GU [ ]SP	[ ]N [ ]VL [ ]F [ ]G [ ]E	5M[ ] <10	100M[ ] <10
[ ]TR [ ]RW	[ ]AS	jyr[ ] jdg[ ] jsb[ ] IN	[ ]GU [ ]WR	[ ]N [ ]VL [ ]F [ ]G [ ]E	[ ]<25	[ ]<100
[ ]CK	[ ]CD	jyr[ ] jdg[ ] jsb[ ] AF	[ ]EN [ ]SP	[ ]N [ ]VL [ ]F [ ]G [ ]E	[ ]<50	[ ]<200
	[ ]GD	jyr[ ] jdg[ ] jsb[ ] OT	[ ]EN [ ]WR	[ ]N [ ]VL [ ]F [ ]G [ ]E	[ ]<100 Fm	[ ]>500

Children's History over 16:

7	8	9	10	11
[ ]SP [ ]MU	[ ]PS [ ]HS	jyr[ ] jdg[ ] jsb[ ] US	[ ]GU [ ]SP	[ ]N [ ]VL [ ]F [ ]G [ ]E	5M[ ] <10	100M[ ] <10
[ ]TR [ ]RW	[ ]AS	jyr[ ] jdg[ ] jsb[ ] IN	[ ]GU [ ]WR	[ ]N [ ]VL [ ]F [ ]G [ ]E	[ ]<25	[ ]<100
[ ]CK	[ ]CD	jyr[ ] jdg[ ] jsb[ ] AF	[ ]EN [ ]SP	[ ]N [ ]VL [ ]F [ ]G [ ]E	[ ]<50	[ ]<200
	[ ]GD	jyr[ ] jdg[ ] jsb[ ] OT	[ ]EN [ ]WR	[ ]N [ ]VL [ ]F [ ]G [ ]E	[ ]<100 Fm	[ ]>500

Children #2 #2 over 16:

7	8	9	10	11
[ ]SP [ ]MU	[ ]PS [ ]HS	jyr[ ] jdg[ ] jsb[ ] US	[ ]GU [ ]SP	[ ]N [ ]VL [ ]F [ ]G [ ]E	5M[ ] <10	100M[ ] <10
[ ]TR [ ]RW	[ ]AS	jyr[ ] jdg[ ] jsb[ ] IN	[ ]GU [ ]WR	[ ]N [ ]VL [ ]F [ ]G [ ]E	[ ]<25	[ ]<100
[ ]CK	[ ]CD	jyr[ ] jdg[ ] jsb[ ] AF	[ ]EN [ ]SP	[ ]N [ ]VL [ ]F [ ]G [ ]E	[ ]<50	[ ]<200
	[ ]GD	jyr[ ] jdg[ ] jsb[ ] OT	[ ]EN [ ]WR	[ ]N [ ]VL [ ]F [ ]G [ ]E	[ ]<100 Fm	[ ]>500

Children #3 over 16:

7	8	9	10	11
[ ]SP [ ]MU	[ ]PS [ ]HS	jyr[ ] jdg[ ] jsb[ ] US	[ ]GU [ ]SP	[ ]N [ ]VL [ ]F [ ]G [ ]E	5M[ ]	100M[ ]
[ ]TR [ ]RW	[ ]AS	jyr[ ] jdg[ ] jsb[ ] IN	[ ]GU [ ]WR	[ ]N [ ]VL [ ]F [ ]G [ ]E		
[ ]CK	[ ]GD	jyr[ ] jdg[ ] jsb[ ] AF	[ ]EN [ ]SP	[ ]N [ ]VL [ ]F [ ]G [ ]E		
			[ ]EN [ ]WR	[ ]N [ ]VL [ ]F [ ]G [ ]E		

Your Father History:

7	8	9	10	11
[ ]SP [ ]MU	[ ]PS [ ]HS	jyr[ ] jdg[ ] jsb[ ] US	[ ]GU [ ]SP	[ ]N [ ]VL [ ]F [ ]G [ ]E	5M[ ] <10	100M[ ] <10
[ ]TR [ ]RW	[ ]AS	jyr[ ] jdg[ ] jsb[ ] IN	[ ]GU [ ]WR	[ ]N [ ]VL [ ]F [ ]G [ ]E	[ ]<25	[ ]<100
[ ]CK	[ ]CD	jyr[ ] jdg[ ] jsb[ ] AF	[ ]EN [ ]SP	[ ]N [ ]VL [ ]F [ ]G [ ]E	[ ]<50	[ ]<200
	[ ]GD		[ ]EN [ ]WR	[ ]N [ ]VL [ ]F [ ]G [ ]E	[ ]<100 Fm	[ ]>500

Your Mother History:

7	8	9	10	11
[ ]SP [ ]MU	[ ]PS [ ]HS	jyr[ ] jdg[ ] jsb[ ] US	[ ]GU [ ]SP	[ ]N [ ]VL [ ]F [ ]G [ ]E	5M[ ]	100M[ ]
[ ]TR [ ]RW	[ ]AS	jyr[ ] jdg[ ] jsb[ ] IN	[ ]GU [ ]WR	[ ]N [ ]VL [ ]F [ ]G [ ]E		
[ ]CK	[ ]GD	jyr[ ] jdg[ ] jsb[ ] AF	[ ]EN [ ]SP			

Complete This Questionnaire For Indo-American Surat - Bulsar Districts Patidars

Column 12: How often do the women of your family wear traditional Indian clothing? AL- Always, MO- Most Of the times, HF- Half of the time, OW- Once a While, N- Never

આપના ઘરની સ્ત્રીઓ કેટલી વખત ઈન્ડિયન ટ્રેડિશન વસ્ત્રો સામાન્યતઃ પહેરે? AL- કાયમ, MO- મોટે ભાગે, HF- પચાસ ટકા. OW- ક્યારેક, N- કદી નહિ.

Column 13: Occupation: PA- Previous, PR- Present: SE- Self Employed (motel etc.) ET- Engineer/Technician/Professional, BM- Manager/Office work, SL- Sales, F- Farmers, HS- Health/Medical svcs, SR- Services, PS- Prod'n/semi skilles, OT.

ધંધા બાબત : PA- પહેલાનો PR- હાલનો : SE- પોતાનો પોતે (મોટેલ વિ.) ET- એન્જિનિયર-ટેકનિશિયન-પ્રોફેશનલ, BM- મેનેજર- ઓફિસ, SL- સેલ્સ, F- ફાર્મ, HS- મેડિકલ સર્વિસ, SR- સર્વિસ, PS- સેમીસ્કિલ, OT-બીજા.

Column 14: If you owned: What type of business? RE- Real Estate, PS- Professional Services, SL- Sales agents etc., SR- Services, CS- City and State of Business. No. of (Em)- Employees,(excluding You)

જો આપનો પોતાનો ધંધો હોય તો તે કયા પ્રકારનો (RE, PS, SL ,SR) અને કયા(CS) શહેર અને સ્ટેટમાં? આપ કેટલાં ઈલ્લા (Em)કામદારો ?

Column 15: Reason for Starting Business. ER- Enterpriser Relative, WE- Work Experince, PT- Professional Training, BR- Borrowed From Relative/friends, LN-Loan

ધંધા શા કારણે ER -તમા ધંધામાં હતા. WE- પચાસમ અનુભવ હતો. PT-પ્રોફેશનલ ટ્રેનિંગ,BR -મિત્ર સગાનો સહાય, LN-લોન.

Please answer in the following boxes (check marks) એક માટે કરી કૃપા કરી જે જવાબ આપોમાં જવાબો આપો

	12	13	14	15
Your History (Head of House) આપની હિસ્ટ	[ ] AL [ ] MO [ ] HF [ ] OW [ ] N	[ ] PA/PR [ ] SE [ ] ET [ ] BM [ ] PA/PR [ ] SL [ ] F [ ] HS [ ] PA/PR [ ] SR [ ] PS [ ] OT	[ ] RE [ ] CS [ ] None Em [ ] PS [ ] CS [ ] <5 [ ] SL [ ] CS [ ] <15 [ ] SR [ ] CS [ ] <50	[ ] ER [ ] WE [ ] PT [ ] BR [ ] LN
Wife's History પત્નીની હિસ્ટ	[ ] AL [ ] MO [ ] HF [ ] OW [ ] N	[ ] PA/PR [ ] SE [ ] ET [ ] BM [ ] PA/PR [ ] SL [ ] F [ ] HS [ ] PA/PR [ ] SR [ ] PS [ ] OT	[ ] RE [ ] CS [ ] None Em [ ] PS [ ] CS [ ] <5 [ ] SL [ ] CS [ ] <15 [ ] SR [ ] CS [ ] <50	[ ] ER [ ] WE [ ] PT [ ] BR [ ] LN
Children's History over 16 #1 બાળકોની હિસ્ટ	[ ] AL [ ] MO [ ] HF [ ] OW [ ] N	[ ] PA/PR [ ] SE [ ] ET [ ] BM [ ] PA/PR [ ] SL [ ] F [ ] HS [ ] PA/PR [ ] SR [ ] PS [ ] OT	[ ] RE [ ] CS [ ] None Em [ ] PS [ ] CS [ ] <5 [ ] SL [ ] CS [ ] <15 [ ] SR [ ] CS [ ] <50	[ ] ER [ ] WE [ ] PT [ ] BR [ ] LN
Children #2 over 16 બાળક #2	[ ] AL [ ] MO [ ] HF [ ] OW [ ] N	[ ] PA/PR [ ] SE [ ] ET [ ] BM [ ] PA/PR [ ] SL [ ] F [ ] HS [ ] PA/PR [ ] SR [ ] PS [ ] OT	[ ] RE [ ] CS [ ] None Em [ ] PS [ ] CS [ ] <5 [ ] SL [ ] CS [ ] <15 [ ] SR [ ] CS [ ] <50	[ ] ER [ ] WE [ ] PT [ ] BR [ ] LN
Children #3 over 16	[ ] AL [ ] MO [ ] HF [ ] OW [ ] N	[ ] PA/PR [ ] SE [ ] ET [ ] BM [ ] PA/PR [ ] SL [ ] F [ ] HS [ ] PA/PR [ ] SR [ ] PS [ ] OT	[ ] RE [ ] CS [ ] None Em [ ] PS [ ] CS [ ] <5 [ ] SL [ ] CS [ ] <15 [ ] SR [ ] CS [ ] <50	[ ] ER [ ] WE [ ] PT [ ] BR [ ] LN
Your Father's History: આપના પિતાની હિસ્ટ	[ ] AL [ ] MO [ ] HF [ ] OW [ ] N	[ ] PA/PR [ ] SE [ ] ET [ ] BM [ ] PA/PR [ ] SL [ ] F [ ] HS [ ] PA/PR [ ] SR [ ] PS [ ] OT	[ ] RE [ ] CS [ ] None Em [ ] PS [ ] CS [ ] <5 [ ] SL [ ] CS [ ] <15 [ ] SR [ ] CS [ ] <50	[ ] ER [ ] WE [ ] PT [ ] BR [ ] LN
Your Mother History: આપના માતાની હિસ્ટ	[ ] AL [ ] MO [ ] HF [ ] OW [ ] N	[ ] PA/PR [ ] SE [ ] ET [ ] BM [ ] PA/PR [ ] SL [ ] F [ ] HS [ ] PA/PR [ ] SR [ ] PS [ ] OT	[ ] RE [ ] CS [ ] None Em [ ] PS [ ] CS [ ] <5 [ ] SL [ ] CS [ ] <15	[ ] ER [ ] WE [ ] PT [ ] BR [ ] LN

Complete This Questionnaire For Indo-American Surat - Bulsar Districts Patidars

	16	17	18
Q U E S T I	What is the Ethnicity of your Friendship net work ? MI- Mostly Indians, MX- Indian/US Mix, OI- Only Indian, US- Only US, SL- Speaks same Language	Best describe your Annual Income (optional) : A- <10K, B- <20K, C- <30K, D- <40K, E- <50K, F- <60K, G- <70K, H- $70,000 and up.	How satisfied with each of these features of Your life : LT- Leisure Time, JC- JOb, Education and Career, LL- Love Life, FS- Financial Security, (choose one each for the above) . VH- Very Happy, S- Satisfied, M- Medium, SW-Somewhat Satisfied, NS- Not Satisfied.
O N s	તમારો મિત્ર વર્ગ કઇ જાતિનો છે ? MI- મોટે ભાગે હિન્દિઓ, MX- મ્યુઅસ હિન્દિઅન, OI - માત્ર હિન્દિઓ, US- માત્ર ન્યુ.એસ., SL- એક જ ભાષા બોલતા.	તમારે આવકની વાર્ષિક આવક(કોઇ વિકલ્પ) A <૧૦ હજાર B < ૨૦ C <૩૦ D <૪૦ E < ૫૦ F < ૬૦ G < ૭૦ H > ૭૦ કે વધારે.	આપ ત્રિવે જીવનના લક્ષણો સાથે કેટલા સંતુષ્ટ છો ? LT- (ફિત સમય, JC- જોબ અને ડિગ્રિઅર અને આવખાર. LL- લવ લાઇફ. FS- ફાઇનાન્સિઅલ સેકચુર. VH- ખૂબ સંતુષ્ટ. S- સંતોષ, M- મધ્યમ-સંતોષ, SW-આંશિક સંતોષ, NS- સંતોષ નથી.(દરેકમાંથી એક એક માર્ક કરો.)

Please answer in the following boxes (check marks)

	16	17	18
Your History (Head of House) આપનો ઇતિહાસ	[ ] MI [ ] US [ ] MX [ ] SL [ ] OI	A [ ]<10 B [ ]<20 C [ ]<30 D [ ]<40 E [ ]<50 F [ ]<60 G [ ]<70 H [ ]>70	LT [ ]VH [ ]S [ ]M [ ]SW [ ]NS JC [ ] [ ] [ ] [ ] [ ] LL [ ] [ ] [ ] [ ] [ ] FS [ ] [ ] [ ] [ ] [ ]
Wife's History પત્નીનો ઇતિહાસ	[ ] MI [ ] US [ ] MX [ ] SL [ ] OI	A [ ]<10 B [ ]<20 C [ ]<30 D [ ]<40 E [ ]<50 F [ ]<60 G [ ]<70 H [ ]>70	LT [ ]VH [ ]S [ ]M [ ]SW [ ]NS JC [ ] [ ] [ ] [ ] [ ] LL [ ] [ ] [ ] [ ] [ ] FS [ ] [ ] [ ] [ ] [ ]
Children's History Over 16 #1 બાળકનો ઇતિહાસ	[ ] MI [ ] US [ ] MX [ ] SL [ ] OI	A [ ]<10 B [ ]<20 C [ ]<30 D [ ]<40 E [ ]<50 F [ ]<60 G [ ]<70 H [ ]>70	LT [ ]VH [ ]S [ ]M [ ]SW [ ]NS JC [ ] [ ] [ ] [ ] [ ] LL [ ] [ ] [ ] [ ] [ ] FS [ ] [ ] [ ] [ ] [ ]
Children #2 #2 Over 16 બાળકો	[ ] MI [ ] US [ ] MX [ ] SL [ ] OI	A [ ]<10 B [ ]<20 C [ ]<30 D [ ]<40 E [ ]<50 F [ ]<60 G [ ]<70 H [ ]>70	LT [ ]VH [ ]S [ ]M [ ]SW [ ]NS JC [ ] [ ] [ ] [ ] [ ] LL [ ] [ ] [ ] [ ] [ ] FS [ ] [ ] [ ] [ ] [ ]
Children #3 over 16	[ ] MI [ ] US [ ] MX [ ] SL [ ] OI	A [ ]<10 B [ ]<20 C [ ]<30 D [ ]<40 E [ ]<50 F [ ]<60	LT [ ]VH [ ]S [ ]M [ ]SW [ ]NS [ ] FS [ ] JC [ ] [ ] [ ] [ ] [ ] LL [ ] [ ] [ ] [ ] [ ]
Your Father's History: આપના પિતાનો ઇતિહાસ	[ ] MI [ ] US [ ] MX [ ] SL [ ] OI	A [ ]<10 B [ ]<20 C [ ]<30 D [ ]<40 E [ ]<50 F [ ]<60 G [ ]<70 H [ ]>70	LT [ ]VH [ ]S [ ]M [ ]SW [ ]NS JC [ ] [ ] [ ] [ ] [ ] LL [ ] [ ] [ ] [ ] [ ] FS [ ] [ ] [ ] [ ] [ ]
Your Mother History: આપના માતાનો ઇતિહાસ	[ ] MI [ ] US [ ] MX [ ] SL [ ] OI	A [ ]<10 B [ ]<20 C [ ]<30 D [ ]<40 E [ ]<50 F [ ]<60	LT [ ]VH [ ]S [ ]M [ ]SW [ ]NS [ ] FS [ ] JC [ ] [ ] [ ] [ ] [ ] LL [ ] [ ] [ ] [ ] [ ]

Complete This Questionnaire For Indo-American Surat - Bulsar Districts Patidars

Legend:
Q U E S T I
O - ર N - વા s - લો

	19	20	21
	Parents ? Is it easy (E) or Hard(H) to find person with qualities you want in an ideal mate for your child ? *Children* ? Is it easy or hard to find person with qualities You want in an ideal mate ? E- Easy, SW- Some What hard, H- Hard.	*For unmarried people*: Do You like dating ? VM- Very Much for, LS- Like Some What, DS- Dis like Somewhat, DB-Don't Believe. *Parents* What is your opinion your children dating ?	*Children*. What Qualities are you mainly interested in your future spouse ; *Parents* , what qualities mainly do you look for your children's spouse ? PL- Person's looks and fun loving ?, IT- Intelligent, FS- Financial Status, TV- Shares traditional values.(choose-one from each) MP- MOst Important MD- Medium NP- Not Imp
	વડીલો? આપના બાળકોને લાયક પાટૅનૅર શોધવામાં આપને સરળતા અથવા મુશ્કેલી પડે. કૃનૅ? આપને આપના બાળકો લાયક લગ્ન પાટૅનૅર મુશ્કેલી પડે ? E- સરળ. SW- કંઇક અંશે અઘરૂ. H- અઘરૂ.	આપ ડેટીંગ માં માનો છો ? VM- બહુ જ માનો, LS-થોડૉ માનો, DS-થોડૉ ન માનો, DB- ન માનો.	વડીલો? આપના બાળકોના. અને. કૃનૅઓ? આપના ભવ્ય પાટૅનૅર માં આપ ઝંખો છો ? PL- વ્યક્તિનો દેખાવ. IT- તેજસ્વીતા. FS- આર્થિક સ્થિતિ. TV- સમન દૃષ્ટિકોણ. (દરેક માંથી એક પસંદ કરો) MP-અતિ મહત્વનૂ. MD- મધ્યમ. NP- મહત્વનૂ નહી.
	આ માટે કરી નિશાન ખાનામાં ખાલી જગા	**Please answer in the following boxes (check Marks)**	
Your History (Head of House) આપની હિસ્ટ	[ ] E [ ] SW [ ] H	[ ] VM [ ] LS [ ] DS [ ] DB	[ ] PL [ ] MP [ ] MD [ ] NP [ ] IT [ ] MP [ ] MD [ ] NP [ ] FS [ ] MP [ ] MD [ ] NP [ ] TV [ ] MP [ ] MD [ ] NP
Wife's History પત્નીની હિસ્ટ	[ ] E [ ] SW [ ] H	[ ] VM [ ] LS [ ] DS [ ] DB	[ ] PL [ ] MP [ ] MD [ ] NP [ ] IT [ ] MP [ ] MD [ ] NP [ ] FS [ ] MP [ ] MD [ ] NP [ ] TV [ ] MP [ ] MD [ ] NP
Children's History over 16 બાળકોની હિસ્ટ	[ ] E [ ] SW [ ] H	[ ] VM [ ] LS [ ] DS [ ] DB	[ ] PL [ ] MP [ ] MD [ ] NP [ ] IT [ ] MP [ ] MD [ ] NP [ ] FS [ ] MP [ ] MD [ ] NP [ ] TV [ ] MP [ ] MD [ ] NP
Children #2 બાળક #2 over 16 બાળકોની હિસ્ટ	[ ] E [ ] SW [ ] H	[ ] VM [ ] LS [ ] DS [ ] DB	[ ] PL [ ] MP [ ] MD [ ] NP [ ] IT [ ] MP [ ] MD [ ] NP [ ] FS [ ] MP [ ] MD [ ] NP [ ] TV [ ] MP [ ] MD [ ] NP
Children # 3 over 16	[ ] E [ ] SW [ ] H	[ ] VM [ ] LS [ ] DS [ ] DB	[ ] PL [ ] MP [ ] MD [ ] NP [ ] TV [ ] [ ] IT [ ] MP [ ] MD [ ] NP [ ] FS [ ] MP [ ] MD [ ] NP
Your Father's History: આપના પિતાની હિસ્ટ	[ ] E [ ] SW [ ] H	[ ] VM [ ] LS [ ] DS [ ] DB	[ ] PL [ ] MP [ ] MD [ ] NP [ ] IT [ ] MP [ ] MD [ ] NP [ ] FS [ ] MP [ ] MD [ ] NP [ ] TV [ ] MP [ ] MD [ ] NP
Your Mother History: આપની માતાની હિસ્ટ	[ ] E [ ] SW [ ] H	[ ] VM [ ] LS [ ] DS [ ] DB	[ ] PL [ ] MP [ ] MD [ ] NP [ ] TV [ ] [ ] IT [ ] MP [ ] MD [ ] NP [ ] FS [ ] MP [ ] MD [ ] NP

Complete This Questionnaire For Indo-American Surat - Bulsar Districts Patidars

	22		23		24
Q U E S T I O N S	*Children* ? How important to you that your future spouse, and for *Parent's* ? How Important to you that future spouse of your children be from: AP- from Any Patidar group, OC- from your Own Cast, AI- Any Indian, AR- Any Race.(choose one each from above) MP-Most Imp, IP-- Some Imp, NP-Not Important		What is the source of family conflicts betw'n parents & children from the following : AC - Arrange/Choice Marriage, CC- Career Choice , PC- Parental Control, CB- Children's Behaviour.(choose one from each) MP- Most Imp.,IP-Important, NP-Not Imp.		1 .Would you say that your health is Generally: E- Excellent, G- Good, F- Fair, P- Poor. 2. Any one in the family suffers with : D- Diabates , HB- High Blood pressure, HD- Heart Disease, AR- Arthritis, OT- Other
સ વા લો	વડીલો આપ તેમજ આપના બાળકો તેમના લગ્ન પાર્ટનર માટે ઇચ્છો કે ? AP- તેઓ પટેલ જ્ઞાતિના હોય. OC-આપની પોતાની જ પેટા જ્ઞાતિના હોય. AI-કોઇ પણ ઇન્ડિયન હોય. AR- કોઇ પણ જાતિ પમે? MP-ખૂબ જરુરી. IP- થોડુ જરુરી. NP-જરુરી નહિં.		ફેમિલીના વાલી/બાળકોના મતભેદોની અસર કુટબને થાય છે.અહીં આપને કઇ લાગુ પડે ? AC- એરેન્જ પસંદગી મેરેજ. CC- કેરીઅર (ભણતરની) ચોઇસ. PC-પેરન્ટ કંટ્રોલ (દરેકમાંથી એક પસં કરો)CB-બાળકોની વર્તણુક. (MP, IP, NP)		૧-આપને શું લાગે? આપની તંદુરસ્તી : E- ખૂબ સારી G-સારી. F-મધ્યમ. P- ખરાબ. ૨- આપનામાંથી કોઇને D- ડાયાબીટીસ. HB- હાય બ્લડ પ્રેસર. HD- હાર્ટ ડીસીસ. AR- આથરાઇટીસ.- વા. OT- બીજી કોઇ વ્યાધી ખરો?
	ચેક માર્ક કરી નીચેના ખાનાઓમાં જવાબો આપો		Please answer in the following boxes (check marks)		
Your History	[ ] AP	[ ] MP [ ] IP [ ] NP	[ ] AC	[ ] MP [ ] IP [ ] NP	1. [ ] E [ ] G [ ] F [ ] P
(Head of House)	[ ] OC	[ ] [ ] [ ]	[ ] CC	[ ] [ ] [ ]	
આપની વિગત	[ ] AI	[ ] [ ] [ ]	[ ] PC	[ ] [ ] [ ]	2. [ ] D [ ] HB [ ] HD [ ] AR [ ] OT
	[ ] AR	[ ] [ ] [ ]	[ ] CB	[ ] [ ] [ ]	
Wife's History	[ ] AP	[ ] MP [ ] IP [ ] NP	[ ] AC	[ ] MP [ ] IP [ ] NP	1. [ ] E [ ] G [ ] F [ ] P
પત્નીની વિગત	[ ] OC	[ ] [ ] [ ]	[ ] CC	[ ] [ ] [ ]	
	[ ] AI	[ ] [ ] [ ]	[ ] PC	[ ] [ ] [ ]	2. [ ] D [ ] HB [ ] HD [ ] AR [ ] OT
	[ ] AR	[ ] [ ] [ ]	[ ] CB	[ ] [ ] [ ]	
Children's	[ ] AP	[ ] MP [ ] IP [ ] NP	[ ] AC	[ ] MP [ ] IP [ ] NP	1. [ ] E [ ] G [ ] F [ ] P
History	[ ] OC	[ ] [ ] [ ]	[ ] CC	[ ] [ ] [ ]	
over 16 # 1	[ ] AI	[ ] [ ] [ ]	[ ] PC	[ ] [ ] [ ]	2. [ ] D [ ] HB [ ] HD [ ] AR [ ] OT
બાળકોની વિગત	[ ] AR	[ ] [ ] [ ]	[ ] CB	[ ] [ ] [ ]	
Children #2	[ ] AP	[ ] MP [ ] IP [ ] NP	[ ] AC	[ ] MP [ ] IP [ ] NP	1. [ ] E [ ] G [ ] F [ ] P
બાળક #2	[ ] OC	[ ] [ ] [ ]	[ ] CC	[ ] [ ] [ ]	
over 16	[ ] AI	[ ] [ ] [ ]	[ ] PC	[ ] [ ] [ ]	2. [ ] D [ ] HB [ ] HD [ ] AR [ ] OT
	[ ] AR	[ ] [ ] [ ]	[ ] CB	[ ] [ ] [ ]	
Children #3	[ ] AP	[ ] MP [ ] IP [ ] NP [ ] **AR** [ ]	[ ] AC	[ ] MP [ ] IP [ ] NP [ ] **CB** [ ]	1. [ ] E [ ] G [ ] F [ ] P
	[ ] OC	[ ] [ ] [ ]	[ ] CC	[ ] [ ] [ ]	
over 16	[ ] AI	[ ] [ ] [ ]	[ ] PC	[ ] [ ] [ ]	2. [ ] D [ ] HB [ ] HD [ ] AR [ ] OT
Your Father History:	[ ] AP	[ ] MP [ ] IP [ ] NP	[ ] AC	[ ] MP [ ] IP [ ] NP	
	[ ] OC	[ ] [ ] [ ]	[ ] CC	[ ] [ ] [ ]	1. [ ] E [ ] G [ ] F [ ] P
આપના પિતાની વિગત	[ ] AI	[ ] [ ] [ ]	[ ] PC	[ ] [ ] [ ]	2. [ ] D [ ] HB [ ] HD [ ] AR [ ] OT
	[ ] AR	[ ] [ ] [ ]	[ ] CB	[ ] [ ] [ ]	
Your Mother's History:	[ ] AP	[ ] MP [ ] IP [ ] NP [ ] **AR** [ ]	[ ] AC	[ ] MP [ ] IP [ ] NP [ ] **CB** [ ]	1. [ ] E [ ] G [ ] F [ ] P
	[ ] OC	[ ] [ ] [ ]	[ ] CC	[ ] [ ] [ ]	
આપની માતાની વિગત	[ ] AI	[ ] [ ] [ ]	[ ] PC	[ ] [ ] [ ]	2. [ ] D [ ] HB [ ] HD [ ] AR [ ] OT

Complete This Questionnaire For Indo-American Surat - Bulsar Districts Patidars

	25	26	27	28
Q U E S T I O N S	How would you compare your life in US with your past life in your motherland ? E- Excellent, G- Good, F- Fair, P- Poor	How often do you get together with (Fr) Friends (RI) Relatives. OW-Once a Week, FM- Few times a Month, OM- Once a Month, NO- Not at All (choose one for each)	1. How often do you experience feelings of : (LL) Lonliness? LT–a Lot, ST–Some Time, R- Rarely, N- Never. 2. Do you (SC)- Smoke Cigarett ? D- Daily, OW- Once a While, N- Never.(choose one each for above)	Who are the most important people to you ? PT-Parents, T - Teachers, RS - Saints, FR- Frie'ns/ Reltv's. (CHOOSE ONE EACH) MP-Most Imp, IP-Imp., NP- Not Important
Please answer in the following boxes (check marks)				
Your History (Head of House)	[ ] E [ ] G [ ] F [ ] P	Fr [ ] [ ]OW [ ]FM [ ]OM [ ]NO RI [ ] [ ]OW [ ]FM [ ]OM [ ]NO	1. [ ] LL [ ]LT [ ]ST [ ]R [ ]N 2. [ ] SC [ ]D [ ]OW [ ]N	[ ]PT [ ]MP [ ]IP [ ]NP [ ]T [ ]MP [ ]IP [ ]NP [ ]RS [ ]MP [ ]IP [ ]NP [ ]FR [ ]MP [ ]IP [ ]NP
Wife's History	[ ] E [ ] G [ ] F [ ] P	Fr [ ] [ ]OW [ ]FM [ ]OM [ ]NO RI [ ] [ ]OW [ ]FM [ ]OM [ ]NO	1. [ ] LL [ ]LT [ ]ST [ ]R [ ]N 2. [ ] SC [ ]D [ ]OW [ ]N	[ ]PT [ ]MP [ ]IP [ ]NP [ ]T [ ]MP [ ]IP [ ]NP [ ]RS [ ]MP [ ]IP [ ]NP [ ]FR [ ]MP [ ]IP [ ]NP
Children's History over 16 #1	[ ] E [ ] G [ ] F [ ] P	Fr [ ] [ ]OW [ ]FM [ ]OM [ ]NO RI [ ] [ ]OW [ ]FM [ ]OM [ ]NO	1. [ ] LL [ ]LT [ ]ST [ ]R [ ]N 2. [ ] SC [ ]D [ ]OW [ ]N	[ ]PT [ ]MP [ ]IP [ ]NP [ ]T [ ]MP [ ]IP [ ]NP [ ]RS [ ]MP [ ]IP [ ]NP [ ]FR [ ]MP [ ]IP [ ]NP
Children #2 #2 over 16	[ ] E [ ] G [ ] F [ ] P	Fr [ ] [ ]OW [ ]FM [ ]OM [ ]NO RI [ ] [ ]OW [ ]FM [ ]OM [ ]NO	1. [ ] LL [ ]LT [ ]ST [ ]R [ ]N 2. [ ] SC [ ]D [ ]OW [ ]N	[ ]PT [ ]MP [ ]IP [ ]NP [ ]T [ ]MP [ ]IP [ ]NP [ ]RS [ ]MP [ ]IP [ ]NP [ ]FR [ ]MP [ ]IP [ ]NP
Children #3 over 16	[ ] E [ ] G [ ] F [ ] P	Fr [ ] [ ]OW [ ]FM [ ]OM [ ]NO RI [ ] [ ]OW [ ]FM [ ]OM [ ]NO	1. [ ] LL [ ]LT [ ]ST [ ]R [ ]N 2. [ ] SC [ ]D [ ]OW [ ]N	[ ]PT [ ]MP [ ]IP [ ]NP [ ]T [ ]MP [ ]IP [ ]NP [ ] [ ]MP [ ]IP [ ]NP
Your Father's History:	[ ] E [ ] G [ ] F [ ] P	Fr [ ] [ ]OW [ ]FM [ ]OM [ ]NO RI [ ] [ ]OW [ ]FM [ ]OM [ ]NO	1. [ ] LL [ ]LT [ ]ST [ ]R [ ]N 2. [ ] SC [ ]D [ ]OW [ ]N	[ ]PT [ ]MP [ ]IP [ ]NP [ ]T [ ]MP [ ]IP [ ]NP [ ]RS [ ]MP [ ]IP [ ]NP [ ]FR [ ]MP [ ]IP [ ]NP
Your Mother's History:	[ ] E [ ] G [ ] F [ ] P		1. [ ] LL [ ]LT [ ]ST [ ]R [ ]N 2. [ ] SC [ ]D [ ]OW [ ]N	[ ]PT [ ]MP [ ]IP [ ]NP [ ]T [ ]MP [ ]IP [ ]NP [ ]RS [ ]MP [ ]IP [ ]NP

BIBLIOGRAPHY

Abraham, Sen et al. *India: the Rough Guide*. London: Rough Guides, 1996.

Agarwal, Priya. *A Passage from India: Post-1965 Immigrants and their Children*. Palos Verdes: Yuvati Publication, 1991.

Agarwal, Vijay. "Problems with Parents." *India-West*. October 1996.

Aruberg, Lenora. "Raising Children Bilingually: the Pre-School Years." *Orange County Register*, September 17, 1994.

"Asian-American Health Forum." *State of Asian-Pacifics Today*. California Department of Health Services, 1992.

Azores, Tania, and Paul Ong. "Health Professionals on the Front Line." *The State of Asian-Pacific America: Economic Diversity, Issues and Policies Public Policy Report*. Los Angeles: LEAP—Asian Pacific American Public Policy Institute and UCLA Asian American Studies Center, 1994.

Barringer et al. "Asian and Pacific Islanders in the United States." *Asian American Almanac*. United States Census, Population Bureau. New York: Russell Foundation, 1993.

Batter, Karin. "A Gift of Language." *Los Angeles Times*, October 4, 1995.

Baxi, Chandrakant. *Mahajati Gujarat*. Ahmedabad and Bombay: Navbharat Sahitya Mandir, 1994.

—. *Pitru Bhumi Gujarat*. Bombay: Navbharat Sahitya Mandir, 1983.

Bhakta, Dudhiben L. *Vividh lagna gitos*. Vyara, India: Anand Printing, 1993.

Bhatt, Dr. Kantikumar. *Jivanji Maharaj and Bhakta Samaj*. Rajpipla, India: Pinakin Prakashan, 1982.

Brandnock, Robert. *India Handbook*. London: Footprint Handbooks, 1996.

Brennan, Jennifer. *The Cuisines of Asia: Nine Great Oriental Cusines by Technique*. New York: St. Martin's, 1984.

Brown, Dr. Robert. *Music and Musicians*. India: Wesleyan University Press, 1989.

Burgess, Tyrrel, Richard Layard, and Pitambar Pant. *Manpower and Educational Development in India*. Parmar Director of Information, Government of Gujarat, 1986.

Cain, Bruce. "Acquisition of Partisanship by Latinos and Asian Americans." *Statistical Records of Asian Americans*, May 1991.

Canada, Virendra. "Will Gujurati Language Vanish by 2012 in Foreign Countries?" Ahmedebad and New Jersey: Gujarat Samchar, September 1997.

Census of India. Bulsar District, 1981.

Census of India. Surat District, 1981.

Chan, Sucheng. *Asian Americans: An Interpretive History*. New York: Twayne Publishers, 1991.

Chandrasekera, Archanna. "Dealing with Interfaith Marriages." *India-West*, September 22, 1995.

Charotariya Patidar Seva Samaj International Directory (1994-1995).

Chavez, Leo. *Shadowed Lives: Undocumented Immigrants in American Society*. International Thomson Publishing, 1997.

Chhaya, Romeshchandra S. *Bharatani Vasti Ganatri*. "Bulsar Jillo." Census of India, Bulsar District. Ahemadabad: Gujarat State, 1981.

—. *Bharatani Vasti Ganatri*. "Surat Jillo." Census of India, Surat District. Ahemadabad: Gujarat State, 1981.

Chinai, Radhika. "On Living in India." *India-West*, September 29, 1995.

Christian, Susan. "Single in Orange County—Breaking the Dating Tradition." *Los Angeles Times*, September 12, 1994.

Choice Hotels International Hospitality Franchise System. Phoenix: Choice Hotels International, Inc.

Clinton, President William. "AAHOA on the Hill." *AAHOA—A Magazine Dedicated to Asian American Hoteliers.* Atlanta: the Nelson Advantage Inc., December 1996.

Crohn, Joel. *Mixed Matches: How to Create Successful Interracial, Interethnic, and Interfaith Relationships.* New York: Ballantine Books, 1995.

Debu, Kersi K. *Our Navsari: Charcha Patri Mandal, Navsari.* Ahmedabad: Bhargavi Printers, 1994.

Desai, Mahadevbhai. *The Story of Bardoli.* Navjivan: Ahmedabad, 1929.

Desai, Suresh. *Our Navsari: Charcha Patri Mandal.* Navsari: Dialogue Organization, 1994.

Elliot, Robert Barkan. *Asian and Pacific Islander Migration to the U.S.* West Port: Greenwood Press, 1992.

Emmers, Steve. "Single in Orange County: Looking for Love in the 90's." *Los Angeles Times,* September 11, 1994.

Farley, Reynolds, and Walter Allen. *Color Line and Quality of Life in America.* New York: Oxford University Press, 1989.

Fillmore, Lily Wong, Peter Kiang, and Vivian Lee. "Preschool and Native Language Loss." *MABE Newsletter.* Massachusetts Association for Bilingual Education 2 (1991).

Gall, Susan, and Irene Natividav. *Asian American Almanac: A Reference Work on Asian Americans in the U.S.* Detroit: Gale Research, 1995.

Gall, Susan B., and Timothy Gall. *Statistical Record of Asian Americans.* Detroit: Gale Research, 1993.

Gokul, Ramesh. "Family Values and Business." *India Post,* March 7, 1997.

Gordon, Susan. *Asian Indians.* U.S.: Franklin Watts, 1990.

Guillermo, Tessie. "Health Care Needs and Service Delivery." *The State of Asian Pacific America.* Los Angeles: LEAP—Asian Pacific American Policy Institute and UCLA Asian American Studies Center, 1994.

Gupta, Vandana. "Impressions of India: Close Bonds." *India-West,* September 18, 1992.

Haiti, Sheba. "Nara's Beat: Doctor of the 90's." *India Journal,* March 1996.

Haney, Daniel. "Culture-Science." *The Orange County Register,* February 19, 1995.

Harish, Pattni. "A Pioneer Asian American Hotel Owner." *AAHOA—A Magazine Dedicated toAsian American Hoteliers,* 1993.

Helm, Leslie. "Capers Jones, Boston Based Software Productivity Consultant." *Los Angeles Times,* November 1993.

Hindu Matiya Patidar Samaj Directory 1994-95. Rancho Santa Fe: Hindu Matiya Patidar Samaj Inc.

Hindu Matiya Patidar Samaj Directory 1997. Rancho Santa Fe: Hindu Matiya Patidar Samaj Inc.

Hing, Bill Ong. "Immigration Policy: Making and Remaking Asian Pacific America." *The State of Asian Pacific America.* Los Angeles: LEAP—Asian Pacific American Public Policy Institute and UCLA Asian American Studies Center, 1993.

Hing, Bill Ong. *Making and Remaking Asian America Through Immigration Policy, 1850-1990.* Stanford: Stanford University Press, 1993.

Imahara, Kathlyn. "Language Rights Policy." *The State of Asian Pacific America.* Los Angeles: LEAP—Asian Pacific American Policy Institute and UCLA Asian American Studies Center, 1993.

INS Advanced Reports, 1989.

INS Annual Report, 1969.

INS Statistical YearBook.

International Who's Who in Community Service, 3rd Ed. Cambridge, U.K.: International Biological Center, 1979.

Kang, Elliot. "Marketing to Asian Minorities" (1995) quoted in "American Demographics." *AD/MT Home Page*. New York City: Cowles Business Media, 1997.

Kar, Snehendur B., Kevin Campbell, Armando Jimenez, and Sangeeta Gupta. *Amerasia Journal* 21 (1995-1996). Los Angeles: Asian American Studies Center, UCLA.

Kelleher, Kathleen. "Married with Benefits." *Los Angeles Times*, February 3, 1996.

Kiang, Peter N., and Vivian Wai-Fun Lee. "Exclusion or Contribution? Education K-12 Policy." *The State of Asian Pacific America: Issues to the Year 2020*. Los Angeles: LEAP—Asian Pacific American Public Policy Institute and UCLA Asian American Studies Center, 1993.

Labich, Kenneth. "Can Your Career Hurt Your Kids?" *Fortune*, May 30, 1991.

Lavina, Melwani. "The Joys and Challenges of Growing up in Intercultural Families." *India-West*, January 20, 1995.

Leauva Patidar Samaj of U.S.A Directory 1997. Berea, KY: Leauva Patidar Samaj of USA Publishing.

Lee, Lilly. "A Demographic Study of Asian Pacific Population in Los Angeles County: American Born and Foreign Born by Ethnic Group, L.A. County, 1980." *Pacific Rim Profile Technical Report*. Los Angeles: Asian Pacific Research and Development Council, United Way, Inc., 1985.

Leonard, Karen. *Making Ethnic Choices: California's Punjabi Mexican Americans*. Philadelphia: Temple University Press, 1992.

Leonard, Karen B. and Chandra S. Tibrewal. "Asian Indians in Southern California: Occupations and Ethnicity." In *Immigration and Entrepreneurship: Culture, Capital, and Ethnic Networks*. New Brunswick: Transaction Publishers, 1993.

Lessinger, Johnna. "The Indian Immigrant Experience," quoted in "Policy on New Communities: South Asians in the United States with a Focus on Asian Indians," Sucheta Mazumdar. *The State of Asian Pacific America*. Los Angeles: LEAP—Asian Pacific American Public Policy Institute and UCLA Asian American Studies Center, 1993.

Library of Nations. Time Life Books: Time Inc., 1986.

Lugailla, Terry. "Marital Status and Living Arrangements." *India-West*, May 24, 1996.

Macwan, Heerva. "My Culture is Also My Religion." *India Journal*, July 17, 1998.

Magnet, Margaret. "The American Family: Children in Crisis." *Fortune*, August 10, 1992.

Mahu, Shobha. "Hindu Marriage." *India Journal*, February 9, 1996.

Malkani, Manish. "On Ideal Mates." *India-West*: July 26, 1996.

Manish, Puri. "Focus on Youth." *India-West*, July 1995.

Mar, Don and Marlene Ki. "Historical Trends." *The State of Asian Pacific America: Economic Diversity: Issues and Policies: A Public Policy Report*. Los Angeles: LEAP—Asian Pacific American Public Policy Institute and UCLA Asian American Studies Center, 1994.

Marino, Vivian. "How to Follow in Mom and Pop's Footsteps." *Los Angeles Times*, October 22, 1996.

Matiya Patidar World Directory, 1993.

Matsuda, Mari. "Voice of America: Accent, Anti-Discrimination Law, and

Jurisprudence for the Last Reconstruction." *Yale Law Journal* (1991).

Maynard, Cindy. "Meet your Executive Committee." *AAHOA Hospitality Magazine*, April 1999.

Mazumdar, Sucheta "Ethnic Niches: Creating Jobs that Fuel Immigrant Growth." *New York Times*, January 12, 1993.

—. "Long Road from Home." *The State of Asian Pacific America: Policy on New Communities*. Los Angeles: LEAP—Asian Pacific American Public Policy Institute and UCLA Asian American Studies Center, 1993.

—. "Policy on New Communities: South Asians in the United States, with a Focus on Asian Indians." *The State of Asian Pacific America*. Los Angeles: LEAP—Asian Pacific American Public Policy Institute and UCLA Asian American Studies Center, 1993.

Mechling, Elizabeth. "Commentary." *Los Angeles Times*, April 7, 1993.

Mekvan, Subbarov Ratikumar. "Archeological Exploration in Mahival." In *Gaurvarshali Patidar of Mahagujarat*. Baroda: Ridhi Sidhi Publication, 1991.

Melendy, H. Brett. *Asians In America: Filipinos, Koreans, and East Indians*. Boston: Twayne Publications, 1976.

Mill-Man, Joel. "Other Americans: The Rise of the Asian American Hotel Owners: How Immigrants Renew Our Country, Our Economy, and Our Values." *AAHOA Hospitality*, December 1997.

Mogelonsky, Marcia. "American Demographic AD/MT home page, opinion by Elliot Kang, Kang and Lee Advertising, 1997." In *Marketing to Asian Minorities*. New York City: Cowles Business Media. *American Demographic Magazine* 6 (1995).

Montaner, Carlos Alberto. "Talk English—You are in the U.S." In *Language Loyalties: A Sourcebook on the Official English Controversy*, edited by James Crawford. Chicago: University of Chicago Press, 1992.

Narain, R. Kamna. "In Step with the Unbridgeable Generation Gap." *India-West*, March 3, 1995.

Professor Narshihbhai. "Who Were the Predecessors of the Motel Occupation?" In *Gujarat Samachar*. New Jersey: Gujarat Chamar, March 5, 1995 and March 14, 1995.

Natali, Jagdish, and Dhirubhai Bhavan. *Shree Moraribapuni Ram Katha*. Auckland, New Zealand: Logan Campbell Center,1988.

National Data for Health Statistics, 1994. Washington, D.C.

The New World Book of Patels. Halbert's Family Heritage, 1997.

Nyrop, Richard F. *India: A Country Study*. Washington D.C.: American University, 1986.

O'Reilly, Brian. "The New Face of Small Business: Executive Life." *Fortune*, May 2, 1994.

Omi, Michael. "Out of the Melting Pot and into the Fire: Race Relations Policy." *The State of Asian Pacific America*. Los Angeles: LEAP—Asian Pacific American Public Policy Institute and UCLA Asian American Studies Center, 1993.

Ong, Paul. "Asian Americans in Los Angeles: Entrepreneurship and Enclave Economy—Alternative Business Development." In *Beyond Asian American Poverty: Community Economic Development Policies and Strategies*. Los Angeles: LEAP—Asian Pacific American Public Policy Institute and UCLA Asian American Studies Center, 1993.

—. "Inner City Community." In *Beyond Asian American Poverty: Community Economic Development Policies and Strategies*. Los Angeles: LEAP—Asian Pacific American Public Policy Institute and UCLA Asian American Studies Center, 1993.

Ong, Paul, and Evelyn Blumenberg. "Scientists and Engineers." *The State of Asian*

Pacific America: Economic Diversity, Issues and Policies: A Public Policy Report. In *Beyond Asian American Poverty: Community Economic Development Policies and Strategies.* Los Angeles: LEAP—Asian Pacific American Public Policy Institute and UCLA Asian American Studies Center, 1994.

Ong, Paul, and Suzanne Hee. "Work Issues Facing Asian Pacific Americans: Labor Policy." *The State of Asian Pacific America.* In *Beyond Asian American Poverty: Community Economic Development Policies and Strategies.* Los Angeles: LEAP—Asian Pacific American Public Policy Institute and UCLA Asian American Studies Center, 1993.

Ong, Paul and Suzanne Hee. "Economic Diversity." *The State of Asian Pacific America: Economic Diversity, Issues and Policies. A Public Policy Report.* In *Beyond Asian American Poverty: Community Economic Development Policies and Strategies.* Los Angeles: LEAP—Asian Pacific American Public Policy Institute and UCLA Asian American Studies Center, 1994.

Panchapakesan, Karthik. "NRIS—A Diverse Diaspora Growing." *India-Post,* April 10, 1998.

Parikh, Purusottam L. *Kanbe-ksatriyas Utpati and etihas (Origination and History).* Ahmedabad: Umiya Prakashan, 1986.

Parmar, V.R. *Gujarat.* Ahemadabad: Government of Gujarat, March 1992.

Patel, Arvind R. "Marriage: Perspective for Parents." In *Patidar in Foreign Lands,* edited by Videshoma Patidar. Ahmadabad: Dharti Vikas Mandal, 1994.

Patel, Chandrakant D. *History of the Patels.* Auckland, New Zealand: 1975.

—. "Unanimity with Mind: English Mixing of ABC." *Naya Padakar, Purti Edition,* November 22, 1996.

Patel, Gokaldas Sombhai, and Mahendrabhai Gokalbhai. *Gujaratna Kurmi Kshtriya Patidaroni History.* Ahmadabad: Mahendrabhai Patel, 1989.

Patel, Kunverji V., and Premanand S. Shyam. *Matiya Patidar Samaj Directory* V and VII (1989-1990).

Patel, Dr. Mafatlal. *Videshoma Patidar (Patidar in Foreign Land).* Ahemadabad: Dharti Vikas Mandal, 1994.

Patel, Dr. Mangubhai. *Gaurava Gatha.* Ahemadabad: Patidar Research Center, 1991.

—. *Patidaroni Gaurava Gatha.* Ahmedabad: Patidar Research Center, 1993.

Patel, Ranjan, and Ramesh Patel. *Hindu Marriage Ceremony.* North Dartmouth, MA: Charotaria Leauva Patidar Samaj, 1995.

Patel, Surendra C. "Ethnomusicology." *India Music and Musicians Magazine* (1971); and in *India: the Ultimate Fantasy Souvenir Book.* India: Wesleyan University Press, 1989.

Patel, Vasant G., and Bhupendra Joshi. "Ame Leauva Patidar." *Leauva Patidar Samaj of California First Convention Magazine* (1997).

Potts, Michael. "Study of Indo-Americans Reveals Contradictions." *India-West,* May 24, 1996.

Prasad, Shivani. "Say What? On Language." *India–West,* February 2, 1996.

Puri, Manish. "Focus on Youth." *India –West,* July 1995.

Rahul, Jacob. "Overseas Indians Make it Big." *Fortune,* November 15, 1993.

Reejhsinghani, Aroona. *Vegetarian Wonders from Gujarat.* Mumbai: Jaico Publishing House, 1997.

Rice, Louis. "Children in Crisis." *Fortune,* August 10, 1992.

Roan, Shari. "Parents: Beyond the Birds and the Bees." *Los Angeles Times,* February 16, 1993.

Robinson, Denton. "Society's Message: Don't be Too Fruitful. Families: Despite Criticism, Some Parents No Longer Believe that Two Children Are Enough." *Los Angeles Times*, 1996.

Rushdie, Salman. *The Satanic Verses*. New York: Penguin, 1989.

Samaj, Darpan. "A Message to Indo-American Youth." *Leauva Patidar Samaj of USA Magazine* (1995).

Scott, E. Reckard. "$80 Million Deal Close on Sale of Anaheim Hotel: Tourism: O.C.'s Tushar Patel is Said to Be Near to Acquiring the Convention-Oriented Marriott, the City's Third Largest Facility." *Los Angeles Times*, April 29, 1999.

Sehgul, Puneet. "Arranged Marriage." *India-West*, April 14, 1995.

Seth, Jagdish. "Dahyabhai Patel: The Grand Patriarch of Hospitality." *AAHOA: India Post Supplemental*, March 19, 1999.

Shah, Bharat. "Importance of Gujurati Language to Be Alive Overseas." Ahmedabad and New Jersey: Gujarat Samchar, 1997.

Shah, Neil. "India, More Than Just Poverty." *India-West*, May 26, 1996.

Shah, Preeti. "H.P. Rama Reveals Successful Strategies." *India–West*, February10, 1995.

Sheely, Gail. *New Passages: Mapping Your Life Across Time*. New York: Random House, 1995.

Sherman, Stratford P. "America Won't Win Till It Reads More." *Fortune*, November 18, 1991.

Shree Ramkabir Bhakta Samaj of U.S.A. Directory, 1996.

Slack, Susan Fuller. *Oriental: Appetizers and Light Meals*. Los Angeles: HPBooks, 1998.

Smith, Bradford. *Portrait of India*. New York: Lippincott, 1962.

Smith, Lee. "How the Average American Gets by: Census Research: Who We Are." *Fortune*, October 21, 1991.

Smith, Tom. *A Report on the Socio-Economic Status of Ethnic Groups in the United States*. Chicago: University of Chicago Press, 1992.

Snehendu, Kar, Sangeeta Gupta, Kevin Campbell, and Armando Jimenaz. *Invisible Americans: An Exploration of Indo-American Quality of Life*. 25th *Commemorative Issue of the Amerasia Journal*. In "Study of Indo-Americans Reveals Contradictions," by Michael Potts. *India-West*, May 24, 1996.

Sole, Yolanda. "Bilingualism: Stable or Transitional? The Case of Spanish in the U.S." *International Journal of Social Languages* 84 (1990).

Sowell, Thomas. *Race and Culture: A Worldview*. New York: Basic Books, 1994.

Tamari, Julie. "Cultural Balancing Act Adds to Teen Angst: Asian American Youths Face Perils of Adolescence While Coming to Grips with Issues of Identity." *Los Angeles Times*, July 13, 1998.

Thaker, Suvarnaand, and Sucheta Mazumdar. "The Quality of Life of Asian Indian Women in the Motel Industry." *South Asia Bulletin* 2:1 (1998).

Tharoor, Shashi. *India From Midnight to the Millennium*. New York: Arcade Publishing, 1997.

Trsn, Tini. "Culture." *Los Angeles Times*, June 8, 1998.

Unger, Sanford J. *Fresh Blood: The New American Immigrants*. New York: Simon and Schuster, 1995.

U.S. Bureau of the Census. *1983 and 1984 Census of Population Subject Reports*. Washington, D.C.: United States Government Printing Office.

U.S. Bureau of the Census. *1990 Census of Population and Housing Data Paper Listing* (CPH-L133).

U.S. Bureau of the Census. *1992 Characteristics of Business Owners*. Washignton, D.C.: United States Government Printing Office.

U.S. Bureau of the Census. *1996 Statistical Abstract of the United States: The National Data Book*. Washington, D.C.: United States Government Printing Office.

U.S. Bureau of the Census. *1997 Current Population Reports: School Enrollment and Educational Attainment in the U.S.* Washington, D.C.: United States Government Printing Office.

U.S.-Canada Bhakta Directory 1996. Los Angeles: Ram Kabir Bhakta Samaj of USA.

U.S. Commission on Civil Rights. "Civil Rights Facing Asian Americans in the 1990's." Washington, D.C.: United States Government Printing Office, 1992.

U.S. Congressional Record. 66 Congress, Session 1 (1919), 7606-07.

U.S. Department of Commerce, Bureau of the Census. *Statistical Abstract of the United States*. Washington, D.C.: U.S. Government Printing Office, 1980 and 1990.

U.S. Department of Justice, Immigration and Naturalization Service. 1967 and 1969 Memorandum. In *Migration in Professions and Related Fields*. "Fiscal 1967," Chart 3; "Fiscal 1969," Chart 3.

U.S. Immigration and Naturalization Service, *1991 Statistical YearBook*, Table 20.

U.S. Immigration and Naturalization Service, *1995 Statistical Year Book*.

Van Buren, Abigail. "What Every Teen Should Know." Illinois: Phillips-Van Buren, Inc., 1993.

Vasant, Aruna. "Little Hoover Commission: Meeting the Challenge of Language Diversity: A Report from BW Associates, Department of Education, Berkeley, CA," *India–West*, November 10, 1995.

Viswanathan, Ed. *Am I a Hindu?: The Hinduism Primer*. San Francisco: Halo Books, 1992.

Wang, L. Ling-chi. "Higher Education Policy." *The State of Asian Pacific America*. Los Angeles: LEAP—Asian Pacific American Public Policy Institute and UCLA Asian American Studies Center, 1993.

Warner, Deborah. "For Moms Only." *Orange County Register*, September 1996.

Worldwide Bhakta Directory, 1991-1992.

Yoshitomi, Gerald. "Asian American Art in the Year 2020: Art Policy." *The State of Asian Pacific America*. Los Angeles: LEAP—Asian Pacific American Public Policy Institute and UCLA Asian American Studies Center, 1993.

—. *National Task Force on Presenting and Touring the Performing Arts: An American Dialogue*. Washington, D. C.: Association of Performing Arts Presenters, 1993.

NOTES

1.   Darpan Samaj, former principal from India, "A Message to Indo-American Youth," in *Leauva Patidar Samaj of USA Magazine* (Kentucky: Leauva Patidar U.S.A. Surat, Bulsar, and Navsari Districts, 1995).

2.   Priya Agarwal, *A Passage from India: Post-1965 Immigrants and their Children* (Palos Verdes: Yuvati Publication, 1991), 37.

3.   Robert Brandnock, *India-Handbook* (London: Footprint Handbooks, 1996), 137.

4.   Sen Abraham, et al., *India: the Rough Guide* (London: Rough Guides, 1996), 610-611.

5.   1981 Census of India, Surat District.

6.   Kersi K. Debu, "Navsarini Tarikh and Tavarikh" in *Our Navsari: Charcha Patri Mandal, Navsari* (Ahmedabad: Bhargavi Printers, 1994), 33.

7.   See Navsari District's map, by Anand Sahitya Publisher in Ahemadabad, India.

8.   Suresh Desai, *Our Navsari: Charcha Patri Mandal* (Navsari: Dialogue Organization, 1994), 33-35.

9.   Richard F. Nyrop, *India: A Country Study* (Washington, D.C.: American University, 1986), 120, 22, 25, 33, 79, 80, 220-82, 344.

10.   Subbarov Ratikumar Mekvan, "Archeological Exploration in Mahival," in *Gaurvarshali Patidar of Mahagujarat* (Baroda: Ridhi Sidhi Publication, 1991), 8.

11.   Gokaldas Sombhai Patel and Mahendrabhai Gokalbhai, *Gujaratna Kurmi Kshtriya Patidaroni History* (Mahendrabhai Patel: Ahmadabad, 1989), 141,196,197, 205.

12.   My research indicates that the term could be derived from French or Hindi, with the meaning of "one who sold cakes and tarts" or "handyman in the village," respectively. However, there may be other meanings handed down over the generations in separate Patel families.

13.   Chandrakant D. Patel, *History of the Patels* (Auckland, New Zealand, 1975). Concluded from the books kept by the "Baroths"—a priestly caste–and "Vahivanchas"—bards who keep the records of genealogical trees. Matiya Patidar Samaj Directory (1989), 2-4.

14.   Mahadevbhai Desai, *The Story of Bardoli* (Navjivan: Ahmedabad, 1929), 86.

15.   Dr. Mangubhai Patel, *Gaurava Gatha* (Ahemadabad: Patidar Research Center, 1991), 86, 94.

16.   *The New World Book of Patels* (Halbert's Family Heritage).

17.   Ibid.

18.   See Appendix G: IAPFM U.S. Distribution.

19.   Kunverji V. Patel and Premanand S. Shyam, *Matiya Patidar Samaj Directory* (U.S.: Matiya Patidar Samaj, 1989-1990), vols. V and VII.

20.   Dr. Kantikumar Bhatt, *Jivanji Maharaj and Bhakta Samaj* (Rajpipla, India: Pinakin Prakashan, 1982), 55-56.

21.   Karen Leonard, *Making Ethnic Choices: California's Punjabi Mexican Americans* (Philadelphia: Temple University Press, 1992), 30.

22.   Susan Gordon, *Asian Indians* (New York: Franklin Watts, Inc, 1990), 9.

23.   Susan B. and Timothy Gall, *Statistical Record of Asian Americans* (Detroit: Gale Research, 1993), 411, Table 515.

24.   H. Brett Melendy, *Asians in America* (Boston: Twayne Publishers, 1976), 207.

25.   Bill Ong Hing, *Making and Remaking Asian America Through Immigration Policy, 1850-1990* (Stanford: Stanford University Press, 1993), Table 982.

26.   U.S. Congressional Record, 66 Congress, Session 1 (1919), 7606-07, in Melendy, 208.

27.   Barringer et al., "Asian and Pacific Islanders in the United States," in *Asian American Almanac* (U.S. Census Population Bureau, New York: Russell Foundation, 1993), 25-26.

28.   *1969 INS Annual Report*, Tables 6.6B and 7A, 40-48; *INS Statistical Year Book*, Tables IMM 2.6 and 3.1, 33-37; *1989 INS Advanced Reports*, Table 4.

29.   Gordon, 22.

30.   Mazumdar, in *The State of Asian Pacific America* (1993), 38.

31.   Leo Chavez coined this term for illegal immigrants who cross the Mexican-California border in his famous book, *Shadowed Lives: Undocumented Immigrants in American Society* (International Thomson Publishing, 1997).

32.   Ibid.

33.   Leslie Helm, "Capers Jones, Boston-Based Software Productivity Consultant," *Los Angeles Times*, November 1993.

34.   Ibid.

35.   Salman Rushdie, *The Satanic Verses* (New York: Penguin, 1989), 168.

36.   Jacob Rahul. "Overseas Indians Make it Big," *Fortune*, November15, 1993, 169, 120, 172, 174.

37.   Ibid., 170.

38.   President William Clinton, "AAHOA On The Hill," *AAHOA—A Magazine Dedicated to Asian American Hoteliers* (Atlanta: The Nelson Advantage Inc., December 1996) 24, 25, 27.

39.   Data source: U.S. Department of Justice, Immigration and Naturalization Service Memorandum, *Migration in Professions and Related Fields*, "Fiscal 1967," Chart 3; "Fiscal 1969," Chart 3.

40.   Compiled from Robert Bakan Elliot, *Asian and Pacific Islander Migration to the U.S.*,Table 4 and 74,75,140; and from INS public use tapes, 1972-1985.

41.   Susan Gall and Irene Natividav, *Asian American Almanac: A Reference Work on Asian Americans in the U.S.* (Detroit: Gale Research, 1995), 15-16.

42.   Sucheta Mazumdar, "Policy on New Communities: South Asians in the United States, with a Focus on Asian Indians" in *The State of Asian Pacific America* (Los Angeles: LEAP—Asian Pacific American Public Policy Institute and UCLA Asian American Studies Center, 1993), 291.

43.   Pattni Harish, "A Pioneer Asian American Hotel Owner," *AAHOA* (1993), 6-7.

44.   Vivan Marino, "How to Follow in Mom and Pop's Footsteps," *Los Angeles Times*, October 22, 1996, D21.

45.   U.S. Immigration and Naturalization Service, *Statistical Year Book*, 1991, Table 20, 66.

46.   Marcia Mogelonsky, *American Demographic Magazine* 6 (1995).

47.   See Mazumdar, "Policy on New Communities," 292.

48.   Compiled from Lee Smith, "How the Average American Gets by: Census Research: Who We Are," *Fortune*, October 21, 1991, 55.

49.   *Choice Hotels International Hospitality Franchise System* (Phoenix, AZ: Choice Hotel International Inc.); Preeti Shah, "New High-Flying Hoteliers," *India-West*, May 31, 1996, B1.

50.   *Leauva Patidar Samaj of U.S.A Directory 1997*, for Surat, Bulsar, Navsari Districts (Berea, KY: Leauva Patidar Samaj of USA Publishing).

51.   *U.S.A.-Canada Bhakta Directory 1996* (Los Angeles: Ram Kabir Bhakta Samaj of USA).

52.   *Hindu Matiya Patidar Samaj Directory 1997*; *Matiya Patidar World Directory 1993* (Rancho Santa Fe, CA: Hindu Matiya Patidar Samaj Inc.).

53.   *Charotaria Leauva Patidar Seva Samaj International Directory, 1994-95* (North Dartmouth, MA: CLPS, USA).

54.   Brian O'Reilly, "The New Face of Small Business: Executive Life," *Fortune*, May 2, 1994, 82.

55.   Karthik Panchapakesan, "NRIS—A Diverse Diaspora Growing," *India-Post*, April 10, 1998, S2.

56.   Mogelonsky.

57.   The following section is compiled by the author and adapted from the *AAHOA* magazine article by Joel Mill-Man, "Other Americans: The Rise of the Asian American Hotel Owners: How Immigrants Renew Our Country, Our Economy, and Our Values," in *AAHOA Hospitality* (December 1997), 26, 27, 29, 31, 33, 35.

58. Ibid.
59. Ibid.
60. Ibid.
61. Ibid.
62. These articles are quoted by AAOHA author, but references were not given.
63. Ibid.
64. Ibid.
65. Joel Mill-Man, "Other Americans: The Rise of the Asian American Hotel Owners: How Immigrants Renew Our Country, Our Economy, and Our Values" in *AAHOA Hospitality* (December 1997), 33.
66. Ibid.
67. Ibid.
68. U.S. Bureau of the Census, *Characteristics of Business Owners, 1992*; Ong and Hee, "Economic Diversity," 49.
69. Ong and Hee, "Economic Diversity," 47-51.
70. Ibid.
71. Ibid.
72. Ong and Hee, "Economic Diversity," Table 2, 36.
73. According to Hee, for Census 1990.
74. Rahul, 169.
75. Dr. Arun Jain, in "Asian-Indian Americans," *American Demographics Magazine* (1995), 3.
76. Compilation from Pattni Harish, "A Pioneer Asian American Hotel Owner" (1993), 6-7; and abstract from Professor Narshihbhai Gujarati's article, "Who Were the Predecessors of the Motel Occupation?" in *Gujarat Samachar* (New Jersey: Gujarat Samachar), March 5,1995, P6 and March 14, 1995, P6.
77. Jagdish Seth, "Dahyabhai Patel: The Grand Patriarch of Hospitality," in *AAHOA: India Post Supplemental*, March 19, 1999, 50.
78. Ibid.
79. Ibid.
80. Author's note: I also bought a small motel at the same time in Anaheim, CA. I have had the same motel after twenty-six years and some others with joint venture.
81. Preeti Shah, "H.P. Rama Reveals Successful Strategies," *India–West*, February10, 1995, C56.
82. E. Reckard Scott, "$80 Million Deal Close on Sale of Anaheim Hotel: Tourism: O.C.'s Tushar Patel is Said To Be Near To Acquiring the Convention-Oriented Marriott, the City's Third Largest Facility," *Los Angeles Times*, April 29, 1999, C16.
83. Ramesh Gokul, "Family Values and Business," *India Post*, March 7, 1997, B18.
84. *International Who's Who in Community Service*, 3rd Ed. (Cambridge, U.K.: International Biological Center, 1979).
85. Chandrakant Patel, "Unanimity with Mind: English Mixing of ABC," *Naya Padakar, Purti Edition*, November 22, 1996, Appendix.
86. Cindy Maynard, Ed., "Meet your Executive Committee," *AAHOA Hospitality Magazine*, April 1999, 36-39.
87. Ibid.
88. Ibid.
89. Ibid.
90. Ibid.
91. Ibid.
92. Ibid.
93. "Family" here refers to a group of two or more persons related by blood, marriage, or adoption and residing together in the same household.

94. Denton Robinson, "Society's Message: Don't be Too Fruitful. Families: Despite Criticism, Some Parents No Longer Believe that Two Children Are Enough" in *Los Angeles Times*, 1996.

95. Kenneth Labich, "Can Your Career Hurt Your Kids?" *Fortune*, May 30, 1991.

96. Robinson, "Society's Message."

97. U.S. Bureau of the Census, *Unpublished Data and Statistical Abstract, 1996; the National Data Book*, Table 1326.

98. Reynolds Farley and Walter Allen, *Color Line and Quality of Life in America* (New York: Oxford University Press, 1989), 144-145.

99. Bill Ong Hing, "Immigration Policy" in *The State of Asian Pacific America* (Los Angeles: UCLA Asian American Studies Center, 1993), 132.

100. Micheal Omi, "Race Relations Policy" in *SAPA* (1993).

101. See *1997 Leauva Patidar Samaj of U.S.A.; 1996 U.S.A Canada Bhakta Directory, 1997; Hindu Matiya Patidar Samaj U.S.A Directory, 1994-95; Charotariya Leauva Patidar Samaj_International Directory.*

102. U.S. Bureau of the Census, *1990 Census of Population and Housing Data Paper Listing* (CPH-L133) and Summary Tape File 3C, *The Statistical Abstract of the United States*, 1996.

103. Peter N. Kiang and Vivian Wai-Fun Lee, "Exclusion or Contribution? Education K-12 Policy," in *The State of Asian Pacific America: Issues to the Year 2020* (Los Angeles: LEAP—Asian Pacific American Public Policy Institute and UCLA Asian American Studies Center, 1993), 39-40.

104. Lily Wong Filmore et al, "When Learning a Second Language Means Losing the First," in *Early Child Researchers Quarterly*, 1993, 39.

105. Paul Ong, "Inner City Community," in *Beyond Asian American Poverty: Community Economic Development Policies and Strategies* (Los Angeles: LEAP—Asian Pacific American Public Policy Institute and UCLA Asian American Studies Center, 1993), 34.

106. Chandrakant Baxi, in *Pitrubhumi Gujarat* (Bomaby: Navbharat Sahitya Mandir, 1983).

107. Virendra Canada, "Will Gujarati Language Vanish by 2012 in Foreign Countries?"; and Bharat Shah, "Importance of Gujarati Language To Be Alive Overseas," both in *Gujurat Samchar* (September 1997).

108. Aruna Vasant, "Little Hoover Commission: Meeting the Challenge of Language Diversity: A Report from BW Associates, Department of Education, Berkeley, CA," *India–West*, November 10, 1995.

109. A report from BW Associates, Department of Education, Berkeley, CA, cited in *India West*, November 10, 1995.

110. Ibid.

111. Karin Batter, "A Gift of Language," *Los Angeles Times*, October 4, 1995.

112. Ibid.

113. Ibid.

114. Lenora Aruberg , "Raising Children Bilingually: The Pre-School Years," *The Orange County Register*, September 17, 1994.

115. Quote from Dr. Arun Jain, in "Asian-Indian Americans," *American Demographics Magazine* (1998), 6.

116. Lilly Lee, Table 8E, p.175 and Table 19C, Charts 9, 50.

117. Shivani Prasad, "Say what? On Language," *India–West*, February 2, 1996, B19.

118. Ling-chi Wang, "Higher Education Policy," in *The State of Asian Pacific America* (Los Angeles: LEAP—Asian Pacific American Public Policy Institute and UCLA Asian American Studies Center, 1993), 49, 52, 54.

119. U.S. Commission on Civil Rights, "Civil Rights Facing Asian Americans in the 1990's" (Washington, D.C.: United States Government Printing Office, 1992), 97.

120. Deborah Warner, "For Moms Only," *Orange County Register*, September 1996.

121. Tom Smith, *A Report on the Socio-Economic Status of Ethnic Groups in the United States* (Chicago: University of Chicago Press, 1992).

122. United States Bureau of the Census, 1983 and 1984, *Census of Population Subject Reports* (Washington D.C.: United States Printing Office).

123. Gall and Natividav, 14.

124. Lee, Table 14, p.76.

125. Julie Tamari, "Cultural Balancing Act Adds to Teen Anguist; Asian American Youths Face Perils of Adolesence While Coming To Grips with Isues of Identity," *Los Angeles Times*, July 13, 1998, A10.

126. Ibid.

127. United States Bureau of the Census, *1996 Statistical Abstract of the United States: The National Data Book* (Washington D.C.: United States Government Printing Office), Table 297; and from the New York Institute of International Education.

128. Manish Puri, "Focus on Youth," *India-West*, July 1995.

129. Parsottam Patel, in a speech delivered by President Radha Krishna Mandir to Gujarati Society Balmandir on Gujarati School Day, Norwalk, Los Angeles, 1994.

130. Tini Trsn, "Culture," *Los Angeles Times*, June 8,1998.

131. Elizabeth Mechling, "Commentary," *Los Angeles Times*, April 7,1993.

132. Mari Matsuda, "Voice of America: Accent, Anti-Discrimination Law, and Jurisprudence for the Last Reconstruction" *Yale Law Journal* (1991), 1329.

133. Priya Agarwal, 48.

134. Ibid.

135. Ibid.

136. Snehendu Kar, Sangita, Shypra et. al, "Amerasia Journal: 25th Issue," *India-West*, May 24, 1996.

137. Shari Roan, "Parents: Beyond the Birds and the Bees" in *Los Angeles Times*, February 16, 1993, E10.

138. Ibid; data from the Center for Population Options, 1993.

139. R. Narain, "In Step with the Unbridgeable Generation Gap," *India-West*, March 3, 1995.

140. Susan Christian, "Single in Orange County," *Los Angeles Times*, September 12, 1994.

141. Manish Malkani, "On Ideal Mates," *India-West*, July 26, 1996, B18.

142. Susan Christian, "Single in Orange County."

143. Heerva Macwan, "My Culture Is Also My Religion," *India Journal*, July 17, 1998.

144. Compiled and translated from Vasant G. Patel and Bhupendra Joshi's article, "Ame Leauva Patidar," in *Leauva Patidar Samaj of California First Convention Magazine* (Los Angeles, 1997), 53-61.

145. Dudhiben L. Bhakta, *Vividh lagna gitos* (Vyara, India: Anand printing, 1993), 1, 28, 63, 70, 110.

146. Ranjan and Ramesh Patel, *Hindu Marriage Ceremony* (North Dartmouth, MA: Charotaria Leauva Patidar Samaj, 1995), 10-11.

147. Arvind R. Patel, Marriage Perspective for Parents." In Patidar in foreign lands, edited by Videsoma Patidar, Ahmadabad: Dharti Vikas Mandal, 1994.

148. Melwani Lavina, "The Joys and Challenges of Growing up in Intercultural Families," *India-West*, January 20, 1995.

149. "Grahastha": One who has a good family life.

150. Puneet Sehgul, "Arranged Marriage," *India-West*, April 14, 1995.

151. Emmers.

152. Lily Wong Fillmore, Peter Kiang, and Vivian Lee, "Preschool and Native Language Loss," *MABE Newsletter* (Massachusetts Association for Bilingual Education 2, 1991), 39.

153. Tessie Guillermo, "Health Care Needs and Service Delivery" in *The State of Asian Pacific America* (Los Angeles: LEAP—Asian Pacific American Policy Institute and UCLA Asian American Studies Center, 1994), 63.

154. Susan Christine, "Single in Orange County—Breaking the Dating Tradition," *Los Angeles Times*, September 12, 1994.

155. Vijay Agarwal, "Problems with Parents."

156. Priya Agarwal, 27.

157. Ibid, 42.

158. Neil Shah, "India, More Than Just Poverty," *India-West*, May 26, 1996.

159. Previous three quotes from Radhika Chinai, "On Living in India," *India-West*, September 29, 1995, B25.

160. Vandana Gupta, "Impressions of India: Close Bonds," *India-West*, September 18, 1992.

161. Bruce Cain, "Acquisition of Partisanship by Latinos and Asian Americans," *Statistical Records of Asian Americans*, May 1991.

162. Jagdish Natali and Dhirubhai Bhavan, *Shree Moraribapuni Ram Katha* (Auckland, New Zealand: Logan Campbell Center,1988), 35

163. Ibid.

164. Dr. Robert Brown, *Music and Musicians* (India, 1989), 6-9.

165. The text was extracted from Surendra C. Patel, "Ethnomusicology," in *India Music and Musicians* magazine (Wesleyan University, 1971); and *India: The Ultimate Fantasy Souvenir Book* (1989), 7-8.

166. Gerald Yoshitomi "Asian American Art in the Year 2020: Art Policy,"in *The State of Asian Pacific America* (Los Angeles: LEAP—Asian Pacific American Public Policy Institute and UCLA Asian American Studies Center, 1993), 103.

167. Dr. Mafatlal Patel, *Videsoma Patidar* (Dharti Vikas Mandal, 1994), 201-204.

168. *World Vaishnava Association and American Hindus Against Defamation* (Los Angeles: *India Post*, April 1999). Also, *Member Organizations* (Los Angeles: *India Journal*, January, 1999), A14.

MAPS

Surat District

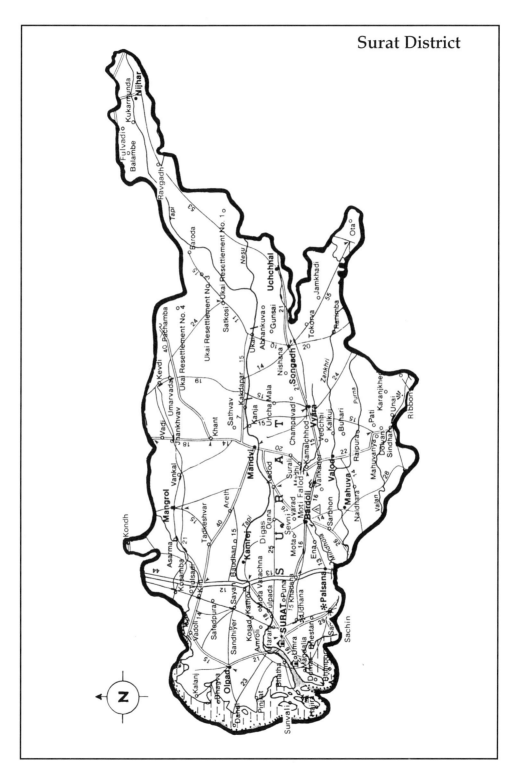

165

Navsari District

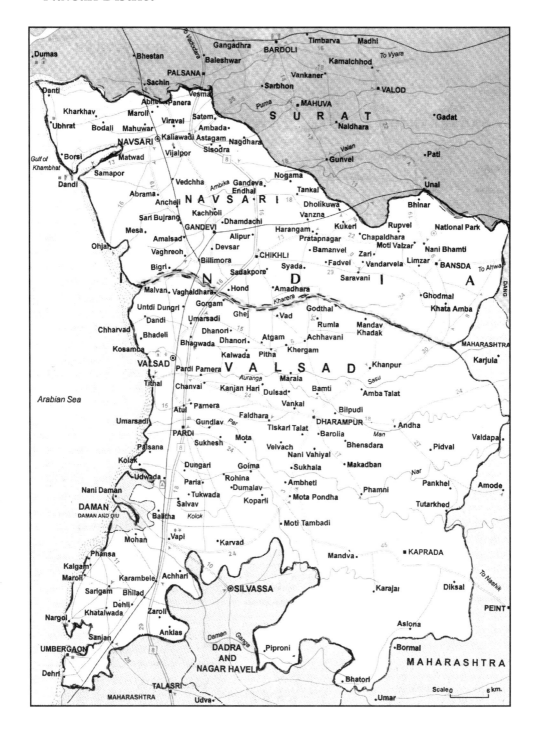

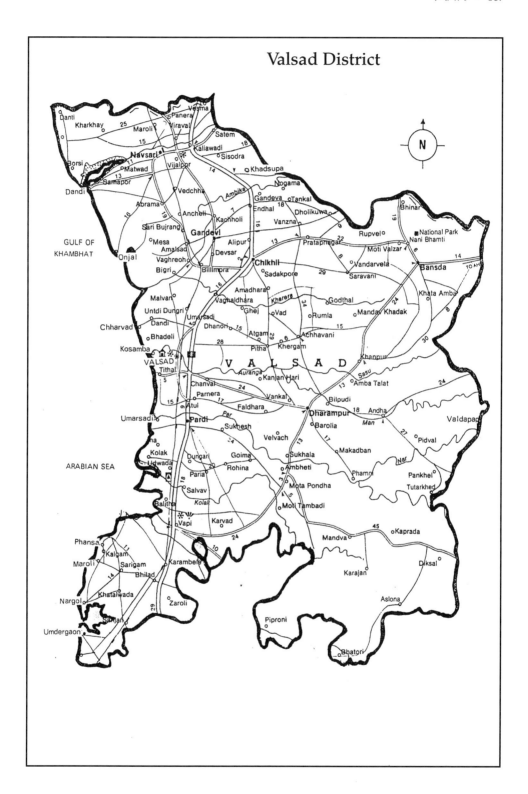

Valsad District

.

DHANSUKH and Jyotsna - CABRillo
SAN DIEGO, CA.